COLLECTED PLAYS
Volume Four

Brian Friel

COLLECTED PLAYS

Volume Four

Edited by Peter Fallon

FABER & FABER

Gallery Books

Collected Plays: Volume Four
is first published in paperback and in a clothbound edition
by The Gallery Press and in paperback by Faber and Faber Limited
in 2016. Originated at The Gallery Press.

The Gallery Press
Loughcrew
Oldcastle
County Meath
Ireland

Faber and Faber Limited
Bloomsbury House,
74-77 Great Russell Street,
London, WC1B 3DA
England

ISBN 978 1 85235 676 7 *paperback*
     978 1 85235 677 4 *clothbound*

A CIP catalogue record for this book
is available from the British Library.

Collected Plays: Volume Four receives financial assistance
from the Arts Councils of Ireland.

Contents

THE
LONDON
VERTIGO

Based on a play

THE TRUE BORN IRISHMAN

or

THE IRISH FINE LADY

by Charles Macklin

MacLochlainn's Vertigo

The desire to metamorphose oneself, to change everything utterly
— name, beliefs, voice, loyalties, language, ambitions, even
one's appearance — secretly excites most people at some stage
of their lives and is as old as Adam. It is an element in the dream
that charms young people into a career in acting. It is the private
delirium that middle-aged writers are especially vulnerable to:
to obliterate that whole past of botched and failed and embarrassing work and to begin afresh and anonymously with a few
simple markings on a white sheet of paper. And of course the
desire is a delusion. There are no new beginnings with new
identities, as Cathal MacLochlainn, the eighteenth-century actor
and playwright, discovered. But his attempt at transmogrifica-
tion is interesting for two reasons. The first is that he set about it
with calculation and precocious acumen while he was still only
a boy, long before he knew the pain of failure as a writer or as an
actor. The second is that he pulled it off. Well, almost.

MacLochlainn was born some time during the last decade of
the seventeenth century in the townland of Gortanarin in the
parish of Cloncha in the Inishowen peninsula in the very north
of County Donegal. Various birth-years are offered — 1690, 1693,
1699. Even as an old man (he died in 1797 when he may have
been anything from ninety-eight to one-hundred-and-seven) he
never attempted to clear up the confusion, perhaps because the
actor liked to be ageless, more likely because the writer preferred
the past to be blurred. His background was poor peasant, his
religion Catholicism, his only language Irish. Very early in life he
recognized that an Irish-speaking Catholic peasant from north
Donegal did not possess the very best qualifications for success
in eighteenth-century Ireland. He emigrated to England. He
learned English and spoke it with an English accent. He changed
his name to Charles Macklin. He invented a background of
wealth and land in County Down. He converted to Protestantism.
And the metamorphosis brought abundant success. London and
Macklin loved one another. Before he was thirty he had a considerable reputation as a budding playwright and a rising star
on the English stage. He became a friend of Garrick and
Edmund Burke and Henry Fielding, was smiled on by royalty,

was celebrated by Alexander Pope after the poet had seen his Shylock ('This is the Jew / That Shakespeare drew'), became famous for his Macbeth and his Iago and his own hugely popular *Love à la Mode*.

He was in his sixties when he wrote his first play with an Irish theme, *The True Born Irishman*, a satirical look at Irish Anglophiles; and one marvels at Macklin's ease and assurance in his new identity, so confident that he would now attempt to write out of a discarded persona. The play opened at the Crow Street Theatre, Dublin, on May 14th, 1761. Perhaps predictably Irish audiences received it warmly.

The plot is simple. Nancy O'Doherty, wife of Murrough O'Doherty (played by Macklin himself), a pompous and ponderous Dublin burgher, has been to London for the coronation of George III. During her brief visit she has been smitten by 'the London vertigo', a sudden and dizzy conviction that London is the very heart of style and wit and good fortune and excitement. When the play opens she has recently returned to dreary Murrough O'Doherty.

Macklin wants her to be an absurd and ludicrous figure. He achieves this — without a hint of irony, it would seem — by two devices: the lady, now ashamed of her Irish name, O'Doherty, has decided to call herself Mrs Diggerty; and she now speaks a patois in a posh accent that her husband can scarcely understand. 'London — Dublin — don't neem them together!' she says. 'After London everything I set my eyes on here gives me the *ennui* and the *contre cure*. The streets are mean, the houses dirty, the people ridiculous. And the women! None of the *non chalance*, none of that *jenny-see-quee* we have in London. And everything sounds so strange here! Even the very dogs when they bark, I swear they bark wit' a brogue!'

O'Doherty, distressed by his wife's lunacy, enlists the help of her brother and together they hatch a plot to restore her to sanity and thorough Irishness. By a series of complicated and cruel manoeuvres Macklin has Mrs Diggerty cured of her vertigo, properly humiliated before her friends and reconciled to decent Dublin domesticity. Simultaneously and almost certainly unwittingly Macklin has written his own biography as comedy/farce.

Six years passed before he brought *The True Born Irishman* to

London. It opened in Covent Garden on November 28th, 1767. Circumspect as ever Macklin retitled the play *The Irish Fine Lady* just in case the original title might have a hint of coat-trailing for his English audience. But the play did not travel. Whatever the reason the night was a disaster. And when the curtain came down Macklin rushed on to the stage in panic. 'Ladies and gentlemen,' he pleaded, 'I am very sensible that there are several passages in this play which deserve to be reprobated and I assure you that they shall never offend your ears again.' One can almost hear the terrified voice and the clipped Donegal vowels. Later, when he had composed himself, he said to a friend, 'I believe the audience are right. There is a geography in humour as well as in morals, which I had previously not considered.' What he meant by a geography in humour is clear enough; a geography in morals is nicely ambiguous. Anyhow *The Irish Fine Lady* was withdrawn after that one performance.

I have worked on Macklin's text with affection and respect. I have pruned his script vigorously, mainly by compressing his three acts into one and by reducing his cast of fourteen to a cast of five. (The missing nine appear only briefly in his Act 2 and Act 3 and he uses them not to energize his central theme but as contemporary stereotypes who make leisurely and amusing social comment on mid-eighteenth century Ireland; in other words to stroke his audience.) But I trust — I believe — I have done neither structural nor aesthetic damage to the script. And in excuse for my ruthless culling of his cast I plead the stern economics of late twentieth-century theatre. Indeed my hope is that a lean and less discursive text may be more attractive to theatre companies today and better suited to our impatient stage.

My reason for renaming the play *The London Vertigo* is that this title both signposts the play's theme and hints at the fate the author himself so eagerly embraced.

This may not be Macklin's best play — *The Man of the World* or *Love à la Mode* claims that place. But it is a very considerable piece of work from an almost completely self-made man and it gave me pleasure to work on it — a kind of *comhar* or cooperation or companionship with a neighbouring playwright.

Brian Friel

13

Characters

MURROUGH O'DOHERTY, self-assured Dublin burgher
KATTY FARREL, family servant
TOM HAMILTON, slow-thinking and pompous lawyer
MRS DIGGERTY, O'Doherty's wife
COUNT MUSHROOM, typical 18th-century fop, stage-English in accent and manner

Time and Place

An afternoon and evening in September 1761. The drawing room in Murrough O'Doherty's Dublin home.

The London Vertigo was first produced by the Gate Theatre, Dublin, at Andrews Lane Theatre, on 23 January 1992, with the following cast:

MURROUGH O'DOHERTY   John Kavanagh
KATTY FARREL   Antoine Byrne
TOM HAMILTON   Eamon Morrissey
MRS DIGGERTY   Gemma Craven
COUNT MUSHROOM   John Hurt

Directed by   Judy Friel
Designed by   Monica Frawley
Lighting by   Rupert Murray
Choreography by   Geri O'Kelly

for Owen, Emer and Chrissie

MURROUGH O'DOHERTY *is dozing on a chair, an open book on his lap.*
Enter KATTY FARREL, *the maid.*

KATTY Mr O'Doherty, sir. Mr O'Doherty.

O'DOHERTY Mm? Mm? Yes? What is it?

KATTY Your brother-in-law gives his compliments to you, Mr O'Doherty.

O'DOHERTY Yes, Katty? Yes? Yes?

KATTY Counsellor Hamilton, the barrister.

O'DOHERTY Yes?

KATTY He gives his compliments to you, sir.

O'DOHERTY Splendid, Katty. Thank you.

KATTY He's on his way upstairs.

O'DOHERTY What's that you have in your hand?

KATTY A card for my mistress — from Madam Mulrooney.

O'DOHERTY Pray let me see it. 'Mrs Mulrooney makes her compliments to Mrs Murrough O'Doherty and likewise to Mr Murrough O'Doherty and hopes to have the favour of their company on Sunday 17th instant to play at cards, sup and spend the evening with Count Mushroom, Lady Kinnegad, Lord Ballybeg, Captain Kilmaine, Major Bellaghy, Lady Belmullet — ' Here, Katty. Take this to your mistress. I have nothing to say to it.

KATTY Very well, Mr O'Doherty.

She exits.

O'DOHERTY (*To audience*) Mrs Mulrooney! She's another of the fine ladies of this country who, like my wife,

17

is sending her soul to the devil and her husband to jail as fast as she can. Mr Mulrooney, the boob, has scarce a thousand pounds a year in the world; yet he spends above two thousand in equipage — in other words on a carriage and servants — on jolly parties and high living besides what his fool of a wife loses to that female-sharper, my Lady Kinnegad; which, if I may judge by my own wife, is at least a good two thousand more; so that by the rule of subtraction, take four thousand pounds a year out of one thousand pounds and in a very little time nothing will remain but the jail — or a fast packet boat to France. Money! Money! They think it grows on trees, these women!

Enter COUNSELLOR HAMILTON.

HAMILTON Murrough! I'm extremely glad to see you.
O'DOHERTY By my faith and so am I you, too, Tom. You are most welcome, brother-in-law. Odzooks, give us a kiss, man.

They embrace.

I give you my honour I am as glad to see you in Dublin at this juncture as I should to see a hundred head of fat bullocks upon my own land all ready for Ballinasloe fair.
HAMILTON That is a great compliment from you, brother. (*To audience*) Fat bullock — curious image.
O'DOHERTY A very true compliment, I assure you. (*To audience*) All beef — no brains.
HAMILTON And I see by the newspapers that my sister is returned from the Coronation frolics.
O'DOHERTY (*To audience*) George III.
HAMILTON (*To audience*) September 22nd, 1761.
O'DOHERTY (*To audience*) London.
HAMILTON (*To audience*) England.

O'DOHERTY ⎱ (*To audience*) God bless His Majesty.
HAMILTON ⎰

O'DOHERTY She has returned with a vengeance.

HAMILTON What's the matter?

O'DOHERTY Returned with a distemper that will soon affect the whole nation. It is called the Irish Fine Lady's Delirium — or the London Vertigo.

HAMILTON What may that be?

O'DOHERTY The devil an inhabitant in Jonathan Swift's Hospital for Lunatics is in a worse pickle than she is.

HAMILTON (*To audience*) Opened here in Dublin four years ago.
'He gave the little wealth he had
To found a house for fools and mad.'

O'DOHERTY If you were to hear her when the fit is upon her — oh, she is as mad — the devil a thing in this poor country but what gives her the spleen and the vapours. Then such a frenzy of admiration for everything in England! And among the rest of her madness she has brought back — (*he looks around and lowers his voice*) — a new language with her.

HAMILTON A new — ?

O'DOHERTY A new kind of London English that is no more like our Irish English than — than — than a fine gilded carriage is like a Carrickmore cart. What name do you think she went by when she was in England?

HAMILTON What do you mean?

O'DOHERTY What did she call herself over there?

HAMILTON What would she call herself but Nancy O'Doherty!

O'DOHERTY O'Doherty! Oho! Upon my honour, Tom, she startles when she hears the name O'Doherty, and blushes, and is much ashamed as if a man said something bawdy to her. No, no, my friend; my wife, your sister, is no longer the plain, modest, good-natured, domestic, obedient Irish Mrs O'Doherty — in other words the perfect wife;

19

but the travelled, rampant, high-lifed, prancing, English . . . Mrs Diggerty.

HAMILTON Diggerty?

O'DOHERTY Diggerty. Was there ever such impertinence? Nor is that all of your sister's whims and madnesses.

HAMILTON There is more?

O'DOHERTY She wants me to go after a title. Can you imagine! Young Lord Turnabout has hinted to her that if I throw my weight behind him in the coming election a title is mine for the asking. And that piece of information has stirred up such a rage of quality and title in her giddy head that I cannot rest night or day for her importunity!

HAMILTON Good heavens!

O'DOHERTY She would have me desert my friends and sell myself, my honour and my country, as several others have done before me, so that she may sink the ancient name of O'Doherty in the upstart title of Lady Ahohill or Lady Culmore or some such ridiculous nonsense.

HAMILTON (*To audience*) 'Sell my country'! He really means it would cost him money!

O'DOHERTY Oh Tom, Tom, I have many grievances to tell you of but I have one that is even more whimsical than all the rest.

HAMILTON Tell me.

O'DOHERTY I am going to be a cuckold.

HAMILTON My sister? — Your wife? — You mean she is going to — ?

O'DOHERTY There is an English coxcomb just arrived among us in this town who thinks every woman that sees him is in love with him.

HAMILTON Who is this spark?

O'DOHERTY His name is Mushroom, as in . . . mushroom. Maurice Mushroom. Count Maurice Mushroom.

HAMILTON And he lives here, this cuckold-maker?

O'DOHERTY You know those huge estates owned by Lord Oldcastle?

HAMILTON On which your family for generations have had long and very profitable leases?

O'DOHERTY The same. (*To audience*) Is the boob getting saucy?

HAMILTON And have sublet at enormous profit to much less fortunate Irishmen?

O'DOHERTY (*To audience*) Indeed he is! (*To* HAMILTON) Well, my Lord Oldcastle has made this Mushroom his agent in this country and sent him over to settle his affairs here. Now one of the main businesses he must conclude is an agreement between Oldcastle and me on the terms of the leases; and Mushroom and I not being able to agree on the terms, what does the coxcomb do?

Pause.

HAMILTON You and he disagree.

O'DOHERTY (*To audience*) Noodle-brain! (*To* HAMILTON) What he does is this, Tom. He sends my wife a warm billet-doux in which he very gallantly tells her that she shall settle the leases at her own price — only upon the trifling condition that he may be permitted now and again to be the occasional lord of her ladyship's matrimonial manor.

HAMILTON So he just wants occasional lodgings here, Murrough?

O'DOHERTY In a manner of speaking — yes. (*To audience*) Close to genius, wouldn't you say?

HAMILTON That is trifling indeed.

O'DOHERTY Do you think so? (*To audience*) Himself — his sister — all the Hamiltons — mahogany heads!

HAMILTON And pray, what says my sister to all this?

O'DOHERTY She knows nothing of it.

HAMILTON But she got Mushroom's letter, did she not?

O'DOHERTY I intercepted it — with the help of Katty Farrel. And with Katty's assistance I have carried on a correspondence with the fellow in my wife's name — unknown to her, of course. And by that means I shall not only detect and expose the fellow but get an excellent bargain of the leases which are to be signed this very day!

HAMILTON But, Murrough, you couldn't accept the leases upon those terms.

O'DOHERTY Could I not? (*To audience*) And he's a barrister! Question is: how did the noodle ever qualify?

HAMILTON (*To audience*) Forging letters in my sister's name! Lord Counterfeit!

O'DOHERTY (*To audience*) Of course he'd make a living nowhere else but at the law.

HAMILTON (*To audience*) And involving decent Katty Farrel in his corruption! No wonder our Mama always hated him!

Enter KATTY.

KATTY Sir, Count Mushroom is below.

She exits.

O'DOHERTY I will wait upon him, Katty. Now, brother, you shall see one of the pertest and most conceited impudent coxcombs that has ever been imported into this land or that disgraced humanity.

MUSHROOM (*Off*) My compliments to your lady, Mrs Katty. I will be with her in the twinkling of a star —

O'DOHERTY D'you hear?

MUSHROOM — or in less time than a single glance of her own immortal beauty can pass to the centre of an amorous heart.

O'DOHERTY (*Eyes closed*) Control, Murrough O'Doherty! Control!

Enter MUSHROOM.

MUSHROOM My dear Diggerty, I kiss your hand. I am come on purpose to discuss the leases that you and I — (*He sees* HAMILTON) I beg ten thousand pardons — I see you are busy —

O'DOHERTY Indeed, Count, we are not. Tom Hamilton, my wife's brother — Count Mushroom.

MUSHROOM Sir, I feel a superlative happiness in being known to you. I have long expected and long wished for it with a lover's appetite. Therefore, without waiting for the dull advocation of experience or the pedantic forms of ceremony, I beg you will honour me with a niche in your esteem and register me in the select catalogue of your most constant and most ardent friends and admirers.

   Pause.

HAMILTON That's right.

O'DOHERTY (*To audience*) And he'll be a judge some day!

MUSHROOM Give me your hand, Hamilton. It's Tom, isn't it? Yes, it's Tom. Give me your hand, dear Tom Hamilton. You are Diggerty's friend. Diggerty is your friend. Diggerty is my friend. I am Diggerty's friend. So it follows that you and I are destined to be friends since friends of friends must naturally be friends, too. But that's enough. I'll serve you. Say no more. I'll serve you. Rely upon me, friend.

HAMILTON You live in this town, Count?

MUSHROOM Quite *en famille*. I go about everywhere, am of no party but those of love, pleasure and gallantry. The women like me and commend me at cards, tea, scandal and dancing. The men commend me at jolly parties, a late hour, a bottle and hazard —

HAMILTON (*To audience*) 'Hazard' — in other words, dice. You know, a small cube having its faces marked with spots numbering from —

O'DOHERTY They know — they know!

MUSHROOM I love ease, hate ceremony and am at home wherever I go. Correct, Diggerty?

O'DOHERTY To give you your due, Count, you are never bashful in any place.

MUSHROOM   Bashfulness, dear Diggerty, is a mask of ignorance, a disease of the vulgar and uncourtly — what we men of the world are never infected with. But to business, my friend.

O'DOHERTY   Business?

MUSHROOM   The leases, Diggerty. Lord Oldcastle's leases.

O'DOHERTY   Of course.

MUSHROOM   Cards on the table, my friend: My lord is loath to lose you as a tenant just as I am convinced it would be for his interest you should have the lands. So let us sign and seal at once — upon your own terms. For really I think tenants in Ireland want encouragement; they are racked too high; they are indeed; it is a shame they should be racked so high. (*To* HAMILTON) You want encouragement in trade, too — tax concessions — greater incentives — relief in exports — that sort of thing. I'll speak to some people of consequence about it — on the other side.

HAMILTON   On the other side of what?

O'DOHERTY   London, Tom, London.

HAMILTON   Ah. (*To* MUSHROOM) Will you?

MUSHROOM   Upon my honour. The moment I return.

O'DOHERTY   You English politicians promise us the devil and all while you are among us. But the moment you get to the other side you have devilish bad memories.

HAMILTON   You seem to like Ireland, sir?

MUSHROOM   A damn fine country, Tom. Upon the whole, take you all together, you are a damned honest tory rory, rantum scantum, dancing, singing, laughing, boozing, jolly, friendly, fighting, hospitable people. And I like you mightily.

O'DOHERTY   (*To audience*) Nothing changes, does it?

MUSHROOM   I do upon honour and I believe I shall marry one of your women here, grow domestic and settle among you. But I beg pardon, my dear Diggerty. I must rob you of my company for a moment to pay my duty to your lady. (*Catches*

24

HAMILTON'*s hand*) Hamilton — yours, yours. Give me thy hand, Diggerty. (*To* o'DOHERTY) From this moment set me down as thy unalterable friend. I'll serve you — rely upon me — I'll serve you.

He moves towards the door and pauses there.

MUSHROOM (*To audience*) And now to try my hand at casual lodgings — bed and perhaps board?

He exits. KATTY *enters.*

O'DOHERTY Didn't I tell you? There never was so conceited and so impudent a coxcomb as that puppy! (*To* KATTY) Is your fine mistress dressed yet, Katty?

KATTY The mistress, sir — she — she — (*uneasy in front of* HAMILTON) — she has had a little misfortune, sir.

O'DOHERTY Speak up, Katty. No secrets here.

KATTY You know that bill that came from Covent Garden, from the mercer there?

HAMILTON (*To audience*) In other words, draper.

O'DOHERTY I gave her the money for that two days ago, Katty.

KATTY Lost it all last night — to Lady Kinnegad.

O'DOHERTY My God! All?

KATTY Playing brag.

O'DOHERTY (*To audience*) A kind of poker that's played with — (*Recovering. To* KATTY) She played brag with that sharper?

KATTY And to cover up her excesses she's going to borrow from Count Mushroom.

O'DOHERTY And what collateral has she to — (*We hear* MUSHROOM *and* MRS DIGGERTY *laugh, off*) Don't answer that!

HAMILTON Oh, Murrough, the woman has lost all sense of shame.

O'DOHERTY She is not to borrow from Mushroom, Katty. Here — here — here — give her this. Say you borrowed it from your brother — from a friend — say you —

Enter MUSHROOM *and* MRS DIGGERTY. *She is gaudily dressed and, as Macklin says, 'What a head she has!' — i.e. extravagantly dressed hair.*

O'DOHERTY Ah, my dear.

MRS DIGGERTY Brother, I am veestly glad to see you.

HAMILTON Welcome home from England, Nancy.

MRS DIGGERTY I am imminsely obliged to you, brother.

HAMILTON Did it answer your expectations?

MRS DIGGERTY Ravishingly.

HAMILTON Indeed?

MRS DIGGERTY Transcendently.

HAMILTON I'm glad you —

MRS DIGGERTY Beyond all degrees of compirison. England, brother, England is just veest, imminse, extatic! I never knew life before. Everything there is high, tip top, the *grand monde*, the bun tun —

HAMILTON (*To audience*) Bun tun?

MRS DIGGERTY — and quite, quite teesty.

MUSHROOM She liked it.

HAMILTON And London?

MRS DIGGERTY London? The place of the world, brother!

HAMILTON Then this town, I suppose, is —

MRS DIGGERTY This town? Where? Where? — I've forgot — what's the neem of this place?

O'DOHERTY Dublin.

MRS DIGGERTY Dublin! That's it! Oh dear brother, London — Dublin — don't neem them together. After London everything I set my eyes on here gives me the *ennui* and the *contre cure*. The streets are mean, the houses dirty, the people ridiculous. And the women! None of the *non chalance*, none of that *jenny-see-quee* we have in London. And everything sounds so strange here; everybody talks so peculiar; I scarcely understand them. Even the very dogs when they bark, I swear they bark wit' a brogue.

O'DOHERTY As strong a brogue as your mother, Madge Gallagher from Donegal Town, ever had.

MRS DIGGERTY You are a very rude man to remind me of my mother's family. You know I always despised my mother's family. Didn't I, brother? I hate the very neem of — What was my mother's maiden name?

HAMILTON Gallagher.

MRS DIGGERTY That's it. Gillogher. Hate it. Hate it.

HAMILTON Tell us about the Coronation, sister. No doubt you were there?

MRS DIGGERTY There? O *moundew* — what a quistion! Ax the Count.

MUSHROOM She was everywhere — and with everybody. The court never stirred without her.

MRS DIGGERTY But the highlight of the visit was the feast in the Guildhall. That — was — just — imminse! I went to it with her grace, a friend of mine, and a peerty of the court, as one of the household. And the moment I entered that imminse hall every eye was upon me! So this is the handsome Irish-woman — the famous Irish toast — the cele-brated Mrs Diggerty! I was just brilliant, even more brilliant than I was at the Coronation itself. I was so brilliant that night at the Corona-tion ball that the Count was moved to write a poem about me.

MUSHROOM Oh heavens, madam!

MRS DIGGERTY It's true. And he is one of the prettiest poets we have in England or for that matter in — in — in — what's the name of this — ?

O'DOHERTY Ireland.

MRS DIGGERTY Ireland — that's it! He is by my honour.

HAMILTON I don't doubt the gentleman's talents in the least, sister.

MUSHROOM You are most polite, sir, and the lady is pleased to rally.

O'DOHERTY (*To audience*) In other words — to banter.

MUSHROOM My muse is but a smatterer, a slattern, a mere slipshod lady.

MRS DIGGERTY What I say is true. And to convince you of his worth — (*She produces a paper from her bosom*) —

	will you be so obliging as to read them to my brother?
MUSHROOM	The nod of beauty sways both gods and men and I obey. Gentlemen, the title will at once let you into the whole of what you are to expect in this little production: *An Extempore On The Famous Mrs Diggerty Dancing At Court.*
MRS DIGGERTY	La la loo.
O'DOHERTY	(*To audience*) Oh God.
MUSHROOM	Now attend.

'When beauteous Diggerty leads up the dance
    In fair Britannia's court,
      Then every heart is in a prance
    And longs for Cupid's sport.'

MRS DIGGERTY	'Cupid's sport'! Naughty — naughty!
MUSHROOM	'Beaux ogle and pant and gaze;

      Belles envy and sneer, yet praise,
      As Venus herself were there — '

MRS DIGGERTY	'Venus'! Oh, Count!
MUSHROOM	'And prudes agree it must be she — '
MRS DIGGERTY	It must be Venus herself.
MUSHROOM	'It must be she — or Diggerty.

    It must be she — or Diggerty,
    Or Diggerty, the fair.'

He bows very low to MRS DIGGERTY. *Enter* KATTY.

	That's it, gentlemen; a slight effort of the muse; a mere *jeu d'esprit*.
KATTY	My Lady Kinnegad and my Lady Belmullet have arrived, Mrs O'Doherty.
MRS DIGGERTY	Who is that creature addressing? Nobody of that neem here, my dear.
O'DOHERTY	(*Angrily*) I want to sign those leases now, Count. Now! I'll await you downstairs. Come with me, Katty. I want a word with you.

He goes off with KATTY.

MUSHROOM   With all my heart, Diggerty.

MRS DIGGERTY   You'll return later this evening, Count, won't you? I'm having some titled friends in for cards.

MUSHROOM   Do I breathe? Do I exist? I will but step down, sign the papers and return tonight on the wings of inclination, *ma chère belle sans adieu.*

Exits.

MRS DIGGERTY   *Au revoir.* 'Then every heart is in a prance' — isn't he the most humorous creature, Tom?

HAMILTON   Most.

MRS DIGGERTY   And mighty witty — don't you think so?

HAMILTON   Mighty.

MRS DIGGERTY   'And longs for Cupid's sport.' And so do I! Oh brother, brother, you are looking at a transported woman! *Adieu.*

She rushes off. HAMILTON *is totally bewildered. He stares at the audience for several seconds before he speaks.*

HAMILTON   Compared with her the inhabitants of Swift's Hospital for Lunatics are marvellously sane. Oh the poor woman, she is very far gone and must be pinched to the quick — and shall this very night. Thank heaven our Mama has passed on.

He goes to the door, stops, turns and addresses the audience again.

Bun tun — tory rory — rantum scantum — what do those words mean? Must ask Mirragh — O'Duggerty — O'Murragh — O'Diggerty — Oh God —

He dashes off.
   A short time later. The stage is in darkness.
   Then KATTY *enters and lights candles. Now we*

hear o'doherty *and his wife arguing, off.*

mrs diggerty (*Off*) Reason? Reason? I will have no reason, Mr Diggerty! There can be no reason against what I say! You are the strangest man — not to be a lord! I insist upon it, sir! There is a necessity for a peerage!

katty *exits.*

o'doherty (*Off*) Show me the necessity then and all my objections will vanish.

mrs diggerty (*Off*) Why, sir, I am affronted for want of a title. (*They both enter*) A parcel of upstarts with their crownets upon their coaches, their chairs, their spoons, their handkerchiefs, nay on their very knockers — (*To audience*) in other words on their doors — (*To* o'doherty) creatures that were below me but t'other day are now truly my superiors and have their precedency and are set above me at table.

o'doherty Come, come, my dear. Don't be in such a fluster.

mrs diggerty Can there be anything more provoking to a woman of my teest and spirit than to hear the titles of these ugly creatures bawled in one's ear upon every occasion: 'My Lady Kinnegad's coach here'; 'My Lady Belmullet's chair there'; 'My Lady Ahohil's chariot here'. And what are they all? Upstarts! With Upstart titles! And then consider how vile my neem sounds: 'Mrs Diggerty's servants here'; 'Mrs Diggerty's chair there'; 'Mrs Diggerty's coach here'. It's mean. It's beggarly. I can't bear it. The very thought of it makes me ready to burst my stays and almost throws me into hysteria.

She flings herself on the couch and howls.

o'doherty Now, now, my dear, don't work yourself up into

a fit.

MRS DIGGERTY My life is miserable. (*Rises*) But I see your design: you have a mind to break my heart. (*Howls*) Yes, you argue and contradict me for no other end; you do everything to fret and vex me.

O'DOHERTY What does that mean?

MRS DIGGERTY Ever since I returned from England to this — this — this —

O'DOHERTY Ireland.

MRS DIGGERTY That's the odious neem. Ever since my unhappy return I have been requesting, begging, praying that you would send to London for a set of long-tailed horses that you know I admire so much.

O'DOHERTY Have you any idea of the cost of — !

MRS DIGGERTY Lady Ballybeg has a set. Lady Kilmaine has a set. Lady Newry has a set. You know very well I detest a short tail. (*To audience*) Don't we all? Every lady of figure loves long tails. Nobody but doctors, lawyers and country merchants have short tails now.

O'DOHERTY Very well, my dear, very well. You will have tails as long as Lord Newry or Lord Ballybeg or whoever. As to the title, if it can be had —

MRS DIGGERTY You know it can be had! Just open your tight purse! Let me hear no more about it — for a title I will have. I can't bear being plain Mrs Diggerty any longer.

> *Again she howls and throws herself on the couch. Enter* KATTY.

KATTY Is Mrs O'Doherty ill, sir?

O'DOHERTY Very ill — with distemper.

> *He takes* KATTY *aside.*

Well, Katty?

KATTY Everything's in hand, sir.

O'DOHERTY The house is empty?

KATTY Yes, sir.

O'DOHERTY Her card friends all gone?

KATTY Everybody's left, sir. They promise to return in an hour.

O'DOHERTY Good. And Mushroom?

KATTY He got out of his carriage at the gate and crept back to the house.

O'DOHERTY Where is he now?

KATTY In the back parlour. Dressing himself in my lady's clothes.

O'DOHERTY That you provided.

KATTY On your instructions, sir.

O'DOHERTY Shhh! I know. I know. How did you persuade him?

KATTY I told him, if he were sighted, he would pass as a laundry woman. (*She laughs*)

O'DOHERTY Shhh!

KATTY You never saw a man — a woman — so eager, sir.

O'DOHERTY Please, Katty.

KATTY Bursting with expectation — in a manner of speaking.

O'DOHERTY Katty, please.

KATTY He's ten times fonder of himself as a woman than he was as a man — if that's possible.

O'DOHERTY I will cure him of his passion for himself and for all Irish women as long as he lives. Here comes her brother. Let us get out of their way for he is resolved to startle the lady and waken her — if possible. They will have a very sharp brush, I reckon. Mushroom's turn comes later.

They exit. HAMILTON *enters.*

HAMILTON Sit up and pay attention to me, Nancy. (*To audience*) Brothers sometimes have stern duties to perform. Sister, I have words for you.

MRS DIGGERTY Can't you see I'm in no state to — ?

HAMILTON Immediately, madam! This very instant! You are not ignorant that your husband took you without a fortune. You know, too, that by the marriage articles, upon a separation or your husband's death you are entitled to only £100 a year. Now, madam, I am commissioned to inform you that the doors are open and that the stipulated sum will be paid punctually —

MRS DIGGERTY You're not — ?

HAMILTON For know that neither your husband's love, my affection, nor a residence in this house can be enjoyed by you another hour — but on the hard condition of a thorough reformation.

MRS DIGGERTY You're telling me I must — ?

HAMILTON If female vanity will be mad, husbands must be peremptory. (*To audience*) I used that line in court once. The judge commended it. (*To* MRS DIGGERTY) The sums of money you have squandered and those you have been cheated of by your female friends — that is the least offence in your husband's judgement. It is your pride, your midnight revels, insolence of taste, rage of precedency that grieve him; for they have made you the ridicule of every flirt and coxcomb, and the scorn and pity of every sober person that knows your folly. This reflects disgrace upon your friends, contempt upon the spirit and credit of your husband and has furnished whispering suspicion with stories and implications which have secretly fixed an infectious stain upon your chastity.

She jumps to her feet.

MRS DIGGERTY My chastity? I defy the world! I care not what slander says! I will rely upon my innocence! (*To audience*) That was a bit hasty, wasn't it?

HAMILTON It is not sufficient to rely on innocence alone, madam. Women must not only be innocent, they must appear so, too. (*To audience*) This play was written over two hundred years ago. Times —

33

MRS DIGGERTY unfortunately — have changed.

MRS DIGGERTY I don't know what you mean by all this, brother. I beg you will explain.

HAMILTON I will. Know, then, that the coxcomb Mushroom —

MRS DIGGERTY Mushroom?

HAMILTON — took some hints your liberty had given him —

MRS DIGGERTY I gave him hints? Brother, you — !

HAMILTON — and like a true man of intrigue not only returns your hints with a letter of gallantry but bribes your own woman to deliver it.

MRS DIGGERTY Katty? I will turn her out — !

HAMILTON But the maid, instead of carrying the letter to you, delivers that and many others to her master —

MRS DIGGERTY To dear Murrough? (*To audience*) The bitch!

HAMILTON — who in your name, hand, style and sentiment has answered them all and carried on an amorous correspondence with the gentleman —

MRS DIGGERTY Mushroom?

HAMILTON — even up to an assignation. And now at this very instant the spark is preparing for that happy interview.

MRS DIGGERTY With my husband? Tom, I — !

HAMILTON With you, sister. Not only that but he has made the whole town confident of his good fortune.

MRS DIGGERTY Oh Lord!

HAMILTON Now judge what your husband, your brother and your friends must think of her whose conduct could entitle a coxcomb to such liberties.

MRS DIGGERTY I shall make no defence, brother. The story shocks me. Help me. Advise me. (*To audience*) Well, I'm caught, amn't I? (*To* HAMILTON) Only say what I shall do to be revenged upon this fellow for his impudence and what will convince my husband and you, Tom, and all the world of my innocence — and I will do it. Oh, Tom, you have given such a stirring to my heart and such a trouble and trembling as it never felt before.

HAMILTON It is the stirring of virtue, sister.

MRS DIGGERTY   Is it?

HAMILTON   Encourage it.

MRS DIGGERTY   I will — I will.

HAMILTON   For tears of repentance are the brightest ornaments a modern fine lady can be decked in.

MRS DIGGERTY   (*To audience*) Wouldn't he give you an ache in the jerkin?

O'DOHERTY   (*Off*) I shall be in here, Katty. The moment he makes a move, bring me word.

KATTY   (*Off*) I shall, sir.

MRS DIGGERTY   It's Mr Diggerty. Oh, brother, I am ashamed to face him.

Enter O'DOHERTY.

O'DOHERTY   Well, Tom, have you spoken to her?

HAMILTON   There she is, sir, bathed in tears of humility and repentance, as she should be.

MRS DIGGERTY *howls*.

O'DOHERTY   Oh, you've gone too far, brother. You shouldn't have made her cry. Nancy, child, turn round and don't be crying there.

MRS DIGGERTY   I'm ashamed to look you in the face, sir. (*Howls*)

O'DOHERTY   Had I been here, brother, I assure you you should not have made her cry.

MRS DIGGERTY   My errors I acknowledge — (*Howls*)

O'DOHERTY   Nancy —

MRS DIGGERTY   — and for the future it will be the business of my life to — to — to — (*Howls*)

O'DOHERTY   No more — not another word — no more. If you have settled everything with your brother, that is sufficient. Turn round and give me a kiss. Let us be friends at once. (*They kiss*) There. In that kiss now let all tears and uneasiness subside in you as all fears and resentment shall die in me.

HAMILTON   I must have my kiss of peace, too. (*They kiss*) I own I have been a little severe with you but your disease did require sharp medicine.

O'DOHERTY Now, Nancy, I have a favour or two to beg of you.

MRS DIGGERTY Command them, Murrough.

O'DOHERTY The first thing I ask is that you sack that French cook and let us have the food that every ordinary Irishman has.

MRS DIGGERTY He goes tomorrow. (*To audience*) Back to the frying pan.

O'DOHERTY Then let us be rid of your London English with your neems and your teestys and your veestlys and your imminselys.

MRS DIGGERTY They're dispinsed with — dispensed with now.

O'DOHERTY And above all things, pray never again call me Diggerty. My name is Murrough O'Doherty and I am not ashamed of it. But that damned name Diggerty, my dear it — it — it dements me.

MRS DIGGERTY Then upon my honour, Murrough O'Doherty, you'll never be demented again.

Enter KATTY.

(*To audience*) That wasn't too bad after all — was it?

KATTY Mr Mushroom is on his way up, sir.

O'DOHERTY In my lady's clothes?

MRS DIGGERTY What's this?

KATTY Yes, sir.

MRS DIGGERTY Mushroom? — In my clothes?

KATTY And looking very pretty, madam.

MRS DIGGERTY (*To* O'DOHERTY) Has he gone suddenly *soufflé*?

O'DOHERTY Gone what?

MRS DIGGERTY You know — (*she gestures*) — *soufflé*.

HAMILTON (*To audience*) In other words — made fluffy with beaten egg whites and then heated in an oven until it puffs up.

O'DOHERTY Mushroom? Not that toadstool! Detain him for a moment, Katty.

KATTY *leaves.*

(*To* MRS DIGGERTY) Go to your room. I'll come
and instruct you how to behave.

MRS DIGGERTY   Anything to be avenged on that — that pup!

She exits.

O'DOHERTY   Leave me with him, Tom. We mustn't prevent
that man from making me a cuckold.

HAMILTON   Be sure you make the gentleman smart.

Exits.

O'DOHERTY   (*To audience*) I'll make him smart. And smarter.
Impudent rascal — to make a cuckold of an
Irishman — take our own trade out of our own
hands! And a branch of business we pride ourselves so much in, too. Why, sure that and the
manufacture of linen are the only free trades
we have. (*Moves to door. Stops*) 'Soufflé' — never
heard that term before. Must be a London usage.
(*Moves again. Stops*) Where would she have heard
it? Damn.

He hears KATTY *and* MUSHROOM, *off, and quickly
exits.*

KATTY   (*Off*) I protest I should not have known you, sir.

MUSHROOM   (*Off*) Don't you think I make a handsome woman,
Mrs Katty?

They are now both onstage.

KATTY   You are a perfect beauty, sir — madam. I'll go
and see if the coast is clear and tell my mistress
you are come.

MUSHROOM   Tell her my soul is all rapture, ecstasy and transport and rides upon the wings of love.

KATTY *exits.*

(*To audience*) A man must speak nonsense to these creatures or they will not believe he loves them. Trouble is — all these Irish women love me. I'll have more intrigues in this country than I shall know what to do with. Old Diggerty here, when I tire of her, I'll bring her across to England and bequeath her to my Lord Oldcastle.

MRS DIGGERTY *and* KATTY *enter.*

(*To* MRS DIGGERTY) My angel! My goddess!

MRS DIGGERTY It's not — is it? — Count Mushroom?

MUSHROOM The same. All aquiver. Oh my delight —

MRS DIGGERTY But if my husband should discover you —

MUSHROOM Love despises all dangers when such beauty as yours is the price. (*To* KATTY) See we're not distracted. (*To* MRS DIGGERTY) Come to me. Now. Now.

MRS DIGGERTY But your attire, Count — can your passion be sincere?

MUSHROOM Dear creature, do but lay your hand upon my heart — here — here — here — feel what an alarm of love and gratitude it beats. Now, madam, let's retire to your chamber. We may be interrupted here.

KATTY (*Off*) You can't speak to her now, sir.

O'DOHERTY (*Off*) Why not?

MRS DIGGERTY It's Mirragh — O'Duggerty — O'Murragh — O'Diggerty!

MUSHROOM Oh God!

KATTY Because she is ill, sir.

O'DOHERTY All the more reason I must see her.

MRS DIGGERTY Oh, Mr *Soufflé*, I am deeply compromised.

MUSHROOM Mr Who?

KATTY *runs on.*

KATTY Madam, run down the back stairs! Quick!

MRS DIGGERTY *Adieu*, my dear.
KATTY Run! Run!

> MRS DIGGERTY *hoists up her skirts and runs off.*
> MUSHROOM *hoists up his skirts and is about to follow.*

MUSHROOM I'm going, too.

> KATTY *catches the tail of his dress and holds him back.*

KATTY Oh, no, you're not, sir.
MUSHROOM Let go of me, Mrs Katty.
KATTY Hold on a second, sir.
MUSHROOM Let me go, Katty.
KATTY You're safer here, sir.
MUSHROOM What are you doing, woman?
KATTY Protecting you, sir.
MUSHROOM Katty, please — !
KATTY You and your lady mustn't be seen together.
MUSHROOM Excellent thinking!
KATTY Leave it all to me. You stay here. I'll put out the candles. (*She does*) He will take you for my mistress.
MUSHROOM But if he —
KATTY Pretend to be very ill. Mimic a fine lady that has the vapours or the colic.
MUSHROOM Oh my God — !

> *Enter* O'DOHERTY *with a pistol.*

O'DOHERTY Ah! You're in the dark, my dear. Why is that?
KATTY My mistress is very ill and cannot bear the light.
O'DOHERTY What's her complaint?
MUSHROOM⎫ The colic.
KATTY⎰ The vapours.
O'DOHERTY There's no cure in the dark, Katty. Light the candles.

MUSHROOM No, no, no candles. No lights, dear, please. No lights.

KATTY She has a headache as well as the vapours —

MUSHROOM And the colic.

KATTY And lights increase the headache and the colic —

MUSHROOM And the vapours.

KATTY Let her sit in the dark and she'll be well soon. Are you feeling better now, madam?

MUSHROOM A great deal. But no lights, please, no lights, no lights.

O'DOHERTY (*Softly*) If you prefer no lights, my sweet, then you will have no lights.

MUSHROOM Thank you, my dear.

O'DOHERTY Leave us, Katty. I have some special business with your mistress.

MUSHROOM Special business?

O'DOHERTY Very intimate business, my soul.

MUSHROOM Don't leave, Katty! I have the colic, sir. And the vapours, sir. And, sir, *I have a very bad headache.* (*As* KATTY *leaves*) Katt-eeeee!

O'DOHERTY Now, my dear, I want to talk to you about something that has given me utmost unease, nay indeed the utmost torture of my mind. My dear, I am jealous.

MUSHROOM Jealous?

O'DOHERTY As are half the husbands of the town; and all occasioned by one man — that coxcomb Mushroom.

MUSHROOM He is a very great coxcomb indeed.

O'DOHERTY And a great jackanapes.

MUSHROOM A huge jackanapes, my dear; an enormous jackanapes.

O'DOHERTY And a popinjay?

MUSHROOM Mushroom? A popinjay and a mountebank.

O'DOHERTY And a poltroon?

MUSHROOM And a varlet and a malapert and a macaroni. Oh, what a macaroni!

O'DOHERTY (*To audience*) In other words — a fop, a dandy.

MUSHROOM   Mushroom the Macaroni!

O'DOHERTY   That's good. And a libertine, would you say?

MUSHROOM   Indeed I would say a libertine — and a charlatan — and the colic and the vapours and a headache! Oh, how I despise the man!

O'DOHERTY   Do you, my dear?

MUSHROOM   Thoroughly — without qualification!

O'DOHERTY   Though I must own the fellow has something genteel in him.

MUSHROOM   Oh, yes, my dear, he is a very *pretty* fellow — that all the world allows.

O'DOHERTY   But his prettiness will be his ruin.

MUSHROOM   Will it?

O'DOHERTY   For as he makes it his business and his boast to win the affection of women everywhere he goes, and as he has made conquests of several married women in this town —

MUSHROOM   Mere gossip, my dear. (*To audience*) They always blab, the bitches!

O'DOHERTY   — there are half a dozen husbands of us that have agreed —

MUSHROOM *waits.* O'DOHERTY *does not speak.*

MUSHROOM   Agreed?

O'DOHERTY   To poison him.

MUSHROOM   Poison! But that will be murder, my dear.

O'DOHERTY   It will. But before we get to that, one of our company has vowed that if Mushroom ever enters his house again he will put ten inches of cold iron into the rascal's bowels.

MUSHROOM   Bowels?

O'DOHERTY   Can you imagine?

MUSHROOM   I can — I can — Oh God I can!

O'DOHERTY   As for you, my dear, if I ever catch the fellow ogling you, following you around —

MUSHROOM   An old bat like me?

O'DOHERTY   — even smiling at you, I will put the lining of this little pistol into the very middle of his skull.

MUSHROOM Oh-oh-oh!

O'DOHERTY Why are you all in a tremor, my soul?

MUSHROOM I am ill, dear sir —

O'DOHERTY You have the shaking ague. You are all in a cold sweat.

MUSHROOM — mighty, mighty ill, sir.

O'DOHERTY Indeed you are. (*Calls*) Katty! Katty! You must have help immediately.

KATTY *enters.*

Send for Mr Carnage, the surgeon. He must bleed my wife at once.

KATTY Yes, sir.

MUSHROOM Oooooh.

O'DOHERTY And fetch Dr Fillgrave, too. Tell him my wife is very ill and must be blistered.

KATTY *exits.*

MUSHROOM I'm feeling better already. (*To audience*) What the hell shall I do? I'll certainly be discovered now!

O'DOHERTY How are you now, my dear?

MUSHROOM Oh better, better, a great deal.

O'DOHERTY Splendid. I'll have you bled plentifully and ten good rousing blisters laid on by way of prevention. Just sit still and rest until the medical men come. (*To audience*) When I'm finished with him he'll be cured forever of trespassing upon matrimonial premises.

He exits.

MUSHROOM (*To audience*) Oh God, I wish I were out of this damned country! I've often heard of the wild Irish but never believed it until now! Savages! Barbarians! Poison a man for merely having an intrigue with his wife! We never mind such things in England.

Enter KATTY *and* MRS DIGGERTY *with candles.*

MUSHROOM No lights, please, no lights, no lights!

KATTY It's only me, sir, and Mrs Diggerty.

MUSHROOM If you don't get me out of this damned house, madam, I am a dead man.

MRS DIGGERTY I'm distracted — I can't think — my husband suspects I'm —

MUSHROOM He may suspect you. He's going to shoot *me*! Help me!

MRS DIGGERTY Tell him — tell him you came here in that disguise — just to give him a laugh.

MUSHROOM 'Just to give him a — '! The woman's an idiot! Mrs Katty, help me, please! I have got to get out of this place — now!

KATTY The portmanteau trunk. You might be able to fit into it.

MUSHROOM Anything — anything — dear Mrs Katty. My life is in your hands.

KATTY *has now pulled on stage a trunk which she opens.*

If I escape from this damned country, my dear, I promise you you'll never see — Excellent, Mrs Katty. The very thing.

KATTY Get in. Hurry up. My master's coming.

MUSHROOM Will l fit?

KATTY Quick! Quick!

The trunk is on its end so that when MUSH-ROOM *gets into it he is upright. The door is ajar.*

MUSHROOM Put in my clothes — there — cram me in — buckle me up — will I have enough air? Very well, excellent well, Mrs Katty — it will do — snug, snug, damned snug —

Enter O'DOHERTY; *in his hand a naked sword.*

O'DOHERTY What are you doing with that portmanteau?

KATTY Nothing, sir. We're just —

O'DOHERTY What have you got in there?

MRS DIGGERTY It's only a —

> O'DOHERTY *is about to plunge his sword into the trunk.*

O'DOHERTY Speak this minute or I'll put my sword up to the hilt in it.

MUSHROOM Hold, hold, my dear Diggerty!

O'DOHERTY Who's that?

> *Enter* HAMILTON.

MUSHROOM It's I! It's I!

O'DOHERTY Who is 'I'?

MUSHROOM It's Mushroom. Your friend, Mushroom.

HAMILTON What's the coxcomb up to now?

MUSHROOM (*Peeping out the door*) It's the Count — your friend, the Count.

O'DOHERTY The Count, indeed. Or is it the Countess?

HAMILTON Is he going on his holidays?

MUSHROOM I can explain everything, Diggerty.

> O'DOHERTY *shuts the trunk.*

O'DOHERTY I'm sure you can, Mushroom. And I'll give you every opportunity. For we have invited half the town in tonight and they all want a peep at you. Give me a hand here. He's got to be transported downstairs to greet our guests. That's it.

> *One end of the trunk is lifted — and dropped. Another end is lifted (so that* MUSHROOM *is now upside down) — and dropped. The trunk is stood on its end — and tipped over. Throughout all*

this MUSHROOM *squeals in terror* — '*Help! Help!*
Let me out! I'm suffocating! You're killing me!
Help! Help!' Eventually KATTY *and* HAMILTON
and MRS DIGGERTY *drag the trunk off. As they do:*

O'DOHERTY   Careful, there. That's a valuable parcel. And we've
got to keep him healthy at least for a few more
hours. (*To audience*) And that's the end of our
story: How Count Mushroom made himself an
object for a farce. But then if every fine lady and
every coxcomb in this town were turned into a
farce we'd be the merriest people in all Europe.
But ours is over for tonight.
Indeed I think it's fairly ended.
The coxcomb's punished;
The fine Irish lady's mended.

Suddenly MRS DIGGERTY*'s head appears round
the door.*

MRS DIGGERTY   (*Winking broadly at the audience*) For the time
being!

A MONTH IN THE COUNTRY

after Turgenev

Preface

Turgenev called *A Month in the Country* a comedy, just as Chekhov called *The Cherry Orchard* and *The Seagull* comedies. They were not formally categorizing these plays, I believe, but wished to indicate their own amused and ironic attitude to their characters and the situations those characters found themselves in. But I think that to call *A Month in the Country* a comedy today is restricting to the play: it imposes a reading on the text and suggests a response to it that could be inhibiting to actors and audience. *A Month in the Country* is certainly not a tragedy. Neither is it a comedy. Perhaps we should settle for 'a play in five scenes'.

I have attributed to the characters the ages given in T A Greenan's standard text. But I think that all of those parts could and perhaps should be played by slightly older actors. And I trust I will not offend the purists by tinkering with the Russian names and forms of address.

A literal translation of Turgenev's text was done for me by Christopher Heaney. From it I have composed this very free version. In places it may not be reverent to the original but nowhere, I hope, is it unfaithful to its spirit.

Brian Friel

Ivan Turgenev (1818-1883)

Two years before his death, on one of his compulsive return visits to Russia, Turgenev stopped off at St Petersburg to visit Tolstoy and Sonya at Yasnaya Polyana. The date was August 22nd, 1881. It was Sonya's birthday. The house was full of guests. Turgenev was then a celebrated writer with a huge — Tolstoy thought inflated — reputation. To the young guests at the party, most of whom had never been beyond Petersburg, he was mesmerizing, an exotic: well over six feet, handsome, charming, a bachelor, magnificently dressed, multilingual, in this gathering flamboyantly, even aggressively, European; and of course internationally famous. They questioned him about his work, about London, about literary trends, about his Oxford degree. Their hunger and their awe lured him into garrulity and exaggeration. Avoiding Tolstoy's cold eye he launched into witty stories about the latest fashions in Paris. And then suddenly the sixty-three-year-old writer jumped to his feet, threw off his gold jacket, stuck his thumbs into his silk waistcoat and gave an exuberant demonstration of the dance that was all the rage on the French vaudeville stage — the cancan. After a few minutes, breathless and exhausted, he collapsed into an armchair.

That night in his diary Tolstoy, younger than Turgenev by ten years but more knowing by a score, commemorated the event — not his wife's birthday but Turgenev's exhibition. He wrote, 'August 22. Turgenev. Sad.'

The entry was tart but off-centre. Turgenev was not sad. He was confused. All his days he was a ditherer, racked between irreconcilable beliefs and compulsions. An instinctive revolutionary who needed the complacency of conservatism. A Slavophile whose heart loved Russia with an intuitive passion but who offered his mind to Europe to mould. A writer who was never sure whether he was a dramatist, a novelist, a poet or an essayist. A bachelor who throughout his entire life loved the married Pauline Viardot faithfully and without reservation — but who fathered a child by a servant girl and had several casual affairs with discreet women. A dramatist who believed his plays should be read, not performed, and who could not make up his mind whether to call this play *The Student* or *Two Women* or *A Month in the Country*. A sportsman who enjoyed grouse shooting in Scotland and painting in the south of France but who was always haunted by a sense that real life, a life of content and fulfilment, had somehow eluded him but was available elsewhere, if only he could locate just where.

But for all his vacillations the inner man, the assured artist, was organized and practical. With what Graham Greene once called 'admirable domestic economy' he marshalled all these irreconcilables and put them to use in his work. Vacillation, the inability to act decisively, the longing to be other, to be elsewhere, became the very core of his dramatic action. He fashioned a new kind of dramatic situation and a new kind of dramatic character where for the first time psychological and poetic elements create a theatre of moods and where the action resides in internal emotion and secret turmoil and not in external events. We now have a name for that kind of drama: we call it Chekhovian. But in *A Month in the Country* Turgenev had written Chekhovian characters and situations forty-six years before Chekhov wrote his first fully Chekhovian play, *The Seagull*.

A Month in the Country was first performed at the Maly Theatre in 1872, more than twenty years after it was completed. The newness of its form baffled audiences and critics. Because it eluded classification they called it 'old-fashioned' and 'undramatic'. Turgenev had to wait a further seven years for a new production and a warmer reception. Then came Chekhov a decade later; and the new form was crafted to shimmering perfection. The undramatic became the new drama. And in the years to follow *A Month in the Country* found acceptance in the slipstream of Chekhov's astonishing achievement. The term metabiosis in chemistry denotes a mode of living in which one organism is dependent on another for the preparation of an environment in which it can live. The relationship between Turgenev and Chekhov was richly metabiotic. *A Month in the Country* was before its time and moved haltingly across unmapped territory. But it established the necessary environment in which Chekhov could blossom. And once Chekhov had achieved his full stature, once Chekhovian drama was confidently established, the environment was again ready for the reclamation and reassessment and full understanding of Turgenev's pioneering work. So they gave life to each other. And between them they changed the face of European drama.

Brian Friel

Characters

ARKADY SERGEYEVICH ISLAYEV (36), rich landlord
NATALYA PETROVNA (29), his wife
VERA ALEKSANDROVNA (17), Natalya's ward
ANNA SEMYONOVNA ISLAYEVA (58), Arkady's widowed mother
LIZAVETA BOGDANOVNA (37), Anna's companion
HERR SCHAAF (45), German tutor
MICHEL ALEKSANDROVICH RAKITIN (30), family friend
ALEKSEY NIKOLAYEVICH BELYAYEV (21), student/tutor
AFANASY IVANOVICH BOLSHINTSOV (57), neighbouring landowner
IGNATY ILYICH SHPIGELSKY (40), local doctor
MATVEY (43), servant
KATYA (20), servant

Time and Place

The action takes place on the Islayev estate at the beginning of the 1840s. A period of about a day passes between each scene.

Music

John Field (1782-1837)
No. 5 Nocturne in B-flat major: *Andantino*
No. 9 Nocturne in E-flat major: *Andantino*
No. 18 Midi in E major: *Allegretto*

A Month in the Country was first produced at the Gate Theatre, Dublin, on 4 August 1992, with the following cast:

NATALYA	Catherine Byrne
ARKADY	Mark Lambert
VERA	Karen Ardiff
ANNA	Joan O'Hara
LIZAVETA	Susan Fitzgerald
SCHAAF	John Kavanagh
MICHEL	Lorcan Cranitch
ALEKSEY	J D Kelleher
BOLSHINTSOV	John Cowley
SHPIGELSKY	Donal McCann
MATVEY	Mal Whyte
KATYA	Antoine Byrne

Directed by	Joe Dowling
Designed by	Eileen Diss
Costumes by	Dani Everett
Lighting by	Mick Hughes
Music played by	John O'Conor
Stage direction by	Lita O'Connell
Assistant stage managers	Liz Nugent
	Arnold Fanning

for Brian B with love

ACT ONE

Scene One

Summer afternoon in the early 1840s.
The drawing room in the Islayev home on their remote and wealthy
estate. Three doors lead from the drawing room: one right to the rest
of the house; one left to the yard, farm etc; and one centre to the garden
area. (Left and right from the point of view of the audience.)

Upstage left three people are playing Preference (a kind of whist) at
a large table: HERR SCHAAF, *the German tutor of Kolya, the ten-year-*
old son of the house; ANNA SEMYONOVNA, *the widowed head of the*
household; and LIZAVETA BOGDANOVNA, *Anna's companion.*

Downstage left NATALYA PETROVNA *(Arkady's wife, Anna's*
daughter-in-law) is painting. Close to her on a stool sits MICHEL
ALEKSANDROVICH RAKITIN, *a friend of the family. He is staring into*
the middle distance. A book hangs between his legs. He is listening
inattentively to the music coming from an adjoining room.

In the adjoining room VERA ALEKSANDROVNA, *Natalya's ward,*
plays a John Field nocturne on the piano — No. 9 in E-flat major.

SCHAAF *again deals the cards. He then cuts the remainder of the*
pack and holds up the top card.

SCHAAF   Hartz are trumpery.
LIZAVETA   *(So anxious to please)* Sorry? Sorry? I —
SCHAAF   Hartz are trumpery.
LIZAVETA   *(To* ANNA*)* I'm afraid I don't under-
ANNA   He means hearts, my dear.
SCHAAF   *Ja.* Hartz.
LIZAVETA   Ah.
ANNA   The word is trump, Herr Schaaf. Trumpery is a dif-
ferent thing altogether. Trump. Hearts are trump.
SCHAAF   Trump. *Danke schön.* Hartz are trump. *(Pause)* You
come to the front, Lizaveta.

LIZAVETA I beg your pardon? (*To* ANNA) What do I do? (*To* SCHAAF) Sorry, I —

SCHAAF You come to the front.

ANNA I think perhaps he means you lead.

SCHAAF You lead. *Danke schön.*

> KATYA, *demure and knowing, enters with a tray and removes the tea things.*

LIZAVETA Ah, yes — of course — I lead — I lead —

NATALYA (*Softly, with brittle, almost frantic smile*) Dear God — good God — dear, good kind God.

> MICHEL *leans over and squeezes her hand in consolation.*

LIZAVETA Would you like me to lead the four of spades, Madam?

ANNA What I would like, my sweet Lizaveta — (*Controlling herself*) There was a time when playing a game of cards before dinner was one of life's less complex pleasures. (*To* KATYA) And this glass, too, Katya.

KATYA Certainly, Madam.

SCHAAF (*Roguishly*) This tea was *gut*, Katya.

KATYA I'm glad you enjoyed it.

SCHAAF *Schön — sehr schön.*

KATYA You're very welcome, Herr Schaaf.

SCHAAF (*To* ANNA) What is Vera play on piano?

ANNA It's a John Field nocturne, isn't it? (*To* NATALYA) Isn't that John Field, Natalya?

NATALYA Is it? I don't know.

ANNA All of a sudden she's a very mature pianist, your little ward.

NATALYA She should be out in the sun. (*To* KATYA) Tell Miss Vera that's enough practice. Go outside and play games or something.

KATYA Yes, Madam.

ANNA I met John Field in Moscow once — shortly after my husband's death; oh, thirty years ago. A very

handsome man with that angular Irish face. Have
I told you that story, Herr Schaaf?

SCHAAF And he say to you, 'The most interesting women
are widowers.'

ANNA Widows, Herr Schaaf. 'The most interesting women
are widows.' There are times when I think your
vocabulary is wilfully inadequate. And that's my
trick, thank you very much. And now I think I'll
try . . . this.

NATALYA Read some more of Mr Sterne to me, Michel.
We're at page 115.

MICHEL I thought I was boring you.

NATALYA Of course you're not boring me. Please.

MICHEL 'I have dropped the curtain over this scene for a
minute — to remind you of one thing and to inform
you of another. What I have to inform you comes,
I own, a little out of its due course — for it should
have been — '

NATALYA Have you seen Arkady today?

MICHEL At lunch. And this morning down at the dam.

NATALYA Showing off the new sluice gate he invented?

MICHEL It's a very clever design.

NATALYA Bubbling with energy and enthusiasm?

MICHEL Have you seen it?

NATALYA My energetic husband — the dam enthusiast.
Amn't I blessed?

MICHEL Enthusiasm can be a virtue.

NATALYA I think it's a vice.

MICHEL Well of course if it's carried to —

NATALYA Yes, it's a virtue — yes, it's a vice. Don't you know
that nothing bores a woman more quickly than an
excessive desire to please?

MICHEL So you want me to disagree with whatever you —

NATALYA Oh God, I want — I want — I want — (*Controlling
herself and flashing a smile*) I want you to read to
me . . . please . . .

*He spreads his hands and searches for the place in
the book.*

ANNA   Natalya.

NATALYA   Yes?

ANNA   Is little Kolya down at the dam with his father?

NATALYA   He's out in the garden with his new tutor.

ANNA   As long as he has his head covered in that sun.

NATALYA   He'll be fine, Grandmother. Stop fussing.

SCHAAF   (*To* LIZAVETA) Once again hartz.

LIZAVETA   Sorry? (*To* ANNA) Sorry?

SCHAAF   Hartz are trumpery once more.

ANNA   Why should one battle with fate? Hartz are indeed trumpery and once again you come up to the front, Lizaveta.

LIZAVETA   What do you want me to do, Madam?

ANNA   Dear, sweet girl, play a card — play any card at all — what does it matter?

LIZAVETA   All right. I'll hazard the only heart I have.

ANNA   Why not. Hazard away.

MICHEL   Your son has a new tutor?

NATALYA   Got him a few weeks ago — Aleksey Belyayev. See what happens when your back is turned.

MICHEL   Not another randy old goat like Schaaf?

NATALYA   He's twenty-one; open; eager; energetic.

MICHEL   Handsome?

NATALYA   Only just graduated; hungry for the world; and thrilled with himself to have landed a summer job with such exciting people.

MICHEL   Enthusiasm — good!

NATALYA   You won't like him. He hasn't enough grace for you.

MICHEL   He's only twenty-one.

NATALYA   And that's why I like him.

MICHEL   Because he's graceless or because he's twenty-one?

NATALYA   But mostly, I think, because he's so unlike us: he's so . . . unjaded.

MICHEL   So this is going to be another day of little needles, is it?

She takes the book from his hands, leaves it on the floor, and takes his hands affectionately in hers.

NATALYA No, it's not. I'm sorry, Michel. Just talk to me. Not serious talk — silly talk — chatter — gossip. Tell me about your visit to the Krinistins.

MICHEL Real meaty gossip?

NATALYA The meatier the better.

MICHEL Right. Seven months married and already the Krinistins are bored with one another.

She withdraws her hands in shock.

NATALYA Oh God, no! Oh God, that's terrible!

MICHEL Sorry. I shouldn't have —

NATALYA Who told you that? They never admitted that?

MICHEL It was palpable. Bored with each other. Bored with me. And after two days I was bored with them.

NATALYA But you love the Krinistins, Michel.

MICHEL My oldest and closest friends.

NATALYA I don't understand that.

MICHEL That we bored one another? Yes, you do, Natalya. Nobody better.

NATALYA And I won't believe it.

MICHEL That love and boredom aren't perfectly compatible?

NATALYA What does that mean?

MICHEL Maybe even complementary — that's closer to it!

NATALYA I get really angry when you talk like that, Michel. Because you're not talking to me at all: you're playing a private little game of your own. You're like those lace-makers in those gloomy, airless rooms — each one totally isolated, totally concentrated on those minute, complex, subtle little stitches. As if nothing in the world mattered but those ridiculous little stitches.

MICHEL All I suggested was —

NATALYA That's the way we all live here (*everybody in the room*) — making minute, private little stitches. I'm sick of gloomy, airless, constricting rooms.

MICHEL You are angry with me today. Has something happened while I was away?

She looks closely at him for a second; then squeezes his shoulder briefly.

NATALYA You are a kind man and a subtle man and a man of great delicacy. But there are times when I think you know nothing about me.

ANNA And since I have no hartz I cross with the seven of clubs. Which gives me — (*counts*) — four — five — six — seven tricks. And game.

SCHAAF Not game yet.

ANNA Oh, yes. Game now, Herr Schaaf.

SCHAAF (*Very angry, to* LIZAVETA) Why you come forward with spade? You know I have diamond Kaiser!

ANNA Diamond king.

SCHAAF So why you come forward with spade?

LIZAVETA I thought — I don't know — I come forward with spade because I think —

ANNA Please! No post mortems. Thank you kindly, Herr Schaaf — Lizaveta.˙

SCHAAF With Lizaveta Bogdanovna ever again I refuse to couple!

LIZAVETA What do you — !

ANNA I think perhaps you mean to partner, Herr Schaaf. To couple is a different . . . My shawl, please, Lizaveta. Time for a breath of air before we eat.

Suddenly we hear ALEKSEY BELYAYEV *in the distance.*

ALEKSEY (*Very slowly*) One — two — three — four — five — (*very rapidly*) nineteen-twenty-seven-seventy-six-eighty-four — (*very slowly*) ninety-seven — ninety-eight — ninety-nine — one hundred! Here I come, Kolya!

NATALYA (*To* MICHEL) That's him.

ALEKSEY I can smell you! I will eat you up!

NATALYA The new tutor.

MICHEL He cheats.

NATALYA It's a game, Michel — just a game.

And suddenly ALEKSEY BELYAYEV *bursts into the room. He is halfway across the floor before he realizes where he is. Now he stops, freezes with embarrassment and looks from one staring face to the other.*

Nobody rescues him. He begins to withdraw backwards. As he does:

ALEKSEY I'm — I'm sorry — forgive me — Kolya and I — we were playing a game of . . .

ANNA My grandson's not here, young man. Try the gazebo — that's a favourite hiding place of his.

ALEKSEY I'll try that — thank you — I'm really sorry for —

NATALYA Why are you apologizing, Aleksey?

ALEKSEY Because I — thank you — I'm —

He hesitates for a second, then suddenly turns and dashes off.

ANNA Himself and Kolya together — you would scarcely know which was the pupil.

LIZAVETA Indeed, it would be hard to tell.

MICHEL (*To* NATALYA) The new tutor?

NATALYA Aleksey Belyayev. What do you think?

MICHEL Seems a fine young man. Maybe a bit . . . unfinished?

NATALYA We'll finish him, Michel! We'll complete his education! That'll be our game for the summer: Polish the Tutor!

MICHEL He interests you, doesn't he?

NATALYA Interests me?

MICHEL Does he know he has impressed you?

NATALYA Michel, he is only a —

MICHEL He must be very pleased with himself.

NATALYA I have no idea what he thinks or how he thinks. Nor have you. People like Master Belyayev are altogether different from us. We know nothing about them — we're so busy with our little stitches. Trouble is, for all our — (*she mimes lace-making*) —

we know very little about ourselves either. (*She looks at his eager face and tousles his hair*) Just teasing — that's all. And if I can't tease you, who can I tease?

MICHEL (*Looking around*) Any volunteers?

NATALYA Because you know what you are to me, Michel.

MICHEL Tell me again.

NATALYA You know very well. I don't have to say it.

SCHAAF (*To* LIZAVETA) The cat's gone! Who stole the cat? Was it you?

LIZAVETA Cat? What cat?

SCHAAF It was sitting there. Did you stole it?

ANNA Not quite right, Herr Schaaf. The pool of money is called the kitty.

SCHAAF Ah.

ANNA And I took it because I won the last hand.

MATVEY *appears at the door.*

MATVEY Excuse me, please — Doctor Shpigelsky has —

DOCTOR SHPIGELSKY *enters.*

DOCTOR He's here, Matvey. How's the arthritis?

MATVEY A lot better, Doctor, thank you. Those pills are great.

DOCTOR Good. Not interrupting, am I? (*Kisses* ANNA'S *hand*) Afternoon, Madam.

ANNA Welcome, Doctor Shpigelsky.

DOCTOR Thank you. And Lizaveta — (*Kisses her hand*) — Well, if we're not elegant today.

LIZAVETA Doctor!

DOCTOR And Herr Schaaf.

SCHAAF *Guten Tag.*

DOCTOR And the beautiful Natalya Petrovna. (*Kisses her hand*)

NATALYA How are you, Doctor?

DOCTOR How are you?

MICHEL Prickly.

DOCTOR No, she's not! (*A parody of taking her pulse*) Oh,

very fast! But nothing that a good laugh wouldn't cure. Michel, how are you?

MICHEL Managing.

DOCTOR Oh-ho, don't like the sound of that.

NATALYA You have the news of the countryside; bring some fresh air in here; cure us all; give us a good laugh.

DOCTOR Right! A laugh . . . a laugh . . . Yes! The stationmaster told me this one last night. Two farm labourers crawling to work at dawn on Monday morning. One says to the other, 'I am destroyed; I was with this enormously fat woman last night and about five in the morning she caught me by — ' Yes. No, no, that's not funny at all — not a bit. Ever since his wife had those triplets, for some reason that stationmaster has become very coarse . . .

Silence.

In point of fact the story I did intend telling you was about this man who comes knocking at the doctor's door in the middle of the night. 'Doctor, Doctor, please help me: I'm suffering from very bad amnesia.' 'When did you get this?' 'Get what, Doctor?'

Again total silence. LIZAVETA *attempts a polite laugh — it dies too.*

Well, you did encourage me.

ANNA You are a solicitous doctor and that's much more important than being an indifferent comedian. (*She gathers her belongings*) Oh dear; needles in my legs when I sit too long.

NATALYA Then you shouldn't sit too long, should you?

ANNA Indeed . . .

As she exits — to SCHAAF:

Trump — lead — widow — kitty. Got those?

SCHAAF *Ja.* With latitude, Madam.

ANNA With gratitude, Herr Schaaf. One step at a time —
no big leaps. (*To* LIZAVETA) I think I'll lie down for
a while.

LIZAVETA That's a very good idea.

DOCTOR (*As* LIZAVETA *passes*) Brown suits you.

LIZAVETA It's maroon.

DOCTOR Suits you even better.

> *She blushes and exits after* ANNA. SCHAAF *picks
> up his books.* NATALYA *puts away her painting
> materials.* SHPIGELSKY *goes to* MICHEL.

Atmosphere a bit chilly, is it?

MICHEL Is it?

DOCTOR Bit edgy, is she (*Natalya*)?

MICHEL Is she?

DOCTOR Sorry — sorry — read it wrong again. Herr Schaaf,
wie ist Ihres Befinden?

SCHAAF *Wie ist* Ihr *Befinden.*

DOCTOR Ah — *Ihr.*

SCHAAF And in my riposte I respond, 'I am vell.'

> *As* SCHAAF *exits:*

DOCTOR (*To himself*) You are vell. Velly damn good. You
make me velly damn happy . . . Natalya, have you
a second?

NATALYA Yes?

DOCTOR By ourselves.

NATALYA Clean those brushes, Michel. (*To* DOCTOR) What is
it?

DOCTOR Somebody I know quite well — a friend actually
— a very close friend in fact — he has asked me
if I would ask you what — what — what hopes
— plans — you have in mind for the wonderful
pianist.

NATALYA The who?

DOCTOR For your ward. For Vera.

NATALYA What do you mean — plans?

DOCTOR Hopes — expectations — aspirations. What this acquaintance — this friend — asked me to ask you is —

NATALYA He wants to marry her.

Brief pause.

DOCTOR Nail on head.

NATALYA You're really joking now, Doctor Shpigelsky.

DOCTOR Deadly serious.

NATALYA Your acquaintance — your closest friend — wants to marry Vera!

DOCTOR A very genuine proposal.

NATALYA Vera's a child, Doctor!

DOCTOR My friend suggests that —

NATALYA She's barely seventeen!

DOCTOR Nowadays young ladies of seventeen are —

NATALYA And who is this close friend?

DOCTOR Now — now — please — please — one step at a time. And when you think it over you may see that —

He breaks off because VERA *runs on — an entrance like Aleksey's. Her face is flushed and animated.*

NATALYA (*In admonition*) Doctor!

He puts his finger to his lips and smiles at her.

VERA (*To* MICHEL) Have you any glue — or paste — or sticky stuff of any sort?

MICHEL (*Feeling his pockets*) Certainly have, Vera. Never move without it.

VERA You are a clown, Michel!

MICHEL What is it for?

VERA Aleksey and I are making a kite. Well, Aleksey is. For Kolya.

MICHEL (*Leaving*) Leave it to Michel.

He exits.

NATALYA Aren't you saying hello to Doctor Shpigelsky, Vera?
VERA Hello, Doctor.
DOCTOR How are you, young lady?
NATALYA Can't you see how she is? Look at those shoes! What in God's name have you been doing, child?
VERA We were down at the dam. You should see the new sluice gates Arkady designed — they're wonderful. Then we played rounders on the old tennis court. Aleksey's a great runner and he —
NATALYA Aleksey Belyayev's our new tutor.
VERA And now we're making a kite. Aleksey can make a Chinese box kite.

MICHEL *returns.*

MICHEL This one lasts a day. This one lasts forever. (*To* NATALYA) Which one should she take?
NATALYA Just give her some glue, Michel.
VERA Can I have them both?
MICHEL Certainly can.

VERA *kisses him quickly.*

VERA You're great. Thanks. We'll probably use the forever stuff.
NATALYA Careful in that sun, child.
DOCTOR And I have a patient to see. And I've never seen a Chinese box kite. (*To* VERA) May I watch?
NATALYA (*In admonition again*) Doctor!

Again he puts his finger to his lips as he exits with VERA.

DOCTOR Ze velly soul of discletion.

As soon as they leave MICHEL *takes* NATALYA *in his arms from behind.*

MICHEL Something's wrong.
NATALYA Nothing's wrong now.
MICHEL Talk to me about it.

He turns her to face him.

NATALYA I'm so restless, so irritable all day. But I'm fine now. Why are you searching my face like that?
MICHEL Just to look at you is a great . . . happiness.
NATALYA You are the kindest man in the world —
MICHEL Natalya —
NATALYA — and the most gentle and the most considerate and the most understanding. And you're so permanent. What would I do without you?
MICHEL Only you know the answer to that.
NATALYA When I'm with you I feel so centred. Just to be with you — this is the only happiness I want. I mean that with all my heart.
MICHEL Beautiful Natalya.
NATALYA Hundreds of women would envy me, wouldn't they?
MICHEL Thousands! Millions!
NATALYA Oh, yes, they would. To be loved by such a good man? Oh, yes, that must be enviable. Strange, isn't it?
MICHEL I don't know what's strange anymore. I just know I am in love with you.
NATALYA And I love you, too.
MICHEL Do you?
NATALYA Yes, I do. You know I love you. And the moment I say that, the moment I make that acknowledgement, I think . . .
MICHEL Go on.
NATALYA I think: that man has never made me suffer; that man has never made me cry; and if I have never cried because of him, I can't really love him, can

	I? Sounds ridiculous, doesn't it? Is it ridiculous?
MICHEL	Maybe not.
NATALYA	Probably is. I don't know. How long have we known each other?
MICHEL	Years and years and years.
NATALYA	That makes us old friends, doesn't it?
MICHEL	Is that what we are?
NATALYA	But it does, doesn't it? We *are* friends, aren't we?
MICHEL	Let's talk about something else, Natalya. The little shred of happiness I cling to, I feel it slipping away from me.

ARKADY ISLAYEV's *voice, off*:

ARKADY	Tell him to keep the water at that level, Matvey.
MATVEY	(*Off*) Yessir.
NATALYA	Arkady. I can't face him now.
MICHEL	Natalya —
NATALYA	(*Leaving*) Not just at the moment. I'll be straight back.
ARKADY	(*Off*) And we'll not open the gates until the water rises another six inches. (*He enters*) Ah, Michel! And how are you today, Michel? Are you well?
MICHEL	We had lunch together, Arkady.
ARKADY	Had we? Cold partridge! — Of course we had! And we agreed we both prefer partridge to grouse. (*Searching through drawers of cabinet*) Where did I leave . . . ? (*Finds document*) Ah! (*To* MICHEL) The Russian workman never fails to astonish me, Michel. You see that group of men I have down at the weir? As bright and as keen a group of men you could ask for, provided — and maybe this is characteristic of the Russian psyche at every level of society — provided you lead them with intelligence but especially with authority — where's Natalya?
MICHEL	She was around a moment ago.
ARKADY	But leave them for ten minutes without that leadership and — (*claps his hands once*) — chaos! Aston-

ishing, isn't it?

MICHEL Is the new dam nearly finished?

ARKADY This is what I want — I think. Not to be pedantic, Michel, it's a weir, not a dam. And yes, it's almost complete. Why are you laughing at me?

MICHEL Just smiling at the way you —

ARKADY Yes, I suppose I am slightly . . . what am I?

MICHEL I was smiling because you —

ARKADY Yes, I always seem to be simultaneously very busy and very confused, don't I? Yes, I'm not unaware of that. But there was a time — oh, long before you and I became friends — oh, yes, there was a time, strange as it may seem — when —when I was as busy but much, much less confused. Ivan hasn't been here?

MICHEL Who?

ARKADY That new tutor Natalya found somewhere. Ivan something.

MICHEL Isn't his name Aleksey?

ARKADY Whatever. I gave him a simple errand to do and I'm afraid he's —

ALEKSEY *enters.*

Just asking about you, young man. You left the grease gun with the foreman?

ALEKSEY Yes. And now he wants the plans with the blue ribbon.

ARKADY The blue — the blue — the blue — Here we are. That's blue, isn't it? (*Handing the document over*) Good man. You two know each other, don't you?

MICHEL We haven't actually spoken to one another.

ARKADY Ah. Michel Rakitin — Ivan — sorry — Aleksey Belyayev. Why do I keep calling you Ivan? Anyhow. Master Belyayev is teaching our Kolya — what are you teaching him?

ALEKSEY French and English.

ARKADY Exactly — French and English.

NATALYA *enters.*

Ah, Natalya! You look just astonishing. Doesn't my astonishing wife look just . . . astonishing? Give me a kiss. Ah. And guess what has arrived.

NATALYA   What?

ARKADY   Guess.

NATALYA   How can I guess, Arkady?

ARKADY   The new winnowing machine! Outside in the yard! And it is just astonishing. Come out and see it.

NATALYA   I don't understand those machines of yours, Arkady. Michel will go with you.

MICHEL   Yes!

ARKADY   You don't understand machines either, Michel, do you? Doesn't matter. Just to look at this thing is an unqualified pleasure. Astonishing!

> ARKADY *and* MICHEL *leave together.* ALEKSEY *moves to follow them.*

NATALYA   Where are you going?

ALEKSEY   I've got to give this to —

NATALYA   Sit there. You're almost a month here and we haven't had a chance to talk. (*Points to chair*) There.

> *He sits stiffly.*

Have we?

ALEKSEY   Have we — ?

NATALYA   Talked.

ALEKSEY   Oh. Yes — yes — no — no.

NATALYA   I make you uneasy for some reason. Are your parents alive?

ALEKSEY   My mother died when I was a baby.

NATALYA   Your father?

ALEKSEY   He's still alive.

NATALYA   Brothers and sisters?

ALEKSEY   One sister.

NATALYA   Are you and she close?

ALEKSEY We are even though —

NATALYA What's her name?

ALEKSEY Natalya.

NATALYA That's my name.

ALEKSEY Is it?

NATALYA Natalya.

ALEKSEY It's a nice name.

NATALYA You like it?

ALEKSEY It's her name, too — my sister's. Natalya.

NATALYA You've already told me that. Do you love your sister?

ALEKSEY We're very close.

NATALYA How do you find Kolya?

ALEKSEY Great. He's bright and quick and —

NATALYA He thinks you're wonderful. Every night before he goes to sleep he tells me everything you've done together during the day. I think he loves you. Were you and your father close?

ALEKSEY (*Laughs*) My father never looked near us. He was a sort of itinerant labourer — went wherever the work was. And never sober. Natalya and I, we were — I suppose — dragged up by neighbours.

NATALYA You sing very well.

ALEKSEY Me!

NATALYA I heard you in the garden.

ALEKSEY God! When?

NATALYA Yesterday evening.

ALEKSEY Oh my God!

NATALYA One of these days, when we get to know each other a lot better, you'll sing a song for me.

ALEKSEY I really can't —

NATALYA You won't sing for me?

ALEKSEY It's not that I won't — it's just that I —

NATALYA So you will.

ALEKSEY Honest to God, I'm terrible!

NATALYA But you will, Aleksey — won't you?

ALEKSEY If you insist, then —

NATALYA Just one song. That's not a lot to ask, is it? Will you do that? For me?

She holds her hand to him. He takes it. Then in a moment of confusion and warmth kisses it. NATALYA *quickly withdraws it. At the moment of the kiss* DOCTOR SHPIGELSKY *enters. There is general embarrassment. Then* SHPIGELSKY *speaks rapidly.*

DOCTOR Just had a look at old Ivan, the blacksmith . . . You know, while I was in the house . . . two birds — one stone . . . Ninety if he's a day, old Ivan . . . (*To* ALEKSEY) Shpigelsky, local GP. And you're the new tutor. Watched you making a kite out there. Anyhow, at death's door last Saturday, Ivan. But today? Sitting at the kitchen table, knocking back vodka and stuffing himself with pancakes. The doctor's dilemma, young man: if you cure nobody, you're never sent for — consequently no income. Cure everybody, you end up with no patients — consequently no income. What's the solution?

ALEKSEY If you'll excuse me, I've to give this to the foreman.

NATALYA That can wait. We're about to eat and —

VERA *runs on and goes straight to* ALEKSEY.

VERA Come on, Aleksey! We're waiting for you! What's keeping you? Kolya wants you to attach the tail.

NATALYA Calm down, child. What's all the excitement?

VERA Kolya sent me up for Aleksey. (*To* ALEKSEY) Where have you been?

NATALYA *adjusts* VERA's *dress and hair.*

NATALYA Look at the mess you're in. What way is that collar? That's better. Now. We're going to eat. Are you staying the night, Doctor?

DOCTOR May I?

NATALYA You're welcome.

DOCTOR Love to. My old horse is as wheezy as myself. Love to. Thank you.

VERA *and* ALEKSEY *have been whispering and laughing together.*

VERA Just as the swing was at its height, off she came like a ton of bricks.

ALEKSEY Nanny!

VERA Flat on her big fat bottom!

ALEKSEY She did not! Great!

VERA Made a huge crater in the ground!

ALEKSEY Too good for her!

VERA 'Help me! My back's broken!'

NATALYA What's this? Did somebody have an accident?

VERA Nanny fell off the swing.

NATALYA What was Nanny doing on the swing?

VERA Swinging.

NATALYA Vera, please. Was she hurt?

VERA Only her bottom.

VERA *and* ALEKSEY *laugh again.*

NATALYA That swing is dangerous, Aleksey.

ALEKSEY No, it's safe now. I fixed it this morning.

NATALYA Nobody is to play on it again.

ALEKSEY But it's quite —

NATALYA Nobody. Is that understood?

ALEKSEY Yes.

NATALYA You two go ahead into the dining room. We'll join you in a minute.

VERA *and* ALEKSEY *exit.*

Hand me that (*paint*) box, Doctor. About that suggestion of yours.

DOCTOR Suggestion?

NATALYA Your proposition — your friend's proposal.

DOCTOR Ah! About Vera and —

NATALYA Yes. About Vera. Let me think about that, Doctor.

DOCTOR For as long as you like.

NATALYA Yes, I'll give that some thought.

DOCTOR Good.

NATALYA And then perhaps we'll talk.

*She offers him her arm and they go out to the
dining room.*
    End of Scene One.

ACT ONE

Scene Two

The following day. A garden adjoining the house. A birch tree, a gazebo, a garden seat. From the distance the sound of Kolya doing five-finger exercises on the piano.

KATYA is on the stage. Bed sheets on the grass. She is folding them and putting them into a laundry basket. As she does she sings:

KATYA 'There are many . . . ' etc.

MATVEY (*Off, softly*) Katya? . . . Katya?

> *She picks up the sheets and dashes into the gazebo.*
> MATVEY *enters.*

MATVEY (*Urgently, nervously*) Katya? Are you here? Katya, I just want to — You're hiding on me! Why are you hiding on me?

KATYA I'm working, Matvey. Can't you see?

MATVEY We've got to talk, Katya.

KATYA Have we?

MATVEY Yes — yes — yes! (*His arm around her*) You've changed, Katya. What has happened to you?

KATYA You're hurting me.

MATVEY Sorry. (*Releases her*) Something has happened. Did I do something? Say something? Why do you keep avoiding me now?

KATYA Now?

MATVEY Yes — now! There was a time when you were — when I thought you were —

KATYA When you jumped to certain alarming conclusions, Matvey.

MATVEY I'm crazy about you, Katya. You know I am.

KATYA   When you made certain distressing assumptions you had no right to make.

MATVEY   At the dance — and that's only a month ago — you told me that —

KATYA   That I enjoyed your company — on occasion — for brief periods.

MATVEY   Oh God, Katya love, please —

KATYA   We have discussed you at length on several occasions.

MATVEY   Who has?

KATYA   Mother and I.

MATVEY   What does that mean?

KATYA   She says that the gap between our ages — actually the word she used was 'chasm' — it is so large —

MATVEY   I'm only forty-three!

KATYA   And so disquieting —

MATVEY   I'm full of vigour!

KATYA   Indeed so unbridgeable that the possibility of a permanent and a mutually fulfilling relationship between us is — again to use her own word — 'pale'.

MATVEY   If your bloody mother would —

KATYA   Careful!

MATVEY   If we were left alone, Katya —

KATYA   So her advice to me is to give my consideration to gentlemen who are closer to me in years and in temperament and in spiritual disposition.

MATVEY   (*Shocked, awed at this*) Jesus Christ!

KATYA   And the curious thing is she likes you.

MATVEY   I never met the woman in my life, Katya!

KATYA   Well, what she knows about you — what I've told her. Every weekend she enquires about your rheumatism.

MATVEY   You told her about that?

KATYA   Her prediction is that within three years you'll be crippled and — (*She breaks off*) Careful — there's the Hun.

Enter SCHAAF *with a fishing rod.*

MATVEY Damn the Hun!
KATYA Move! Do you want us both sacked!
MATVEY Katya —
KATYA Move!

> *Distraught and irresolute,* MATVEY *dashes off.*
> SCHAAF'*s face lights up when he sees* KATYA. *He*
> *is ponderously coquettish.*

SCHAAF Ah! The beautiful Katya! This is my ravishing!
KATYA (*Sweetly*) Hello, Adam.
SCHAAF Observe — I go to apprehend fish. (*Grabs her*) But
first I apprehend the beautiful Katya. Come with
me.
KATYA Adam, please —
SCHAAF Yes, yes; like last Friday we make lust again beside
the lake?
KATYA (*Afraid of being overheard*) For goodness sake, Adam!
SCHAAF I sing a German song to you: '*Kathrinchen, Kath-
rinchen, wie lieb' ich dich so sehr!*'
KATYA My mother says your songs are lascivious.
SCHAAF Yes? *Gut — gut!* And in Russian that is, 'O Katya,
you are so beautiful, and I love you!'
KATYA Somebody's coming. (*Gathers her laundry*) Later
perhaps?
SCHAAF Yes? We lust later?
KATYA Adam, you're shameless.
SCHAAF (*Delighted*) So my Mama say, too! *Danke — Danke.*
KATYA I'm free after dinner.

> *She dashes off.* ALEKSEY *enters carrying the tail of*
> *the box kite.* SCHAAF *greets him coldly and with a*
> *formal bow.*

SCHAAF *Guten Abend.*
ALEKSEY *Guten Abend*, Herr Schaaf.

> *Now* VERA, *holding the end of the tail of the kite,*
> *enters. And again* SCHAAF *bows formally.*

SCHAAF *Guten Abend*, Fräulein.

VERA *Guten Abend*, Herr Schaaf.

> SCHAAF *exits.* ALEKSEY *dances round the garden,
> parodying* SCHAAF's *bow and accent and manner.
> At first* VERA *laughs; then she joins in.*

ALEKSEY *Guten Abend.*

VERA *Guten Abend.*

ALEKSEY *Guten Abend*, I'm a dandy. *Guten Abend* — also
randy.

VERA *Guten Abend*, you're so agile.

ALEKSEY Body agile, brain more fragile. Do you know I'm
Kolya's tutor?

VERA And perhaps young Katya's suitor?

ALEKSEY *Danke — Danke!* I'm so flatter.

VERA Go catch some fish. That's all that matter.

ALEKSEY *Guten Abend.*

VERA *Guten Abend.*

> *They collapse laughing on the bench seat.*

ALEKSEY I don't trust that man from here to the door.

> VERA *jumps to her feet and looks around anxiously.*

VERA The door? — What door? — Where's the door? —
I see no door.

> *He grabs her and pulls her back on to the seat.*

ALEKSEY Don't you be smart with me, Madam. Just hold
that (*kite*).

VERA I can't see you now.

> ALEKSEY *makes some last adjustments.*

ALEKSEY What do you mean?

VERA I can't see what you're doing.

ALEKSEY *lowers the kite.*

I can now. Listen.

The five-finger exercises have begun again.

Kolya.

ALEKSEY Lizaveta's a bloody sadist, keeping the child stuck at a piano on a day like this.

VERA I played for an hour this morning.

ALEKSEY You like it. He hates it — he told me.

VERA I'm sure she'd rather be outside, too.

ALEKSEY I don't trust her either. She's too sweet.

VERA She's all right. She fancies you.

He grabs her in mock anger.

ALEKSEY You just watch yourself! (*Furtive look around — then whispers in her ear*) Next time you're close to her, look at —

He runs his index finger across his upper lip.

VERA Lizaveta has *not* got a moustache, Aleksey.

ALEKSEY Snuff.

VERA What?

ALEKSEY Little thin snuff line.

VERA God forgive you.

ALEKSEY Bright mustard.

VERA Aleksey!

ALEKSEY And look — so have I. (*He thrusts his mouth towards her face*) Where she kissed me this morning.

VERA God forgive you!

Again horseplay and laughter.

ALEKSEY Careful. You're going to break the kite. I hope this string's strong enough.

VERA Do you fly kites in Moscow?

ALEKSEY My dear child, in Moscow my life is dedicated to scholarship.

VERA Are you very clever?

ALEKSEY Genius.

VERA Really. Are you clever?

ALEKSEY For God's sake! I barely scraped through my finals! You were at school in Moscow, weren't you?

VERA Until last year. Until Natalya took me away.

ALEKSEY Why did she do that?

VERA For company here, I suppose.

ALEKSEY Hasn't she a husband? And a mother-in-law? And a house full of servants? That was selfish of her.

VERA No, it wasn't.

ALEKSEY Interrupting a brilliant academic career?

Again she pushes him playfully.

VERA Aleksey Belyayev, you are one huge clown!

ALEKSEY You like Natalya, don't you?

VERA I love Natalya.

ALEKSEY Yes, I think you do.

VERA You sound surprised.

ALEKSEY All the same you're just a little bit wary of her, aren't you?

VERA Am I? I don't think I am. (*Pause*) What do you think of her?

ALEKSEY (*His response is considered*) I have never been inside a grand house like this — ever in my life. I've never met anybody like her — ever in my life. She . . . she astonishes me.

VERA Does that mean you like her?

ALEKSEY It means that I am . . . a bit in awe of all this and a bit bewildered by her. (*Casual again*) You're really a daughter to her, aren't you, Baby Face?

VERA She and Arkady are the only parents I've ever known. You know I'm an orphan, don't you?

ALEKSEY Yes. I'm half an orphan. My mother's dead.

VERA They say orphans are often drawn to each other; that there's a natural affinity. What do you think?

ALEKSEY Irresistibly. Absolutely no doubt about that. This tail is supposed to be ten times the length of the side. Doesn't look long enough to me.

VERA You have a sister?

ALEKSEY Another Natalya.

VERA What age is she?

ALEKSEY She must be — oh — sixteen — seventeen.

VERA Are we alike at all?

ALEKSEY She's only a baby still. And you're far better looking.

VERA I'm sure.

ALEKSEY Honestly. And much more sophisticated.

Pause.

VERA I wish I were in her place.

ALEKSEY You've never seen our house!

VERA What I meant was —

ALEKSEY It's so small you've got to go sideways in the front door.

She laughs and pushes him again.

Swear to God! And the kitchen's so tiny we take turns to sit in it. (*Another push*) Hi, that was sore! I'm warning you: make sure you marry like Natalya — into big money and a grand house and you'll be happy for the rest of your days.

VERA Promise?

ALEKSEY Hope to die. Who wants to sit in a tiny kitchen all day — alone?

She laughs. The kite is finished.

ALEKSEY Now. All we need is a wind to lift it and a boy to fly it. (*Listens*) He's stopped. Let's see if Mustard Lips has released him.

VERA Here's Natalya and Michel.

ALEKSEY Will we show them our handiwork?

VERA Not now. We'll go. She'll only find some reason for scolding me.

As they go off:

ALEKSEY Why would she do that?

VERA Because she's cranky these days.

ALEKSEY Told you you were a little bit wary of her.

MICHEL *and* NATALYA *enter.*

MICHEL Did you see that? Ran off as soon as they spotted us!

NATALYA She spends far too much time with that young man.

MICHEL That was a bit obvious, wasn't it?

NATALYA And she's still only a child.

MICHEL Seventeen.

NATALYA (*Touching the bench*) It's still warm — where they were sitting.

MICHEL Hot young blood, Natalya.

NATALYA I'm going to have a word with her.

MICHEL Don't tell me you envy them?

NATALYA For God's sake, why should I envy them?

MICHEL Their youth? Their freshness? Their vitality?

NATALYA I'm not quite senile yet, Michel.

MICHEL I suppose I should envy them, too. Trouble is, I don't feel old; I don't feel any age. See those two trees, Natalya? That huge oak at the peak of its vigour and maturity. And beside it — look — that slender young birch, so delicate it may well break under next winter's snows. Yet each has its own perfection. Each is replete in itself — isn't it?

NATALYA You are so eloquent about 'nature', Michel; so sensitive, so responsive to it. 'Nature' must be flattered.

MICHEL Oh, yes; thrilled.

KATYA *enters with another basket of laundry.*

NATALYA But of course you're wrong about 'nature'. Nature is blunt and crude and relentless. Nature cares about nothing except itself — surviving and perpetuating itself. Your exquisite nature is a savage. Busy, Katya?

KATYA Kept going, Madam. Would you like me to get you your parasol?

NATALYA I'm fine, thank you, Katya.

KATYA *exits.*

Another delicate young birch, Michel?

MICHEL The word nature will never cross my lips again.

NATALYA Will it break under the winter snows?

MICHEL Not that one. That's a tough birch. That's a surviving birch.

NATALYA Most young birches are.

MICHEL By the way the doctor has left. He says to thank you for the hospitality.

NATALYA Where has he gone?

MICHEL To do some calls. Have you noticed — himself and Lizaveta seem to have got friendly. Whatever it was he was whispering to her at breakfast she was breaking her sides.

NATALYA What a mask! — The genial country doctor!

MICHEL He's all right, Shpigelsky.

NATALYA He's a huckster.

MICHEL He's not.

NATALYA A mean-minded, ugly-minded, conniving peasant.

MICHEL Natalya, that's — !

NATALYA Will he be back soon?

MICHEL Said he would.

NATALYA Something I wanted to talk to him about.

MICHEL What was that? Sorry — none of my —

NATALYA Don't you know?

MICHEL None of my business.

NATALYA But you do know, don't you?

MICHEL How could I possibly — ?

NATALYA You gaze at me all the time, don't you? You know

every thought in my head — don't you? You analyze everything I think, everything I do — don't you?

MICHEL You should have your parasol.

NATALYA Don't tell me there's a little portion of my mind that you haven't invaded?

MICHEL Natalya —

NATALYA Because if there is then, for all your attentions, for all your scrutiny, you're not nearly as penetrating as I thought you were.

MICHEL Something has happened to you, Natalya.

NATALYA Another brilliant perception?

MICHEL I don't know what it is. All I know is that since I've come back, you've . . . altered. I know — I know — not at all brilliant. But it is obvious, even to me, that for some reason you are deeply unhappy within yourself. And I want you to know that that makes me deeply unhappy, too. And if there is anything I can do, anything at all . . . I don't have to tell you that.

NATALYA What do you think of Bolshintsov?

MICHEL Of who?

NATALYA Bolshintsov! Afanasy Ivanovich Bolshintsov! Who lives fifteen miles north of here! You know? — Our neighbour, Bolshintsov!

MICHEL Of course I know. But —

NATALYA Tell me about him.

MICHEL You know him a lot better than I do. Didn't you tell me he was here playing cards a few weeks ago?

NATALYA Talk about him.

MICHEL Bachelor; large, run-down estate; thick; probably illiterate; an idiot but no fool; cunning — for God's sake, what is there to say about Bolshintsov!

NATALYA He's not thick.

MICHEL Who cares? So I'm wrong again.

NATALYA And he's not illiterate.

MICHEL Wonderful.

NATALYA And the estate isn't neglected.

MICHEL And I'm sure he's charming and entertaining

and industrious. What's the sudden interest in
Bolshintsov?

NATALYA None. Nothing. Just wanted to hear your astute
character analysis.

MICHEL Natalya —

NATALYA And now it's time to decide on the dinner menu.
That sun is hot. I think we'll have lamb this evening.

MICHEL Will I go with you?

NATALYA No, we've had a surfeit of one another, haven't
we? Well, a sufficiency for now.

She exits. The moment she leaves MICHEL'*s façade
of calm, of control, suddenly collapses. He is a man
on the edge of panic. He conducts the following
conversation with himself at a frantic speed.*

MICHEL Oh my God.
Steady, man.
She's slipping away from you.
No, she's not.
You're losing her.
Shut up.
And if you lose her —
I will not lose her!
— you lose whatever happiness you know.
You call this happiness?
I'm talking about your life.
Lose her — lose your life.
You know that, don't you? But then she has never
really loved you.
That's not true!
Affection, maybe; but it never exploded into love.
And why is she giving you hell now? It's the young
tutor, isn't it?
Infatuation; that will pass.
Will it?
Of course it will. She's much too sophisticated for
that — that calf.

Perhaps.

Oh my God.

Why are you lamenting?

Because it's out of my hands, altogether beyond my control. And all I can do is watch — and endure.

You're besotted by her, aren't you?

Yes, I am besotted by her.

If you could only see yourself: you are ridiculous.

Ever since the first day I met her I've never been anything else.

> NATALYA, *now smiling and animated, enters, leading* ALEKSEY *by the elbow. He is flushed — and slightly embarrassed.*

NATALYA I'm telling you — Michel will know. Michel's a very perceptive man. Aren't you, Michel?

MICHEL Michel will know what?

NATALYA Where Aleksey can get gunpowder

MICHEL (*Icy*) In the town.

NATALYA Yes. But where in the town?

MICHEL What's the mystery, Natalya? You buy gunpowder in Kafinsky's every year, don't you?

NATALYA (*To* ALEKSEY) So we'll buy it in Kafinsky's. Thank you, Michel.

MICHEL (*To* ALEKSEY) You're going to make an explosion?

NATALYA An explosion! Michel!

ALEKSEY Fireworks.

MICHEL Sorry?

ALEKSEY Only fireworks. Just fireworks.

NATALYA (*To* ALEKSEY) Go on — tell him.

ALEKSEY And I need some gunpowder —

MICHEL That much I've gathered.

ALEKSEY Not good quality gunpowder — really cheap gunpowder will do —

NATALYA He's too modest to say it himself but Aleksey can make rockets and Roman candles and Chinese squibs.

MICHEL And fishing rods.

NATALYA And fishing rods.

MICHEL And kites.

NATALYA Which we're going to fly in a few minutes.

MICHEL You're a very accomplished young man.

ALEKSEY It's very easy to —

NATALYA Of course he is. (*To* ALEKSEY) Acknowledge it. Wonderfully accomplished. (*To* MICHEL) And do you know what he's going to do next Thursday night?

MICHEL Tell me.

NATALYA On Thursday of next week?

MICHEL Your birthday — I know.

NATALYA You remembered! (*To* ALEKSEY) Told you — he knows everything. (*To* MICHEL) On Thursday of next week we're going to celebrate my birthday with a fireworks display! At night! Out in the middle of the lake! Aleksey can make fireworks that float on water! Won't that be exciting?

Enter SHPIGELSKY *and* BOLSHINTSOV. BOLSHINTSOV
is excited and nervous and smiling resolutely.

Look who's here. I thought you were out on calls?

DOCTOR I've cured everybody. So once again I'll be broke.

NATALYA And Mr Bolshintsov. Welcome.

He bows gauchely.

BOLSHINTSOV Thank you. The doctor brought me with him. And now, since I'm here — Madam, you know me —

NATALYA Yes?

BOLSHINTSOV I'm not a man of much style or grace. So if I can come straight to the point, I'm here because I want —

The DOCTOR *grabs him by the arm.*

DOCTOR I told you, Bolshintsov, I know where it is; I'm bringing you there. (*Confidentially to the others*)

Taken unawares, saving your delicate presence —
chill in the kidneys — very embarrassed. (*Aloud*)
Everything under control in a manner of speaking.
This way, man; straight ahead. Back in a minute.

NATALYA We're about to launch Kolya's new kite. You'll
join us, Doctor?

DOCTOR Wouldn't miss it for the world.

The DOCTOR *pushes* BOLSHINTSOV *off.*

NATALYA You know, when he's dressed up, he's quite a handsome man, Bolshintsov, isn't he? Now. (*To* ALEKSEY)
Kafinsky's — you'll remember that? Anyhow, I'll
send Matvey with you and charge whatever you
need to my account. There was something else we
had to look at — what was it?

ALEKSEY Kolya's progress report.

NATALYA That's it. You're fashioning Kolya, and Michel and
I are polishing —

She looks to include MICHEL. *But he has drifted
upstage and stands with his back to them. For a
few seconds she looks at him, isolated, wretched.
Instinctively she goes to him. She raises her hands
as if to put them consolingly on his shoulders.
Then she glances back at* ALEKSEY *and gives a
short uneasy laugh. Quickly she turns and joins
him.*

There are times when Michel prefers to be alone.

*She holds her hand out to him. Just as he is about
to take it:*

No, no, not my hand, Master Tutor.

ALEKSEY Sorry, I —

NATALYA Not unless I offer it to you. You take my arm.
Taking my hand would signify something different. And that could be altogether misleading.

They exit. For a few seconds MICHEL *is alone on the stage. Then the* DOCTOR *and* BOLSHINTSOV *return.*

BOLSHINTSOV Tell me again —

DOCTOR (*Wearily*) Bolshintsov!

BOLSHINTSOV Just once more — what *exactly* did Natalya say?

DOCTOR 'I don't know Mr Bolshintsov very well — '

BOLSHINTSOV That's right — she doesn't.

DOCTOR 'But he seems a decent sort of man — '

BOLSHINTSOV That's true — I am.

DOCTOR 'And if he wishes to come and see Vera here — '

BOLSHINTSOV She meant here — in this house?

DOCTOR Are you going to let me finish?

BOLSHINTSOV Sorry.

DOCTOR 'If he wishes to see Vera here in this house I will have no objection. Indeed, if he wins her affection — '

BOLSHINTSOV Wins her affection!

DOCTOR 'I will be the first to congratulate them both.'

BOLSHINTSOV (*Elated*) Oh God! Those are her very words?

DOCTOR Hand on heart.

BOLSHINTSOV (*Dejected*) Oh God! What will I say to her? I won't be able to get a word out. Let me tell you a secret, Doctor: never once in my life — never once have I ever . . . been with a girl, ever.

DOCTOR You're not serious!

BOLSHINTSOV So I have no idea how to acquit myself, how to speak, what to say. Maybe I should be very formal, very dignified — what do you say? No, better to be witty, wouldn't it? Yes, that's the tack — witty and debonair — a bit of a lad. Oh God, guide me through this, Doctor, and as well as the three horses I've promised you —

DOCTOR (*In case they are overheard*) Please!

MICHEL *moves off.*

BOLSHINTSOV I'll give you a wagonette as well. Guide me, friend.

DOCTOR The wagonette is new?

BOLSHINTSOV Never on the road.

DOCTOR And the horses?

BOLSHINTSOV Magnificent bays.

DOCTOR I'm your guide. Let's assess what we have. For God's sake, straighten up, man! What age are you?

BOLSHINTSOV What has that got to — ? Fifty-seven.

DOCTOR Size of farm?

BOLSHINTSOV Five hundred acres, give or take a —

DOCTOR Serfs?

BOLSHINTSOV Three hundred and twenty.

DOCTOR Your social graces. Do you play chess?

BOLSHINTSOV No, but I'm a devil at snap!

DOCTOR God! Travel?

BOLSHINTSOV Moscow every autumn — for the pig market.

DOCTOR Music?

BOLSHINTSOV What do you mean?

DOCTOR What instruments do you play?

BOLSHINTSOV When I was a boy I played the mouth organ.

DOCTOR Christ! Dance?

BOLSHINTSOV Me!

DOCTOR Sorry. Languages?

BOLSHINTSOV Russian.

DOCTOR Brilliant. I have to tell you, it's bleak, Bolshintsov. (*Groping around frantically*) Those are your own teeth, are they?

BOLSHINTSOV Yes! Have them all!

BOLSHINTSOV *pulls his lips apart in pride.*

DOCTOR (*With distaste*) Right — right — right — right — right. Now. Our assets are the following — For God's sake, shut your mouth, Bolshintsov! Property substantial. Health — excellent. Appearance — presentable. Widely travelled. Fluent linguist — in our native language. Proficient organist — of the mouth. Money in the bank?

BOLSHINTSOV (*Barely audible*) A little.

DOCTOR Didn't get that?

BOLSHINTSOV A little.

DOCTOR How much?

BOLSHINTSOV I wouldn't tell my mother that, Shpigelsky! Enough
— just say enough.

DOCTOR With regard to the opposite sex, chaste to a saintly
degree.

BOLSHINTSOV That's bad, is it?

DOCTOR No; but in my experience of this whole province
— unique. And my job is to make you sound perfectly . . . normal.

BOLSHINTSOV It's the words, Doctor, the words! What am I going
to say to her? Because if I can't speak, how can I
propose to her?

DOCTOR What you'll say is this —

BOLSHINTSOV In private?

DOCTOR In total privacy. 'Vera, I'm a man of few words — '

> BOLSHINTSOV *silently repeats everything the*
> DOCTOR *says.*

'— but I have watched you for a long time. And I
love you very much. And I want to marry you.
And I want you to know that I love you best of all
in maroon.'

BOLSHINTSOV Where's that?

DOCTOR 'Don't give me your answer now. I'll ask you again
in a week's time — a month's time — a year's time.'

BOLSHINTSOV In a year's time I could be dead!

DOCTOR 'But I do love you very, very much and I know we
could be very happy together.'

BOLSHINTSOV 'And I'm the greatest lecher in the whole province!'

DOCTOR Bolshintsov — !

BOLSHINTSOV Oh Christ! Here they are! (*Quietly, intensely*) And
that was a rotten thing to say.

DOCTOR What was?

BOLSHINTSOV You're my doctor — you know my kidneys are
perfect.

Enter NATALYA, MICHEL, VERA, ALEKSEY *and*

LIZAVETA. ALEKSEY *is carrying the kite and —*
as before — VERA *holds the end of the tail.*

NATALYA Well, you two still here? You look very conspiratorial.

DOCTOR Babes in the wood, Natalya. You all know Bolshintsov, don't you? Aleksey Belyayev, the new tutor.

BOLSHINTSOV We've met. We've had a few chats. From what he tells me, we're a pair of dogs — aren't we?

DOCTOR And Vera you know.

BOLSHINTSOV Certainly do. And if she and I could have a moment of total privacy I'd like —

DOCTOR So what's the big expedition?

NATALYA We're trying out Aleksey's new kite. Isn't it beautiful?

DOCTOR Indeed. What is it made of?

ALEKSEY Balsa wood. From tropical America.

NATALYA That's not the name you told me.

ALEKSEY Maybe I used the Latin name.

NATALYA Did you now. Trying to impress me?

VERA So tell us all the Latin name.

ALEKSEY I will not.

VERA Because you don't know it.

ALEKSEY Ochroma Lagopus.

VERA (*Laughs*) You made that up!

ALEKSEY I'm warning you!

VERA He made that up just now!

General talk and laughter during which:

DOCTOR (*Privately to* LIZAVETA) I like your shoes.

LIZAVETA Do you?

DOCTOR Very stylish.

LIZAVETA They're French.

DOCTOR Beautiful.

NATALYA (*Loudly*) This is an important event; so let's do it with proper formality. I'll lead off with the classical scholar. (*General laughter*) Vera, you and Mr

Bolshintsov come next. Then Lizaveta and the Doctor. And Michel — you'll keep an eye on all of us, will you? Wait! Where's Kolya?

ALEKSEY He's waiting for us down at the granary.

NATALYA Right. Off we go.

BOLSHINTSOV (*To* VERA) I haven't flown a kite for over fifty years, not since —

DOCTOR Move, Bolshintsov! You're holding up the column.

BOLSHINTSOV Sorry.

DOCTOR What are you smiling at, Michel?

MICHEL At myself: tagging along at the rear.

DOCTOR The rear can easily become the front. All you need is a change of direction.

MICHEL I suppose I'll wait for that.

DOCTOR (*To* LIZAVETA) You must come out with me for a run in my new troika.

LIZAVETA When did you get that?

DOCTOR Could arrive any of these days.

LIZAVETA I'd love to, Doctor.

DOCTOR Excellent.

End of Scene Two.

ACT ONE

Scene Three

The following day.

VERA is playing the piano offstage: John Field's Midi No. 18 in E major. The DOCTOR and MICHEL are sitting in the drawing room. They have just had coffee.

DOCTOR   Good coffee. Enjoyed that. The caffeine makes the brain gallop. And nobody makes coffee like the Kenyans. Or maybe you're a Brazilian, are you?

MICHEL   You wanted to talk to me, Doctor?

DOCTOR   Certainly did. Let me take this (*cup*) out of your way. Because of all my good friends you are the most perceptive, the most simpatico. At first I thought I'd go to Arkady and ask his help; but then Arkady isn't quite so astute in these matters as —

MICHEL   You want me to do something for you.

DOCTOR   Aha! No bluffing that razor intelligence! That's why I decided that if anybody could —

MICHEL   Doctor.

DOCTOR   To the point. (*Picks a crumb off MICHEL's knee*) Crumb on knee. Long story short. Bolshintsov has taken an enormous fancy to our young musician.

MICHEL   To Vera!

DOCTOR   Herself.

MICHEL   Bolshintsov!

DOCTOR   Himself.

The music stops suddenly.

MICHEL   Come on, man! Bolshintsov's a stupid old fool and

she's only a child!

Enter KATYA *with fresh coffee. On her heels —
clearly following her and clearly distraught —
comes* MATVEY *carrying logs.*

DOCTOR Inaccurate on both counts, Michel, if I may say
so. She is not a child; and Bolshintsov is neither
stupid, nor old, nor — (*Irritably to* KATYA) What is
it, girl?

KATYA Can I give you some coffee?

DOCTOR None for me. Michel?

KATYA It's freshly made.

MICHEL I'm finished, thanks.

DOCTOR Could we have a little privacy, please? (*To* MATVEY)
Can't that be done later, Matvey? (*To* KATYA) And
take this tray with you.

KATYA Certainly, Doctor.

She picks up the tray and leaves.

MATVEY (*As* KATYA *passes*) You've got to speak to me.

KATYA I've got to do nothing.

MATVEY You can't just ignore me!

KATYA Just watch me.

She sweeps off. MATVEY *stumbles after her.*

DOCTOR Anyhow, my good friend Bolshintsov comes to
me and asks me to speak to Natalya on his behalf.
So I spoke to Natalya. Natalya said no. Then
Natalya said yes. I report back to Bolshintsov.
Bolshintsov is ecstatic! You saw him yesterday —
scarcely coherent with excitement! So far, so good,
I thought. Now move quickly, Doctor. Iron hot —
you know? So this morning I go again to Natalya
and suggest as delicately as I can that now might
be the time for her to have a word in the ear of
young Vera. And how am I received? In one of her

sulks! Barely civil to me! Absolutely refuses to speak to Bolshintsov! And poor Bolshintsov! — He becomes more frantic by the hour! Don't judge him so harshly, Michel. He's reliable, he's rich, he's mad about her — that's a possible basis for marriage, isn't it? And what prospects has Vera in a remote place like this?

MICHEL So?

DOCTOR So what I ask you to do is speak to Natalya on Bolshintsov's behalf. A word from you and that big generous heart of his would dance with joy.

MICHEL What's in this for you, Doctor?

DOCTOR (*Innocently*) What do you mean?

MICHEL You're not matchmaking for nothing.

DOCTOR Oh God, if I had only a fraction of that acumen! All right — cards on table. So that I can minister to the old and the sick in the outlying areas —

MICHEL Doctor!

DOCTOR Bolshintsov is to provide me with . . . new transportation.

MICHEL He's giving you a horse.

DOCTOR In a word.

MICHEL Two horses?

DOCTOR Three.

MICHEL Shpigelsky!

DOCTOR And a wagonette! (*Great burst of laughter*) I'm a rogue, amn't I? I'm not a doctor at all — I'm a quack! (*Voices off*) You'll speak to her for me, won't you?

MICHEL Yes — yes — yes — yes — yes!

DOCTOR Simpatico — mutual.

Enter NATALYA *and* SCHAAF. NATALYA *is flushed, agitated, fiery.*

SCHAAF I request four days — that is all. I will be returned before the end of the week.

NATALYA I have allowed you to go home every month for the past six months, Herr Schaaf. You are abusing that generosity.

SCHAAF But my mama is eighty-five year of age and she loses her strength more and more every day.

NATALYA Your mama has been losing her strength daily ever since you came here.

SCHAAF I am her only masculine child and she —

NATALYA If you go home now, Herr Schaaf, I suggest you take all your belongings with you. I have nothing more to say.

DOCTOR (*Quickly*) Arkady's winnowing machine is the talk of the countryside. Let's go and inspect it, Herr Schaaf. (*He takes* SCHAAF *by the elbow*) See you later.

SCHAAF She is too cold heart.

DOCTOR It's life that's cold heart, my friend. Why don't I look in on your mama one of these days?

> SCHAAF *and the* DOCTOR *exit.* VERA *plays the piano, off: Nocturne No. 5 in B-flat major.*

NATALYA I can't stop Herr Schaaf from running home to his mother and I can't get the doctor to leave. Next thing he'll be seeing his patients here.

MICHEL He's out of favour today?

NATALYA Still trying to match Vera and Bolshintsov, is he?

MICHEL Yes.

NATALYA There's something in that for him. As for Bolshintsov — he's a fool.

MICHEL Yesterday he was in favour, too.

NATALYA Today is not yesterday.

MICHEL For everybody except me.

NATALYA What's that supposed to — ? Oh God, I know — I know — I know; and I'm sorry, Michel; I'm very sorry; please forgive me. Yesterday I was disgraceful. I ate the head of everybody yesterday. But I should never snap at you. I really mustn't.

MICHEL Doesn't matter.

NATALYA Oh yes, it does matter. Because you are the core of my life, Michel. There's nobody in the world I love the way I love you. You believe that, don't you?

MICHEL If you tell me.

He tries to put his arms around her but she evades him — her train of thought is unbroken.

NATALYA I snapped at Lizaveta, too; told her I didn't give a damn about her taking snuff but for God's sake, to snuff openly. Did she think she was fooling any-body, slipping into the toilet every hour and com-ing out with her nose red and her eyes watering?

MICHEL You never — !

NATALYA And poor Grandmother — do you know what I said to her? Oh my God! That she was such a damned domineering mother, no wonder Arkady is such a mess. And the poor woman, her mouth fell open. And she stared at me with such pained eyes. And she was so shocked, so hurt, so wounded, she was beyond tears. And I knew there was no apology I could make; that even if I caught her in my arms, as I wanted to, and said, Sorry — sorry — sorry — sorry, that it would be no good, no good at all.

MICHEL I'm sure she —

NATALYA Maybe I'm going off my head, Michel.

MICHEL Natalya —

NATALYA Maybe I am. I don't mean insane. I mean a kind of temporary . . . derangement. That's possible, isn't it? Am I just slightly demented, Doctor Shpigelsky — not profoundly, not permanently — but today, here, now? Because do you know what I feel, Michel — today, here, now? I feel . . . unhinged.

MICHEL You are perfectly hinged.

NATALYA And dangerously irresponsible — giddy, heady, almost hysterical with irresponsibility. And do you know why I feel like that, Michel? — Michel, my faithful watcher, observer, analyst. Of course you must know. Master Aleksey Belyayev, the gauche young graduate, the tutor of my son, he has taken possession of my head. Ridiculous, isn't it?

I know it is. Ridiculous and at my age pathetic. And here I am telling all this to you, the last person in the world I'd want to hurt. Oh God, Michel, I am the real mess. What's to become of me?

MICHEL I am sorry for you.

NATALYA Can you help me, Michel? Please help me.

MICHEL I told you I thought something had happened, that you had changed. And then when I saw you in the meadow yesterday, when he was flying that damned kite, then I knew for sure.

NATALYA Knew what?

MICHEL I saw you transformed in that meadow yesterday, Natalya. You couldn't take your eyes off him. When he sang, you sang. When he laughed, you laughed even louder. You were so happy — so animated with happiness — that you glowed; your eyes, your skin, your body, your whole personality. And because you existed only for him, only because of him, you became extraordinarily beautiful, more beautiful than I have ever seen you.

NATALYA Yes, yes, yes, he's such an attractive, vital, vigorous young man, and in that meadow yesterday his wild, reckless youth was wonderful, irresistible —

MICHEL I think we shouldn't talk about this any —

NATALYA And that's what I responded to, that's what intoxicated me. But that will pass. I'll sober up. Of course I will, the moment I — Please, Michel, please don't turn away from me.

MICHEL One minute he takes possession of your head; the next he's a passing intoxication.

NATALYA That's all it is.

MICHEL He has intoxicated you or he has possessed you — which?

NATALYA Michel, that's —

MICHEL Does it matter? Who cares?

NATALYA I understand why you're hurt. Give me your hand. I do know why you're angry. But please —

MICHEL Angry? The lapdog angry? The jaded, boring old attendant angry? No, I'm not angry with you! I pity you, for God's sake! You are pitiful, Natalya!

He regrets this immediately. She cries quietly. Pause.

The doctor and Bolshintsov want an answer from you.

NATALYA What?

MICHEL I promised the doctor I would talk to you. He wants you to speak to Vera.

NATALYA Yes . . . all right . . .

MICHEL Will I send her to you? Will you speak to her now?

NATALYA Whatever you think about me, please don't look so coldly at me —

MICHEL Will you speak to Vera now, Natalya?

NATALYA Yes . . . yes . . . (*As he leaves*) Michel!

But he has gone. Now SCHAAF *enters.*

SCHAAF I think about what you say to me. I copulate over it. You are correct. I am in error. Mama I visit too often. So I do not go. I stay.

He bows stiffly and goes off. NATALYA *goes to the mirror, adjusts her hair, makes an effort to control her emotions.* VERA *enters.*

VERA Michel said you wanted me. (*Looks closely at* NATALYA) Are you all right, Natalya?

NATALYA I'm fine, thanks. Just a bit warm. Sit down here beside me. It's time you and I had a 'serious talk'.

VERA What about? Is something wrong?

NATALYA That last piece you played — what was it?

VERA Nocturne in B-flat major.

NATALYA Beautiful. You're really a very accomplished pianist — you know that, don't you?

VERA What's the serious talk about?

NATALYA 'Life' — 'your future' — great issues like that. (*Laughs*) Look at that anxious face! (*Quick hug*) I just want to tell you — to remind you — that this will always be your home and that I will always love you as fully and as openly as if you were my very own daughter. But you know all that, don't you?

VERA Thank you.

NATALYA But we've got to be practical, too — haven't we? You're no longer a child. You're a young woman. And, even though you are an orphan and have no private means, one of these days you're going to find yourself managing your own home. Now, how will that appeal to you?

VERA My own home?

NATALYA Yes! And maybe much sooner than you think. Somebody has asked my permission to marry you, Vera.

> VERA *stares at her in shock; then suddenly covers her face with her hands and sobs.* NATALYA *puts her arms around her.*

NATALYA Here — here — here — here — here. What's all this, for heaven's sake? What's there to cry about?

VERA I'm in your power.

NATALYA You're in my — ! Oh my goodness, will you listen to this baby. There (*handkerchief*). Shhhhh — easy, my love. You are my only daughter, my only darling daughter, and I won't let anyone, anywhere ever say a cross word to her. All right?

VERA Yes.

NATALYA Come closer to me. Put your arm around me. That's better. No, you're not my daughter; we're closer than that. We're sisters. Does that sniff mean yes? I'm your older sister that you love and tell all your secrets to. And supposing she says to you one day, 'Vera, there's somebody who wants to marry you!' what's the first thought that comes into your head? That you're too young? That you never really thought of getting married?

VERA I suppose so . . . yes.

NATALYA But supposing again — just supposing — the man is a good man and a kind man and prepared to wait in the hope that one day — then what would you say?

VERA Whatever you want, Natalya.

NATALYA Stop that! That's not how you speak to your older sister! And it's not what I want, darling; it's what you want. That's all that matters.

VERA Who is he, Natalya?

NATALYA Guess.

VERA I can't.

NATALYA Try.

VERA Have I met him?

NATALYA Yes.

VERA Where?

NATALYA Here.

VERA In this house?

NATALYA You saw him yesterday.

VERA Yesterday?

NATALYA He's not a boy. Who wants a boy? And there may be more dashing men around. But then — it's Bolshintsov.

VERA Bolshintsov!

NATALYA *nods. Suddenly* VERA *bursts out laughing; then* NATALYA.

You're joking me, Natalya!

NATALYA I'm not.

VERA You are — you are — you are!

NATALYA *shakes her head.*

Bolshintsov! Oh my God!

NATALYA *suddenly gets to her feet.*

NATALYA That's it. Serious talk finished. Forget it. Had you

burst into tears, I would have thought, 'Perhaps
. . . maybe'. But the moment you laughed, poor
old Bolshintsov dropped dead!

They both laugh again, NATALYA *hugs* VERA
quickly.

VERA I'm awful, amn't I?

NATALYA All you children — silly geese — you all want to
marry for love.

VERA You married Arkady for love, didn't you?

NATALYA (*Brief pause*) Of course. And all you children are
right. Poor old Bolshintsov — never even came
under starter's orders. And it is awful of us to
laugh at him because he is a kind man and a
generous man. But you're right: can you imagine
tossing about in bed at night, crazed by the
thought of those puffy cheeks?

VERA Or the bald head!

NATALYA Or the bulging stomach! Stop it — stop it! We're a
pair of scamps! But supposing — I'm your sister
again — just supposing he were young — reasonably attractive — wanted to marry you — what
would you say then?

VERA How could I answer a question like that?

NATALYA Because you can't imagine Bolshintsov young and
reasonably attractive — ?

VERA No, no —

NATALYA Or because you're in love with someone else?

VERA No, I'm not.

NATALYA You don't love anybody?

VERA Yes, oh yes. I love you, Natalya.

NATALYA (*Quick hug*) And I love you. Who else?

VERA Kolya. I'm dying about Kolya. And Anna. Even
Lizaveta — with reservations.

NATALYA Arkady?

VERA No reservations. (*Arms wide to indicate a full scale
of love*) That much. You're so lucky.

NATALYA I know. And Michel?

VERA That much, too. (*Slightly smaller*) Maybe that much.

NATALYA The doctor?

VERA Maybe — maybe — maybe; what about — (*smaller still*)? He fancies Lizaveta — (*arms wide again*) — did you know that?

NATALYA And the new tutor?

VERA Aleksey?

NATALYA Aleksey.

VERA Yes, I like Aleksey.

NATALYA Show me.

VERA I couldn't, Natalya. I —

NATALYA (*Arms wide, then wider*) That much? That much? More?

VERA Maybe.

NATALYA More? That much?

VERA (*Very embarrassed*) I couldn't — I just couldn't —

NATALYA (*Arms wide apart*) That much, Vera? Yes, he is an attractive young man, isn't he? If he weren't so shy.

VERA Aleksey shy!

NATALYA Isn't he?

VERA He's certainly not shy! But he's probably afraid of you.

NATALYA Afraid of me?

VERA No, not afraid; not at ease with you — that's what he says. And that's natural enough: you're his employer.

NATALYA But he's . . . at ease with everybody else?

VERA With me he is. And he's such a clown! When we're together we laugh all the time.

NATALYA At what?

VERA At one another — at everything — at nothing. He says all he has to do is — (*she wiggles her little finger*) — and I fall apart. And so I do. You saw him yesterday in the meadow — leaping about and clowning and singing. That's what he's like most of the time. But wait until he's a full month here and he won't be a bit uneasy with you. I've told him that and he does pay attention to me —

even though he calls me Baby Face.

NATALYA I didn't know you were so close.

VERA We're not really close, maybe more like —

NATALYA Oh you are. Oh yes you are.

VERA Do you think so? No, we're not. Well maybe a tiny little bit.

NATALYA Believe me — you are very close.

VERA Do you really think so, Natalya?

NATALYA *puts her arm around her again.*

NATALYA I think so. And you think so, too. And if your older sister were to say to you, 'You are in love with him, Vera, aren't you?' what would you say to her?

NATALYA *gazes into* VERA's *eyes for a long time.*

I know what you would say to her.

She buries VERA's *face in her breasts.*

You are in love, my darling.

VERA Am I?

NATALYA Yes, you are in love.

VERA I don't know what's wrong with me.

NATALYA Oh yes, you are, you poor, poor soul.

VERA I don't know anything anymore, Natalya.

NATALYA And Aleksey — is he in love with you?

VERA How could he be?

NATALYA Because you are very beautiful. Because you are very, very young.

VERA Two or three times he has caught my hand in his hands. And sometimes I have seen him looking strangely at me. But I can't read his eyes. I just don't know. And I wish to God I knew, Natalya. It's not knowing that —

She breaks off because she sees the expression on NATALYA's *face.*

What's the matter? You're very white. Are you all right, Natalya?

NATALYA I'm fine — really — I'm —

VERA I'll get Katya to bring you —

NATALYA (*Very sharply*) You'll get nobody! (*In control again*) It's only the heat. Now, please, go back to your piano and play that nocturne again. Play it for me.

VERA I have annoyed you — have I? You're angry with me because —

NATALYA No, my dear; I'm not at all angry with you. Go back to your music.

VERA Natalya, you know I love you and I wouldn't —

NATALYA Love — love — love — you're so prodigal with that word, child. Leave me. Please. 'Bye.

VERA *leaves reluctantly.*

NATALYA So now you know: they are in love!
Yes, they are in love.
Then God bless them.
Yes, God bless the fools.
You know you're jealous of her.
Jealous of a child?
Oh yes. And for the first time in your life you're in love yourself.
Don't be stupid!
Oh yes; you're in love with Aleksey.
He's afraid of me!
But you are in love with him.
Am I? Oh God, am I mad?
So what are you going to do about it?
He's got to leave. That's the only answer.
But supposing — just supposing — Vera has read it all wrong.
What does that mean?
You know she loves *him*. But you don't really know what he feels about her, do you?
So what?
So she may only imagine he's in love with her.

So — so — so — so — so?
So why not ask him straight out: do you love Vera?
God, I couldn't, could I?
Why not? At this stage what pride have you left?
Very little. None.
Oh God — oh God — listen to yourself, Natalya. If
you're not careful you're going to end up loathing
yourself.

MICHEL *enters. He sits beside her.*

MICHEL I want to apologize, Natalya. There's no excuse for
the way I behaved. Please forgive me. When you
have settled for very little and then you find that
even that is slipping away, you're liable to . . .

He realizes she has not heard a word he has said.

It's me, Natalya. The old lapdog. Remember?

She catches his hand.

Am I forgiven?

NATALYA I have spoken to her, Michel. They're in love.

MICHEL (*Urgently*) And that's why you've got to extricate
yourself, Natalya. Between them you'll be torn
apart.

NATALYA I was prepared to marry her off to an old man just
to be rid of her. What's become of me, Michel?

MICHEL For the first time in years I see things clearly. And
what has to be done is this: I am going to leave,
Natalya — no, listen — please — just listen. For
your sake, my love. Only for your sake. Aleksey
must leave, too. I'll talk to him. I'll take him with
me.

NATALYA Michel, I —

MICHEL For me to talk to you about duty — your home —
Arkady — that would be a bit hollow, wouldn't
it? But with Aleksey and myself out of your life,

in time, in time this terrible disquiet will subside and your life will find an equilibrium again. And in time, my love, in time certain conciliations — reconciliations — all right, maybe they're only resignations — but they will come about and you will find a measure of content, maybe of happiness, again. I promise you.

NATALYA So you're deserting me?

MICHEL No — never. What I'm advising —

NATALYA After you've lectured me on my duties and responsibilities. Wonderful, Michel!

MICHEL What I said was —

NATALYA For God's sake, what's all the fuss about? Have we lost all sense of balance. The house is in turmoil because two stupid young fools are infatuated with one another? Good luck to them, I say. And to you, Michel, I say: Go, friend, go. You are a wonderful support.

MICHEL I am not walking out on you, Natalya. All right — Aleksey goes today — I'll talk to him now; and I'll stay with you until the end of the week, until you feel you're —

NATALYA (*In triumph*) Ah! A cunning lapdog!

MICHEL Natalya —

NATALYA Aleksey goes but Michel stays! 'And in time, my love, in time — '

MICHEL (*Angry*) For God's sake, woman!

NATALYA But let me tell you this: if you say a word to Aleksey, just one word, I'll never speak to you again!

MICHEL All right. But you'll tell him to go?

NATALYA Anything that has to be said to him I'll say it.

MICHEL So you'll tell him to go?

NATALYA That's my business.

MICHEL But you'll tell him to go?

NATALYA (*Shouts*) For God's sake!

MICHEL You're right, Natalya: I don't know what has become of you.

He moves away.

NATALYA Michel, Michel, don't go — please — for God's sake, don't leave me.

> *She rushes to him and embraces him desperately. Through her tears:*

My love — my love — my love — oh my love . . .

> *Enter* ARKADY *and* ANNA, ALEKSEY *between them. He is showing Kolya's drawings in an exercise book.*

ALEKSEY And he did that one last night — horses.
ARKADY They're wonderful horses. Look, Mother.

> *But* ANNA *is staring at* MICHEL *and* NATALYA. ALEKSEY *and* ARKADY *now stare at them.* MICHEL *and* NATALYA *separate quickly.* ARKADY *is suddenly very quiet, very still, almost inaudible.*

ARKADY What — what's all this?
MICHEL It's not at all what you think, Arkady. Trust me.

> ARKADY *stares at him for a few seconds. Then he moves towards* NATALYA.

ARKADY Natalya?
MICHEL As your friend, I —
ARKADY I need some explanation from you, Natalya.
ANNA Arkady —
ARKADY What have you to say to me?
ANNA We can all discuss this at some —
ARKADY I'm talking to you, Natalya.

> *When she does not answer he turns to his mother.*

She won't speak to me.
ANNA She's upset and —

ARKADY Why won't my wife speak to me?

MICHEL It's all perfectly above board, Arkady. I promise you. I'll explain it all to you. I give you my word. We were discussing —

ARKADY (*To* ANNA) His word — he gives me his word.

MICHEL Arkady, believe me — trust me —

ARKADY (*To* ALEKSEY) You are showing me my son's drawings; we walk into this room; I find my wife and the man I believed was one of my closest friends —

MICHEL Arkady, trust me —

ARKADY (*Screams*) For Christ's sake, don't use that word!

ARKADY begins to sob.

MICHEL I do know how distressed you must be —

ANNA I don't think you do, sir. I don't think you have any idea at all — not now nor since you first came to this house.

She takes ARKADY's *arm and leads him off.*

I would like to know what passion is so magnificent it can justify this.

MICHEL *holds the door open.* ANNA *and* ARKADY *leave.* MICHEL *looks quickly, irresolutely at* NATALYA *— and exits too.* ALEKSEY *does not know what to do — Stay? Leave? He decides to go.*

NATALYA (*Icy, imperious*) Where are you going? (*He stops*) It's called a domestic scene. You've seen a few in your time, I'm sure, when your father came staggering home from his labouring job. (*Pause*) I don't have to explain myself to anyone — certainly not to you; but there is nothing between Michel and me. (*Pause*) Vera has told me about you two.

ALEKSEY Told you what? What is there to tell?

NATALYA Don't you know? (*She studies his face*) I really think the boy doesn't know.

She smiles. The icy, imperious manner vanishes.

Why are you so wary of me, Aleksey? Here — sit here beside me. I'll tell you what Vera told me: that she loves you.

ALEKSEY She said that to you!

NATALYA That she is in love with you.

ALEKSEY Oh, God, no. That's awful. God, poor Vera.

NATALYA Poor Vera indeed. But that's what she thinks. And what we must do — since we both love her dearly — we must protect her from as much hurt as possible. You do want to help, don't you?

ALEKSEY Yes, of course I do.

NATALYA Good. So; no more walks alone in the garden; no more of those silly, laughing games you play together — (*she wiggles her little finger*) — no more pranks on the swing.

ALEKSEY I can't change just like that. That would hurt her even more.

NATALYA Are you saying I've misread the whole situation?

ALEKSEY I don't know what you mean.

NATALYA You are in love with each other — is that it?

ALEKSEY No, we're not! No, I'm not! Whatever about her, I'm certainly not! I'll talk to her — tell her she's got it all wrong — as gently as I can. I'll do that just now. Then I'll pack my bag and leave.

NATALYA (*Furiously*) I'll make that decision! (*Calm*) What about your responsibility to Kolya, your duty to me?

ALEKSEY I'll get a substitute. I have a friend who —

NATALYA I'm sorry, Aleksey. If you want to go, then of course go.

ALEKSEY You know that's not what I want. You know very well how much I love it here.

NATALYA But we can't have you performing your duties under duress, can we?

ALEKSEY I'll stay.

NATALYA You'll go — you'll stay. Are you always so fickle?

ALEKSEY I'll stay. Yes, I'll stay as long as you want me to stay.

They look at each other for several seconds and then NATALYA *turns away.*

NATALYA On the other hand perhaps you should go. Let's wait and see. Would you tell Michel I want him? He's probably in the study.

ALEKSEY *moves off.*

One other thing, Aleksey.

He stops.

Don't talk to Vera — not just yet. Leave her in her dream life for the moment.

Now he exits. And suddenly she is wildly triumphant — and uncertain.

So now you know: he doesn't love her!
Yes — yes — yes.
Everything's falling into place!
Is it?
Oh, yes. Meshing — meshing.
And what are you going to say to Michel? To Arkady? To Anna? To Vera? To the world?
I don't give a damn!
You don't care?
Oh yes, I care. But not now — not now!
And him?
Yes, him! Aleksey Belyayev, I love you!
But does he love you?
Time — time — give it time.
And he's staying?
Of course he's staying.

But he really should go.
Should he?
Oh yes — he really must go.
Why must he?
Because if he stays, Natalya . . . (*She hugs herself.*
Her face is alight) . . . if he stays . . . you are lost.

Music: Nocturne No. 5 in B-flat major.
Curtain. End of Act One.

ACT TWO

Scene One

*Afternoon, the following day. The garden as in Act One, Scene Two.
Enter* SHPIGELSKY *and* LIZAVETA, *returning from a walk. He is peeling
an orange.*

LIZAVETA What have you heard?

DOCTOR (*Indifferently*) Nothing.

LIZAVETA You must have heard something?

DOCTOR Not a word. Let's sit down.

They sit in the gazebo.

LIZAVETA Well, whatever happened, the house is crazy today.
The tutor has locked himself in his room — packing his bags, according to Nanny. Now, if she's
right, the question is: has Natalya sacked him or
is he just walking out? And if she has sacked him,
why has she sacked him?

DOCTOR (*Indifferently*) Why?

LIZAVETA Isn't that what we're all dying to know! Was
he getting too amorous — or maybe not amorous
enough for Natalya?

DOCTOR Nasty.

LIZAVETA Yes. Sorry. And Vera went for a walk after breakfast and hasn't been seen since. And the old lady's
getting all her meals sent up to her room. And
Arkady's been out fishing on the lake since before
daybreak!

DOCTOR So?

LIZAVETA Without a fishing rod! I'm telling you — mad, mad,
mad. According to Katya — (*lowers her voice*) —

Katya says what happened was this. Yesterday afternoon the old lady and Aleksey and Arkady just happened to walk into the drawing room — and there they were! — Natalya and Michel!

DOCTOR   There they were what?

LIZAVETA   What just! That's the question!

DOCTOR   You suggest zey ver coupling?

LIZAVETA   God forgive you, they were not!

DOCTOR   He wouldn't be — not that he isn't thinking about it all the time.

LIZAVETA   Ignaty!

DOCTOR   Wouldn't put it past her, though.

LIZAVETA   Now that's nasty.

DOCTOR   Sorry. Orange?

LIZAVETA   Thanks. All the same — Shhh!

> MATVEY *and* KATYA *enter. She is carrying a basket of flowers. He is exuberant and dances in front of her, blocking her way. She is very angry — or pretends to be.*

MATVEY   I knock. The door opens. A sweet little lady with red cheeks and silver hair.

KATYA   God, I really hate you.

MATVEY   'Katya's mother?' 'Yes.' 'I'm Matvey.' 'Ah, Matvey! Welcome, Matvey! Come in! Come in!'

KATYA   I'll never speak to you again.

MATVEY   'Little Katya talks about you all the time. When are you two getting married?'

KATYA   Look, I wouldn't marry you if —

MATVEY   'Come and have dinner with us next Sunday. We'll fix everything up then.'

KATYA   I'll not be there.

MATVEY   'But I'm crippled with rheumatism, dear lady. And I have the wrong spiritual disposition. And what about the chasm between our ages?'

KATYA   You bastard!

MATVEY   'Age? Can't I see you're a splendid, handsome, virile, intelligent man.'

119

KATYA You're a damned liar!

MATVEY 'No wonder little Katya's dying about you.'

KATYA She never said that!

MATVEY 'She never stops talking about you.'

KATYA Get out of my road, you sneaky old . . . pig!

She rushes off. He follows, laughing.

LIZAVETA Well — well — well — well! What d'you make of that?

DOCTOR Cat and curiosity — remember?

LIZAVETA And the word about the house is that herself and Herr Schaaf are a pair. Now he's a real pig — Schaaf.

DOCTOR Matvey has the same idea as myself.

LIZAVETA What idea's that?

DOCTOR What you and I have been skirting around for the past hour and a half.

LIZAVETA (*Coyly*) What have we been skirting around, Ignaty?

DOCTOR If you're going to go all fluttery and simpering on me again, Lizaveta, there's no point in . . . All right. Plain speech. I'm sick of trying to run a bachelor house. You're sick of being a companion to the old bird. We're not getting any younger. Is there any good reason why we shouldn't go ahead with . . . things? All right, we don't know a great deal about one another. But maybe that's no harm. For example, what do I know about you? Tidy appearance; cautious manner; good company to be with when you're not being coy; sharp at times — that tongue can be very bitter —

LIZAVETA Is this kind of analysis really — ?

DOCTOR But that's because you're a spinster. Damned inquisitive — that's another spinsterish thing. But practical, sensible, feet on ground. And you tell me you're a good cook?

LIZAVETA And what do I know about you?

DOCTOR If all you know about me is what they know

about me, then you don't know me at all. 'A
breath of fresh air' — 'comedian' — hah! They're
civil to me because I relieve their boredom. But in
their hearts they hate the peasant in me. And I
clown for them because that masks how deeply I
detest them. Oh, yes — detest them! Let me show
you the Shpigelsky without the mask — well, a
portion of him. Youngest of fourteen. Born in a
mud hovel. Dirt. Cold. Misery. Hungry every day
of my life. Somehow managed to scramble into
an education of sorts and became what you see
— a mediocre doctor with a large practice and
scarcely any money.

LIZAVETA Everyone says you're a good doctor.

DOCTOR I'm not. And if you ever get ill I'll get another
doctor for you. What else is there? A moody man.
Don't talk a lot. But not a jealous man. And I
don't think I'm a mean man. And that's about it:
biography — potted.

LIZAVETA I think you're far too severe on yourself.

DOCTOR Accurate. Because if you agree to marry me you
must know you're not marrying the laughing,
fawning, ingratiating Shpigelsky. You're teaming
up with the bitter, angry, cunning peasant.

LIZAVETA I still think you're much too —

DOCTOR And if you think you could make a life with him,
well and good. What age are you?

LIZAVETA Thirty.

DOCTOR You're forty if you're a day.

LIZAVETA Actually I'm thirty-six.

DOCTOR I'll settle for that. And you should give up that
snuff.

LIZAVETA Snuff! I never — !

He holds up an admonishing finger.

An occasional pinch keeps the head clear. And
you drink!

DOCTOR Point. Snuff away.

LIZAVETA (*Softening*) I'm going to give it up anyway.

DOCTOR A damn good woman, Lizaveta. I like you a lot. But I don't like hanging about. Could I have your answer in — say — a month? Six months? Maybe even a year?

LIZAVETA You'll have it tomorrow morning, Ignaty.

> *He stares at her in amazement. Then a huge smile covers his face.*

DOCTOR Now that's the kind of woman I love! I'm not much good at romantic stuff but maybe this once . . .

> *He takes her hand, bends over it and kisses it. As he does:*

I hope you're not off simpering again?

LIZAVETA I'm not. You are.

> SCHAAF *and* ALEKSEY *enter.* SCHAAF *has* ALEKSEY *by the elbow.* ALEKSEY *looks around for* VERA.

SCHAAF Speak the word again, Aleksey: *Eis, Sah-ne-Eis.*

ALEKSEY *Sahne-Eis.*

SCHAAF *Gut.* And now I tell you how I compose it: from milk fat, from sugar, from gelatin — gelatin, yes?

ALEKSEY Yes.

SCHAAF *Ja.* So I mix them together and I freeze them and then I have *Sahne-Eis* — delicious ice cream.

> *Now he sees the* DOCTOR *and* LIZAVETA.

SCHAAF Ah! Herr Doctor! And Lizaveta!

DOCTOR Herr Schaaf.

> SCHAAF *wags a roguish finger at the* DOCTOR *and* LIZAVETA.

SCHAAF So you make lust in the gazebo, Doctor, yes? Very

gut. Nice hot day for it. And now you all return to go home with me to taste my — Aleksey?

ALEKSEY *Sahne-Eis.*

SCHAAF Excellent. My ice cream. Made with my hand. Lizaveta?

LIZAVETA Lovely, thank you. I didn't know you were a chef, too.

SCHAAF Oh yes, I am great chef — I am great scholar — I am great sportsman with bow and arrow. Did you know, Lizaveta, at university I am prize-winning lecher?

DOCTOR Archer, Herr Schaaf.

SCHAAF Archer — *Danke.* And now we go and eat my *Sahne-Eis.* Aleksey?

ALEKSEY Go ahead. I'll join you in a few minutes.

SCHAAF We eat it on the lawn — *Eis im Freien.* This is very nice on hot day, Doctor. After lust-making.

> *He puts a confident arm around* LIZAVETA — *to her alarm — and leads her and the* DOCTOR *off.*
> ALEKSEY *is alone. He looks around for* VERA. *After a few seconds she enters. Unlike the last time we saw her she is now very still, very controlled. But we have a sense, too, that a breakdown could easily occur.*

VERA Thank you for coming. I was afraid Katya mightn't have got the message to you.

ALEKSEY Have you been crying?

VERA Sunburn. I've been walking for hours, preparing a very important speech I was going to make to you. But now that I'm with you . . .

ALEKSEY You're looking wonderful, Vera.

VERA So you're leaving us, Master Tutor?

ALEKSEY Natalya told you that?

VERA Yes.

ALEKSEY Maybe . . . we'll see . . . nothing's decided.

VERA She says you want to go. Is she telling the truth?

ALEKSEY Well, I thought that — you know — in the circumstances . . . It would be wiser, wouldn't it?

VERA She told you about the talk she and I had?

ALEKSEY Yes.

VERA That I said I was in love with you?

ALEKSEY Yes.

VERA She's so treacherous. She trapped me into saying things I shouldn't have said. And now I've said it again, haven't I?

She begins to cry quietly. He takes her hand in his. She withdraws it.

No, no. I'm fine. Honestly.

ALEKSEY And I love you, too. I really do. D'you know what I'm going to do this winter? Take piano lessons! And this time next year we'll meet somewhere and play duets together and laugh like we —

VERA Please, Aleksey. I'm not Baby Face anymore.

ALEKSEY Of course you're not. You're a very beautiful woman that I have a great, great affection for; that I esteem. Beautiful; and sensitive; and open. I've been here a month; and it's been the happiest month of my life because of you. And the last thing I would want is to see that beautiful, sensitive, open woman hurt in any way at all. That's why I must leave. You know I'm right. Yes, you have my love, Vera, really — whatever the affection of a penniless, jobless graduate is worth . . .

VERA Esteem — affection — love; maybe you're right; maybe they are synonymous; maybe they should be. The fools, the loose-mouths talk only of 'love'. But maybe we should all settle for esteem — just a little esteem. Come on, Aleksey — don't look so anxious. I'm in a mess — a mess — a mess — of course I am. But a mess entirely of my own making. For the first time in my life I had an experience I thought was unique; and I thought everybody must recognize it and rejoice with me. (*Laughs*) A fool. A loose-mouth. No, you're not responsible, Aleksey; you're only a bystander. And for all her deviousness, not her mess either. Of course she betrayed me and I'm angry with her for that. But I'm more sorry for her than angry because she's so confused. She doesn't recognize the unique anymore. Maybe she never did. And now I think she's quite . . . demented.

ALEKSEY Come on, Vera.

VERA You have demented her.

ALEKSEY I have — !

VERA Because she's in love with you.

ALEKSEY For God's sake, Vera — !

VERA And madly jealous of me because she thought you were interested in me. That's why one minute you have to go — the next you stay. That's why she's scheming with the doctor to pair me off with old Bolshintsov.

ALEKSEY You're not serious!

NATALYA *enters and watches them.*

VERA And it all seems quite reasonable to her — because she loves you. That's what love does: makes the unreasonable perfectly reasonable. How do you feel about her?

ALEKSEY Natalya?

VERA Do you love her, Aleksey?

ALEKSEY What are you — !

VERA I think you do.

ALEKSEY If you think I'm going to be —

VERA Yes, you do. I hope it's unique for you.

NATALYA, *smiling resolutely, now joins them.*

NATALYA So there you are! I've been searching all over for you two. (*To* ALEKSEY) You are very disobedient, Aleksey Belyayev: you promised me — no more walks alone in the garden.

ALEKSEY I just happened to —

VERA Aleksey's here because I asked him to join me here.

NATALYA Playing one of your silly laughing games, are you?

ALEKSEY We've just been chatting.

NATALYA I love this old gazebo. Arkady and I used to meet here long ago. It was red then. Your hair needs a wash, darling. I'll do it tonight.

VERA (*Softly*) I always wash my own hair, Natalya.

NATALYA I got a wonderful new shampoo from Paris: Volatile — good name, isn't it? Do you know what I was thinking this morning? If we put the two sides in ringlets we could comb the front —

VERA (*Shouts*) Stop it, Natalya! Stop it!

NATALYA Darling — ?

VERA For God's sake, stop this game-playing! I'm no longer a child, Natalya — nor your ward that you can manipulate —

NATALYA Vera, my love —

VERA Nor your younger sister that you can kiss and worm secrets out of and then betray shamelessly. I am a woman, Natalya, and I am going to be treated like a woman.

NATALYA My darling, you're upset and —

VERA Yes, I am very upset. Aleksey says he is leaving because of me — and that's dishonest. Yes, I love him — you know I love him. But if he goes, it's because of you.

NATALYA Vera —

VERA Because you are in love with him. And that's why you betrayed me — because you thought I was a rival. But I'm not a rival, Natalya — I wish to God I were — but I'm not — I'm not . . .

She suddenly breaks down, looks at them for a second — and then dashes off. ALEKSEY *moves to follow her.*

NATALYA Don't go, Aleksey. Please.

He stops.

Vera is right: I have behaved disgracefully. I'm ashamed of myself. And it is time to stop the game-playing and to muster whatever residue of decency I may still have. So — this is the last time I will see you. Or talk to you. I have made my mind up: you are leaving.

ALEKSEY   I've already packed my —

NATALYA   And she's right, too, about me: I am in love with you. Strange how I can say it so calmly, isn't it? — without embarrassment; almost disinterestedly; so simply, as if it had nothing to do with anguish and despair and pain and a kind of madness. I have been in love with you since the first day you came here. I suppose that was what the game-playing was all about: moving towards that possibility, that discovery, that acknowledgement; and then deviously, frantically trying to protect it. Why am I telling you all this? It's the last thing I should want you to know about me, that I'm calculating and treacherous and — look at me — yes, so ridiculous. No, no, please; you don't have to say anything. Just to have to listen to a declaration of love from a woman you have no interest in, that's difficult enough. Anyhow . . . that's all I have to say . . . (*Brisk*) So. You've packed? Good. You'll leave after lunch. Matvey'll drive you to the town. I'll send you the balance of your salary. We won't meet again. There are going to be no goodbyes.

ALEKSEY   I'm not going.

NATALYA   You are —

ALEKSEY   I won't! I can't! Never in my life have I met a woman like you.

NATALYA   Aleksey —

ALEKSEY   So elegant, so poised, so beautiful —

NATALYA   Please, Aleksey —

ALEKSEY   You have no idea how — how magnificent, how exotic you are to someone like me.

NATALYA For God's sake, stop —

ALEKSEY This house, this style, this grace, this ease, this refinement, this symmetry, this elegance — for a month I pretended that of course I wasn't impressed. But I was overwhelmed — I was in awe, Natalya — mute with awe. And at the centre of all this elegance and grace, there you were — the core, the essence, the very epicentre of it, holding it all in place, releasing, dispensing its wonders. And you noticed me and you spoke to me and you were kind to me — to me! — Aleksey Belyayev, a nobody in shabby clothes holding the delicate hand of this luminous creature.

NATALYA You're leaving tomorrow, Aleksey.

ALEKSEY Yes, yes, yes, Vera's so right, so wise! I am in love with you! And you are in love with me!

He embraces her and swings her round.

Oh my God, you are unique, Natalya! And I am unique! We are both unique!

NATALYA And you'll leave tomorrow?

He kisses her and at the same time swings her round.

You'll leave tomorrow?

ALEKSEY Tomorrow.

Again he kisses her and swings her round.

NATALYA Tomorrow?

ALEKSEY Tomorrow.

Again he kisses her and swings her round.

NATALYA Tomorrow?

ALEKSEY Tomorrow.

Again he kisses her and swings her round.
MICHEL *enters.*

NATALYA Tomorrow.

ALEKSEY Tomorrow — tomorrow — tomorrow.

Again he kisses her and swings her round.

NATALYA No, don't go, Aleksey — don't go — don't ever go. Oh please God, no.

> ALEKSEY *now sees* MICHEL *watching them. He freezes. Now* NATALYA, *seeing* ALEKSEY's *face, turns and sees* MICHEL *too. A few seconds of silence. Then* ALEKSEY *in acute embarrassment runs off.*

MICHEL Thought you were here. Arkady's looking for you. He's just behind me.

NATALYA Well, here I am.

MICHEL So you've made your decision? The young tutor isn't being sent away?

NATALYA I'm not going to be cross-questioned, Michel.

MICHEL And he ran off in embarrassment! But then he's new at the game.

NATALYA (*Looking around*) I had a scarf —

MICHEL And he's bright; give him time; he'll learn to dissemble. Indeed he may be the very man to answer that anguished question of yours, 'What's to become of me?'

NATALYA Did you see a scarf — ?

MICHEL That's the trouble with baring your soul, isn't it? You regret it later. All that inflated language, the emotional palpitations, the heaving passions. I've done it so often myself — in my foolishness. It occurred to me a while ago that we regret most of the things we say and we regret even more all the things we don't say; so that our lives just dribble away in remorse. (*Suddenly regretting his bitterness*)

Natalya, if I could —

Voices, off. MICHEL *breaks off.*

NATALYA (*Urgently*) Have you spoken to Arkady?
MICHEL What about?
NATALYA When he saw us together in the drawing room —
you were to give him an explanation.
MICHEL Yes — no, no, not yet. Don't worry — I'll speak to
him tonight. We've nothing to hide, have we?

Enter ARKADY *and the* DOCTOR.

ARKADY We thought we had lost you, my darling! We've
been searching all —

He stops when he sees MICHEL. *He refuses to look
at him for the rest of the scene.*

NATALYA Is there some mystery? Here I am.
MICHEL So you are . . . yes . . .

Pause.

DOCTOR (*Quickly*) Just telling Arkady about this man who
goes to the doctor —
ARKADY This is very comical — most comical.
DOCTOR 'Doctor, Doctor, I think I'm a pair of curtains.'
'Curtains? Pull yourself together, man!' (*He holds
his head*) I know — I know — I know — I know.

ARKADY *laughs excessively.*

ARKADY Pull yourself together! Because he thinks he's a
pair of curtains!
MICHEL They're getting worse, Doctor.
ARKADY I love them. I'm the best audience you could have.

Brief pause.

DOCTOR One more. This is the last. I promise. 'Doctor, Doctor, I'm in agony. There's a teacher in my eye.'

ARKADY Sorry — missed that — a what?

DOCTOR A teacher.

ARKADY Ah. A teacher. Yes?

DOCTOR 'A teacher? That's not a teacher, you fool! That's a pupil.' (*He spreads his arms*) Shoot me, please — shoot me.

> *A moment's hesitation. Then* ARKADY *laughs excessively again.*

ARKADY A pupil! In his eye! Do you get it? Good one, Doctor! Great one!

> *The laughter dies. Awkward silence.*

(*To* NATALYA) Did I interrupt another discussion?

MICHEL I was telling Natalya —

ARKADY Or just a continuation of the first one? Because whatever it's about, it must be of — of — of universal importance — that's all I can say.

DOCTOR A bit of medical advice for you all.

ARKADY Of universal importance at least.

DOCTOR Dr Schaaf has made ice cream. I've eaten it before. Lethal. (*To* NATALYA) By the way you're having a visitor later, Natalya. Bolshintsov, I'm afraid.

NATALYA I don't want him near this house again.

DOCTOR He's very insistent. And I've said that —

ARKADY If Natalya doesn't want him, Doctor, then let him know he's not welcome here. Nothing more to be said. Now — dinner time! Let's all go and eat.

> *He holds his arm out to* NATALYA. *She takes it. They move off.*

DOCTOR (*To* MICHEL) And we know what our fate is, don't we?

MICHEL Do we?

DOCTOR Oh yes — to bring up the rear.

MICHEL Fine.

DOCTOR Or another way of putting it, Michel: we're hangers-on.

MICHEL Let me tell you something, Doctor — something I regret I haven't said to you before.

DOCTOR And what is that?

MICHEL I am really sick of you.

A huge peal of laughter from the DOCTOR.

DOCTOR Good heavens, isn't that a remarkable coincidence! Because I'm really sick of myself!

End of Scene.

ACT TWO

Scene Two

The drawing room the following morning.
ANNA *is sewing.* ARKADY, *tense and agitated, tries to conceal his unease in activity. He consults a list and passes various documents to* MATVEY.

ARKADY   (*Quickly, sharply*) It doesn't make sense. I just don't understand it. Do you, Mother? Updating survey maps at this time of year — that's a job for winter! (*To* MATVEY) Has the land stewart nothing better to do?

MATVEY   He says —

ARKADY   All right — all right — we'll indulge him. That's the wheat fields (*map*). The birch forest. The paddock area. What else does he want? (*Consults list again*) The lakes. Where are the lakes? Here we are.

MATVEY   And the lower meadows.

ARKADY   The lower meadows.

MATVEY   The new dam.

ARKADY   Weir — weir — weir! Why is everyone so stupid. It's a weir — not a dam.

MATVEY   That's all he wants for the moment.

ARKADY   They must be returned to me before the end of the month, Matvey.

MATVEY   Yessir.

ARKADY   They are not to be left in the bailiff's quarters.

MATVEY   Absolutely not. Trust Matvey. Is it too early for tea?

ARKADY   Mother — tea?

ANNA   No, thanks.

ARKADY   In half-an-hour. That's everything, Matvey, thank you.

MATVEY *hesitates, then goes to* ARKADY *and whispers in his ear.*

ARKADY Can't hear you! Speak up! ·

More whispering.

What for?

More whispering.

What's so very important to you?

More whispering.

We'll see — we'll see — talk to me next week. (*As* MATVEY *departs*) And Matvey — tell Monsieur Rakitin I'd like a word with him. He's in the billiard room.

MATVEY *exits.*

ARKADY Such a strange request. Matvey wants three days off. Never had a day off in his life and now he wants three.

ANNA What for?

ARKADY Something about a wedding, I think. Three full days! He wouldn't know what to do with himself.

ANNA Let him have them, Arkady.

ARKADY I said I'll see; and I will.

ANNA Did I hear you walking about during the night?

ARKADY Did I waken you?

ANNA No, I was reading.

ARKADY Yes, the old mind was thrashing about a bit. So I moved into the nursery. Didn't want to disturb Natalya.

ANNA *puts away her sewing.*

ANNA Michel and you haven't spoken yet?

ARKADY (*Alert*) Sorry?

ANNA Michel hasn't offered you an . . . explanation yet, has he?

ARKADY That's why I've sent for him.

ANNA Ah.

ARKADY Since he hasn't volunteered to give me one, now I'm going to demand one. I am owed an explanation, Mother.

ANNA Of course.

ARKADY And if one isn't offered now, this very morning, then I'll insist on one.

ANNA There may well be a very simple explanation, Arkady; so simple we just can't see it.

ARKADY I'm prepared to listen. I'm not an unreasonable man. But this is my home, Mother; and I am head of this household; and I will not be treated casually by anybody under this roof — not by anybody.

ANNA Of course not.

ARKADY I mean to say — I walk into this room; and there is my wife with this man; and she is sobbing; and all he can say is, 'Trust me. Trust me.' I mean to say, even with the best will in the world, Mother, an explanation is necessary.

> *She looks closely at him. He is on the point of tears. She goes to him.*

ANNA You work too hard. You're getting more like your father.

ARKADY Am I?

ANNA It's a pity you never knew him.

ARKADY I have a vague memory of him.

ANNA He was such a handsome man; and so talented; and so gracious; and so endlessly kind. I loved him very much. Yes; without reservation. And he doted on you. He would have been so proud to have seen you grown up and managing the estate so well — this estate that he fashioned out of a wilderness — gave his entire life to, really . . . And all the years we were married, at the beginning of every month — you wouldn't remember; you were too young — he went to Moscow for three nights; to sell timber or grain; or to buy new horses or equipment. And to visit a lady there that he loved. Her name was Maria, I think. I never saw her but I was told she wasn't at all beautiful. Strange, wasn't it — and he was so . . . so magnificent . . . Every month for almost fifteen years. And throughout all those years he never mentioned her to me and I never mentioned her to him. Because he loved me, too. I know he did. And I loved him very much. Yes; without reservation. So what would there have been to say . . . except wounding things . . . And he would have been so proud of little Kolya.

MICHEL enters carrying a billiard cue.

I'm glad that billiard table's being used again.

MICHEL It's a great table.

ANNA So my husband used to say. But if it weren't for you, Michel, it would be mildewed. You must play more often.

She leaves. MICHEL is on the defensive. He looks at ARKADY who is suddenly embarrassed and pretends to tidy his papers.

MICHEL Matvey said you wanted me. (*Pause*) Do you want to see me, Arkady?

ARKADY You owe me something.

MICHEL Do I?

ARKADY You owe me an explanation.

MICHEL I don't think —

ARKADY I am owed an explanation. You promised me an explanation.

MICHEL   What I said was —

ARKADY   What you said was trust me; that's what you said; trust me; I can explain all this; there is a perfectly simple explanation, you said.

MICHEL   And there is.

ARKADY   And that's what I want to hear — that perfectly simple explanation. I walk in here with my mother and that tutor fellow; and there are you and my wife. And can you imagine — have you any idea at all? — what I felt? — how I felt? — and my mother standing beside me? And then yesterday evening at the gazebo — there you are again — for a second time — for God's sake, for a second time! — and that charlatan Shpigelsky watching and listening and privately sneering and —

          He breaks down. After he recovers:

          I can't talk to you like this, Michel — we've known each other since we were boys — how can I talk to you like this? Oh my God, have you any idea how destroyed I am?

MICHEL   Arkady, I —

ARKADY   Just answer one question — please, please, just one question, please. I really don't want an explanation. For God's sake, what good is an explanation? Just one question, Michel; and please answer it honestly. Are you in love with Natalya?

MICHEL   Yes.

ARKADY   So. There you are. Knew it. So there you are. Knew it for a long time of course. Oh yes. And I don't blame you — blame? — it's not a question of blame for God's sake. No, no; it's — it's understandable; that's what it is; quite understandable; she's such a beautiful woman that naturally men find her attractive; and naturally, of course naturally, naturally — she responds to those attentions. And the trouble is — part of the trouble is — that you and she have so much more in common than she and I have —

oh yes, yes, yes, you have. You're both so intelligent and so well read and so sophisticated. Not that she doesn't love me — I'm not saying that — I know she loves me. But she responds to something in you I haven't got, can't give her. And I think I could have carried on — yes, I know I could — as long as she was, you know — reasonably discreet. But those two occasions, here and at the gazebo — I mean I don't think — I really don't think I should have been subjected to that, Michel. But at the same time it would be wrong of me to deny her her freedom; I won't do that either; I can't crush another person's life. So what we must do, Michel — and Natalya, too — we must try to — to — to find some way of conducting our lives together — the three of us — as best we can — with discretion — without too much hurt — as best we can — however we can . . . That's what we must do . . . please . . .

Pause.

MICHEL I know what we must do, Arkady. I must leave here.
ARKADY Go away?
MICHEL It's the only answer.
ARKADY (*In panic*) Oh, God, no, Michel! Please!
MICHEL By myself, Arkady. Alone.
ARKADY Not with Natalya?
MICHEL Not with Natalya. Alone.
ARKADY But you love her —
MICHEL I'll leave tomorrow. You know I'm right.
ARKADY How will we tell Natalya? Oh God, better you tell her. No, I will. It's my duty. I will.

Impetuously he flings his arms around MICHEL.

God bless you, Michel. You are a very, very good man. Thank you. I said I couldn't deny her her freedom — and I couldn't — how could I? But if I let her go altogether, Michel, I don't think I would survive.

MICHEL   We all survive, Arkady.

ARKADY   Do we? Yes, I suppose we do. Even if we love without reservation.

MICHEL   Especially if we love without reservation.

    ARKADY *embraces him briefly again.*

ARKADY   May God bless you abundantly.

    ALEKSEY *enters.*

ALEKSEY   Sorry. Am I — ?

ARKADY   Come ahead, Ivan — come on.

MICHEL   (*Whispers*) Aleksey.

ARKADY   Sorry — Aleksey. How can we help you?

ALEKSEY   This is a list of French books Kolya will need next term.

ARKADY   Good — splendid. Thank you. Just leave it there. And now, if you'll excuse me —

    He is about to leave, turns, embraces MICHEL *quickly again.*

The astonishing winnowing machine is reluctant to winnow. Maybe that's what makes it astonishing!

    He laughs heartily, nervously, and leaves. MICHEL *goes over to the bookshelf and begins picking out his own books. His manner is brittle and edged with panic.*

MICHEL   I'm going to the town tomorrow. Can I give you a lift?

ALEKSEY   No, thanks.

MICHEL   *Tristram Shandy* — that's my copy. (*Removes the*

bookmark we saw in Act One, Scene One) Never seem to get past page 115. Have you ever read it?

ALEKSEY You're going shopping?

MICHEL Leaving.

ALEKSEY Leaving for good?

MICHEL Business in Moscow. I was sure I had some Dickens here.

ALEKSEY I thought you'd be here until —

MICHEL Between these and the books upstairs I'll have to get an extra trunk.

ALEKSEY Does Natalya know you're leaving?

MICHEL Not yet. She'll be told.

He goes to ALEKSEY *and speaks directly into his face.*

All right, I'll tell you why I'm leaving, Aleksey. Arkady believes I'm in love with Natalya. Asked me straight out. And because he believes that, I have to leave, haven't I?

ALEKSEY Oh God.

MICHEL You'd do the same if you were in my position, wouldn't you?

ALEKSEY Oh my God.

MICHEL I imagine you're a big believer in 'love'. Am I right?

ALEKSEY Oh I — I —

MICHEL Yes you are.

ALEKSEY I've very little —

MICHEL Go on — admit it.

ALEKSEY I believe — I *think* — that if you love a woman and if she loves you — that must be a great happiness, mustn't it?

MICHEL Got it wrong, Aleksey, I'm afraid. All love is a catastrophe. Look at me. An endless process of shame and desolation and despair when you are stripped — you strip yourself! — of every semblance of dignity and self respect; when you grovel in the hope of a casual word or a sly smile or a secret squeeze of the hand. But of course you think: that won't be my experience; poor old Rakitin — all his life he's been a hanger-on, the second man, made for humiliation, invites it with his 'loyalty', his subservience, doesn't he?

ALEKSEY Honest to God, Michel, I never thought of —

MICHEL Let me tell you just one thing. When you find yourself enslaved by love, owned by a woman, then for the first time in your life you will know what real suffering is. Yes; look at me.

He gives a quick dry laugh. Pause.

ALEKSEY I'm very sorry you're leaving, Michel.

MICHEL Thank you. Look after yourself.

ALEKSEY We'll all miss you.

MICHEL For a day.

ALEKSEY Well, I'll miss you. And I really am sorry you've been so . . . hurt.

MICHEL, *embarrassed, quickly ruffles* ALEKSEY's *hair. And then quickly, spontaneously, the two men embrace. As they do* NATALYA *enters carrying a box of chocolates. She is alerted by the display of affection between the two men. She looks quickly from one to the other.*

NATALYA Do you know where I've been for the past half-hour? Sitting under the lime tree in the walled garden gorging myself on these. They're wonderful. (*To* ALEKSEY) Have one.

ALEKSEY Thanks.

NATALYA Have two. Have three. The perfume from that lime tree is so subtle.

MICHEL *has returned to his books.* NATALYA *picks up the* Tristram Shandy.

NATALYA We are never going to get through this *Tristram Shandy*, Michel. So what we've got to do is take ourselves in hand. You'll be a real sweetheart and every night after dinner you'll read me a full chapter — beginning tonight.

MICHEL I'm leaving today, Natalya. In fact — now.

She looks quickly at ALEKSEY *who is suddenly engrossed in Kolya's list.*

NATALYA What do you mean?

MICHEL Going to Moscow. Business.

NATALYA But you'll be back?

MICHEL We'll see. Perhaps. I'll make you a present of the Sterne. Maybe Aleksey'll read it to you.

NATALYA You're not going now — just like that!

MICHEL After I've finished packing. Then I'll say my good-byes.

MICHEL *exits. She tries to conceal her alarm — she laughs.*

NATALYA Typical Michel. Totally unpredictable. God alone knows what goes on in that strange head of his. Now. Give me your hand. I want to tell you my plans. (*She takes* ALEKSEY'S *hand*) This afternoon I'm going to visit my old nanny at a village called Spasskoye. It's about fifteen miles from here. And you are going to drive me. And we are going to have a picnic together on the bank of the —

He suddenly winces and withdraws his hand.

Oh I'm sorry. Did I hurt you?

ALEKSEY No, I'm fine.

NATALYA Don't know my own strength. Are you sure?

ALEKSEY Fine — fine — really.

NATALYA So that's agreed? Good. Can you swim?

ALEKSEY Just about.

NATALYA I'm sure you're a wonderful swimmer. And there's a lovely sandy beach there. And it's a perfect day for a drive.

ALEKSEY   If you'll excuse me, Natalya. I promised Michel I'd help him to pack.

ARKADY   (*Off, calling*) Aleksey! Where are you?

ALEKSEY   (*Calling*) In the drawing room.

NATALYA   So that's agreed?

ARKADY *enters.*

ARKADY   We need help out here. (*To* NATALYA) Oh, I love that dress! You look astonishing in that dress! (*To* ALEKSEY) The winnowing machine's stuck in the mud. Come on, boy. We need your muscle.

ARKADY *exits.*

NATALYA   That's agreed, Aleksey?

ALEKSEY   Yes — yes —

The DOCTOR *and* VERA *enter.*

NATALYA   (*Anxiously*) And we'll leave about three?

ALEKSEY   Fine — yes — yes — fine. (*To* VERA) I'm not running away. I'm needed. I'll be straight back.

ALEKSEY *exits.*

DOCTOR   Have you heard the news, Natalya? Michel's leaving!

NATALYA   Yes.

DOCTOR   Today! Now!

NATALYA   I know.

DOCTOR   Good Lord! Business in Moscow, he says. Well — well — well — well. And what's the commotion in the yard?

NATALYA   The damn winnowing machine — it's stuck again, I think.

DOCTOR   That's the way with those machines: some you winnow, some you lose-ow. (*He holds his head as before*) Sorry — sorry — sorry.

VERA   Aren't we going to get tea this morning?

DOCTOR   Indeed. Good idea.

He goes to the door and calls.

Matvey! Where are you?

NATALYA *speaks softly and intimately to* VERA *who remains icy throughout.*

NATALYA   I'll say it once more and never again. What I did was wrong. I can't explain why I did it. But it's done. And I'm sorry. And I apologize.

VERA   (*To* DOCTOR) If he's in the kitchen he won't hear you.

DOCTOR   (*Louder*) Matvey!

NATALYA   And you've got to stop this childish sulking.

VERA   Why are you so agitated? He does love you. Hasn't he told you yet?

NATALYA   I'm sending him away.

VERA   (*Mirthless laugh*) He goes — he stays — he goes — he stays. You're very unsure of him, aren't you? And what if you lost him now after all that duplicity?

NATALYA   You're a vicious little vixen, aren't you!

NATALYA *leaves. The* DOCTOR *goes to* VERA.

DOCTOR   Either he doesn't hear me or he's ignoring me.

He now sees that NATALYA *is gone. He looks intently into* VERA's *face.*

Do you want to tell me why you're so sad?

She shrugs. He goes through his pantomime of taking her pulse.

Far too fast. Is the heart a bit . . . perturbed? (*Wearily and in self-mockery*) A man came up to me this morning. 'Help me, Doctor. I'm Aikin from Neuralgia.' 'Glad to meet you. I'm Shpigelsky from Gorlovka.' (*Pause*) If the mask fits, wear it, I say.

VERA   Tell me about Bolshintsov, Doctor.

DOCTOR   (*Eagerly*) Happily! What do you want to know? Ask me anything about him — anything at all.

VERA   I've really only one question.

DOCTOR   Very, very well off — I promise you. Owns the biggest farm from here to —

> *He breaks off because* KATYA *enters. She is smiling serenely.*

(*Irritably*) Well — well — what is it, girl?

KATYA   You called, Doctor.

DOCTOR   What for?

KATYA   I can't read minds, Doctor, can I?

DOCTOR   What are you talking about?

KATYA   You called for Matvey. I am here in Matvey's place.

DOCTOR   Yes — tea — tell him to serve tea in here.

KATYA   Matvey is engaged elsewhere, Doctor. But his responsibilities are now my responsibilities and I am very happy to share them with him.

DOCTOR   (*To* VERA) What's the girl ranting about?

KATYA   Tea for two? For three? For everybody?

DOCTOR   If I'm not disrupting your life too much.

KATYA   Not at all, Doctor. It is my pleasure. And Matvey's.

> *She exits.*

DOCTOR   Good God! Touch of sunstroke, maybe. Anyhow — Bolshintsov. Wealthy. Gentlemanly. Considerate. Quite sophisticated — in a rural sort of way. What's your one question?

VERA   If I displeased him, is he the kind of man who would strike me?

The DOCTOR *stares at her in amazement. Then he takes her in his arms as if she were a child and rocks her.*

DOCTOR Never — never — never — never — oh never. Oh my sweet, sad-eyed child, what can I say to you? He's old; and fat; and stupid; so stupid he thinks my jokes are funny. And yes, he's quite well off. And he seems to like you. And he's kind enough, I suppose. What more can I tell you, little one? If I thought for a moment that love was a necessary — even a desirable — ingredient in these matters, then I'd say: pass this up. But since I don't . . . (*He shrugs*) He's bird in hand, I suppose . . .

Pause.

VERA (*Quickly, resolutely*) I'll marry him, Doctor.
DOCTOR You'll wait until —
VERA I said I'll marry him. Tell him I'll marry him.
DOCTOR Vera, you'll —
VERA But I won't wait. It has to be now — as soon as possible. Will you tell him that?

He spreads his hands and nods his head. SCHAAF *enters rapidly, barely hesitating as he dashes through the room.*

SCHAAF You hear the tidings? Michel is exiting — even now as we prattle. (*He takes the* DOCTOR *by the elbow*) Come. We tell him goodbye. Then I go riding. You go riding with me, Doctor?
DOCTOR Sorry, Herr Schaaf. Calls all afternoon.
SCHAAF (*To* ALEKSEY *who enters*) We tell goodbye to Michel. He exits even now as we prattle.

The DOCTOR *and* SCHAAF *both leave.*

ALEKSEY (*To* VERA) I'm glad you're alone.

VERA (*Embarrassed*) I thought you were helping with the — ?

ALEKSEY I was. Then I helped Michel pack. Then I packed my own things.

VERA Why? Are you — ?

ALEKSEY I've got to leave, Vera. Today. Now. You know I have. I had a strange talk with Michel a while ago; and looking at him, listening to him, suddenly there were no more confusions: Get out! — get out! — get out! Do I sound sort of frantic? I suppose I am. Part of my mind is hysterical but part of it is wonderfully lucid. I'm here a month and what happens? Arkady fights with Michel. Michel fights with Natalya. Natalya fights with you. Anna fights with Michel. And in some way I seem to be the cause of it all. And now Michel is leaving. And I'm leaving.

VERA And I'm leaving.

ALEKSEY (*Not listening to her*) Good for you. I'm so far out of my depth, Vera, I can scarcely breathe. Of course they're kind and thoughtful and intelligent people. But honest to God I never want to see any of them ever again.

VERA But you love her, Aleksey.

ALEKSEY That's exactly what I'm saying: that was part of the hysteria, the madness. A Chinese squib — a quick, blinding flash — then nothing.

VERA Nothing?

He catches her hand.

ALEKSEY But it was a good month, too, Vera, thanks to you. A great month. All those laughs — Nanny coming off the swing? — hiding Matvey's wellington in the oven? — remember? — putting pepper in Lizaveta's snuff-box? Terrible to think we'll have forgotten it all by Christmas.

He kisses her casually on the top of the head.

I'm serious about those piano lessons though. Right?
VERA Right.
ALEKSEY I'm leaving now — on foot. Michel's going to pick me up somewhere along the road. (*As he goes*) Be good.

> *He goes quickly to the door — stops — returns to* VERA.

God, the head's really gone. I can't face Natalya. Give her that (*note*), would you? Read it if you like. 'Goodbye' — that's all it says.

> *He runs off. He almost bumps into* SCHAAF *in the doorway. As before,* SCHAAF *is rushing. He holds a pair of riding boots in his hand.*

'Bye, Herr Schaaf.

> ALEKSEY *exits.*

SCHAAF ''Bye?' But I am not going nowhere. ''Bye?' Why does he confuse me? And Katya she hides on me. She was to have polish my boots but she did not. And now she hides.
VERA Did you try the clothes line?
SCHAAF No, no; I look there. She hides on me today. Why is that?

> NATALYA *enters.*

You know where Katya is?
NATALYA No idea.
SCHAAF I try her bedroom — laundry — clothes line — kitchen — her bedroom again — no Katya. And look (*boots*) — still soiled.

> *He goes off.* NATALYA *puts away her painting things. As she does:*

NATALYA I'll be away all afternoon, Vera. Nanny'll look after Kolya but I'd be glad if you gave a hand.

VERA Of course. (*She holds out the note*) For you.

NATALYA You haven't anything else to do, have you?

VERA Nothing.

> NATALYA *holds out her hand to take the note —*
> *and knows instinctively what is in it.*

NATALYA Aleksey?

VERA Yes.

NATALYA He's going?

VERA Yes.

NATALYA He's already gone?

VERA I think so.

NATALYA Oh my God . . . (*Opens note*) 'Goodbye.' The eloquent Aleksey Belyayev . . .

> *She is about to cry. Then with a burst of sudden*
> *passion:*

How dare he, the pup! The jumped-up, baby-faced pup! Who the hell does he think he is! Well he's not walking away like that! I'm not one of his college sluts! He'll go *if* I say he goes! He'll go *when* I say he goes! And who is he to decide I haven't the courage to throw all this up and go with him! If that decision is to be made it'll be my decision — not his! The bastard! (*About to break down*) Oh my God . . .

VERA It's better he's gone. You know that.

NATALYA Everything's in such a mess . . . I'm afraid I can't hold on much longer . . .

VERA Everything'll soon be back to normal.

NATALYA For God's sake, can't you see it's the normal that's deranging me, child?

> ARKADY *enters.*

VERA I'm leaving, too.

NATALYA The sooner the better. I wish you were all gone. I can't tell you how sick I am of all of you.

ARKADY (*Privately to* VERA) How does she know he's going?

VERA (*Puzzled*) He left a note for her.

ARKADY Damn it, we agreed I'd tell her. That was my duty.

He goes to NATALYA *and puts his arm around her.*

It's all right, my darling. Everything's in hand. Michel and I had a wonderfully open talk. I don't want an explanation. I don't need an explanation. All I need is you.

He lifts her head and looks into her face.

Do you hear me, my darling? You are all I need.

Enter KATYA *with a tray.*

(*Sharply*) Not now, girl.

KATYA *takes in the scene and exits.*

Let me tell you what we'll do. You'll lie down for an hour and I'll bring you up a cup of hot choco-late — remember the famous hot chocolate I used to make for you when you were expecting Kolya? And in no time at all you'll be a new woman — a new and even more beautiful woman — in no time at all.

NATALYA Yes. I'll go to my room. (*Removing his supporting hand*) No, please, Arkady. I can manage.

She picks up her paints and is about to leave when MICHEL *enters.*

MICHEL I came to say goodbye.

ARKADY (*Privately*) We agreed I'd tell her, Michel. Now look at the state she's in.

MICHEL I don't think I'm the cause this time, Arkady.

ARKADY Then who — ?

MICHEL Goodbye, Natalya.

No answer.

ARKADY Michel's leaving, my love.

Pause. ARKADY *puts his arm round* MICHEL'*s shoulder and hugs him.*

But he'll be back. I'm insisting on that. We can't afford to lose a good friend like Michel. Amn't I right?

NATALYA *is about to speak, is overcome with tears — and dashes off.* VERA *follows her.*

VERA She'll be fine. Don't worry.

VERA *exits.* ARKADY *tries to cover his embarrassment with bluster.*

ARKADY And I mean that, Michel. You know that. Come and spend Christmas with us! Please. I'd love you to. She would, too. I know she would — We both know she would.

MICHEL Thank you.

ARKADY No, no, my friend; I thank you. What you are doing is . . . noble!

And again he embraces MICHEL. *Suddenly the door opens and in come* LIZAVETA, ANNA, SCHAAF *and the* DOCTOR. *Everybody speaks at the same time.*

DOCTOR Well — where is she?

ARKADY What? Who?

DOCTOR Katya said she was ill.

LIZAVETA Did she faint?

MICHEL If you'll excuse me —

ANNA Natalya, Arkady.

ARKADY Ah. She's gone to her room — to lie down.

LIZAVETA (*To* DOCTOR) Go and have a look at her.

MICHEL Goodbye, Herr Schaaf.

SCHAAF ''Bye? — 'Bye?' — But I am not going nowhere!

DOCTOR She's in her room now?

LIZAVETA Is Vera with her?

ARKADY Perhaps leave her for a while.

ANNA Was it some sort of weak turn?

ARKADY I promise you — she's fine.

MICHEL I'm about to leave, everybody.

ANNA That little Katya exaggerates.

LIZAVETA If I can be of any help?

SCHAAF All day people tell me 'Bye — 'Bye — 'Bye.

ARKADY Goodbye, Herr Schaaf.

SCHAAF But I am not exiting!

ARKADY Ah. Splendid.

ANNA That little maid's been behaving strangely all day.

MICHEL I'm afraid I have to go —

ARKADY *holds his hand up for silence.*

ARKADY Please — please — please — please — please.

DOCTOR Tell me this: how much of that ice cream did she have?

SCHAAF Why do you ask about my — ?

ARKADY Please! Natalya is perfectly well — wonderfully well. Thank you all for your concern. But I promise you there is nothing, nothing at all to worry about. Now. I need help with the accounts. Where's Ivan?

ANNA The blacksmith is illiterate, Arkady you know that.

ARKADY Of course I know the blacksmith is illiterate. I'm talking about Ivan the —

MICHEL He means Aleksey, the tutor.

ARKADY Aleksey! Why do I always get that wrong!

MICHEL Aleksey has just left.

> *This is greeted with general surprise: What?*
> *When did this happen? Why did he go? Did he*
> *say goodbye to you? Does Kolya know?*

SCHAAF He go also? *Mein Gott.* Everybody is 'Bye — 'Bye
— 'Bye.

ARKADY *(Privately)* When did this happen? He's in my
employment! How can he walk out without — ?

MICHEL Shhh. Vera fell in love with him.

ARKADY Our little — ? With the tutor?

MICHEL And I'm afraid he didn't love her. So the kindest
thing he could do was . . .

ARKADY Leave?

> MICHEL *nods.*

Good heavens! Everybody's leaving! Everybody's
being so noble! The world is suddenly becoming
a wonderful place, Michel! (*To* ANNA *who has joined
them*) But now we have another problem, Mother:
who will teach Kolya his French and English?

SCHAAF *(Overhearing)* I will pedagogue him, Arkady. I am
happy. Especially in English.

ARKADY Most kind of you, Herr Schaaf. That's a splendid
suggestion . . . I'm sure . . .

> ANNA *and* MICHEL *find themselves together.*

ANNA This house will suddenly be very quiet.

MICHEL This house is never quiet.

ANNA With you and the young tutor gone? Oh, yes.
Natalya'll especially miss you both.

MICHEL Maybe.

ANNA Strange, isn't it? She has the unqualified love of a
very good man. But for some women — and for
many men — that doesn't seem to be enough.
And instead of that love satisfying, enriching, it
becomes another form of . . . suffocation. So that
all of their life is dissatisfying, even turbulent.

And the people who offer their love without
reservation, even though that love is neither fully
appreciated nor fully reciprocated, they are the
fortunate ones . . . strange as it may seem . . . even
though they don't believe they are . . . . I hope you
have a very good journey, Michel. And I hope you
will come back to us very soon.

The DOCTOR *joins them.*

DOCTOR Are you getting a lift into town?
MICHEL Matvey's driving me.
DOCTOR Because I should be able to do the needful later in
the day. (*Softly*) In a brand new troika — azure blue!
MICHEL You're a real rogue — you know that?
DOCTOR Me! (*Hand on heart*) My entire life is dedicated to
the sick and the poor, Michel.

And he explodes with laughter.

MICHEL Goodbye, everybody. I'm off. 'Bye. 'Bye. 'Bye.

He quickly shakes several hands.

'Bye, Lizaveta.
LIZAVETA Safe journey, Michel.
SCHAAF Travel in health.
MICHEL Thank you. Anna — goodbye.
ANNA Any time you feel like coming back.
ARKADY He knows that, Mother. Come on — I'll see you
off.
DOCTOR We both will.

General goodbyes, and MICHEL, ARKADY *and the*
DOCTOR *leave.*

SCHAAF Michel is a good man. Already I am lonely for him.
My eyes they wish to wet.
ANNA You mean to — Oh, damn!

LIZAVETA *takes out her snuff-box.*

Lizaveta!
LIZAVETA (*Innocently*) Yes?
ANNA What are you doing?
LIZAVETA I am snuffing.
ANNA I will not have you indulge that filthy habit in this house, Lizaveta.
LIZAVETA Then I'll have to say goodbye to this house, won't I?
SCHAAF 'Bye! Another 'Bye! *Mein Gott!*
ANNA And what does that mean?
LIZAVETA Another 'Bye indeed, Herr Schaaf. In three weeks to be exact!
SCHAAF And who stay? Nobody — nobody — nobody!

Enter MATVEY *and* KATYA *with tea trays. They are both beaming and move almost in tandem.*

MATVEY Sorry we're a bit late.
KATYA Not altogether our fault.
MATVEY Tea for everybody?
KATYA We have coffee, too.
MATVEY Katya has made some delicious crumpets.
KATYA Matvey!
MATVEY They're wonderful.
KATYA Don't listen to him. They're simple drop scones.
ANNA Bring everything out to the lawn, Katya.
KATYA My pleasure, Madam. After you.

They all move outside except MATVEY *who tidies the drawing room. Music: Nocturne No. 9 in E-flat major.* BOLSHINTSOV *enters — smiling, uneasy, nervous.*

BOLSHINTSOV Matvey.
MATVEY Ah! You gave me a start. Sir?
BOLSHINTSOV I'm looking for Doctor Shpigelsky.
MATVEY Certainly. I'll get him. He's somewhere around.

BOLSHINTSOV No, no; don't disturb him. Just tell him I've left
the horses and the trap at the back gate.
MATVEY I'll do that. Can I get you something? Tea? Coffee?
BOLSHINTSOV Nothing, thanks. Is that Miss Vera?
MATVEY That's Miss Vera. Terrific, isn't she?

> BOLSHINTSOV, *his face raised, stands listening,*
> *smiling.*

BOLSHINTSOV Nice . . . nice . . .

> MATVEY *exits with his tray. The music continues*
> *for a few seconds; then stops abruptly in mid-*
> *phrase.* BOLSHINTSOV *stands there, his face raised,*
> *still smiling, waiting.*

WONDERFUL
TENNESSEE

Characters

Three married couples all in their late thirties/early forties:

TERRY
BERNA
GEORGE
TRISH
FRANK
ANGELA

Terry is Trish's brother. Angela and Berna are sisters.

Time and Place

Time — the present. The action takes place on a remote pier in north-west Donegal.

Set

A stone pier at the end of a headland on the remote coast of north-west Donegal. The stonework is grained with yellow and grey lichen. The pier was built in 1905 but has not been used since the hinterland became depopulated many decades ago.

The pier extends across the full width of the stage. It begins stage left (the mainland) and juts out into the sea so that it is surrounded by water on three sides — the auditorium, the area stage right, and the back wall. (Left and right from the point of view of the audience.)

From the floor of the pier stone steps lead down to the sea/auditorium. Steps also lead up to the catwalk, eighteen inches wide and about five feet above the floor of the pier. From the catwalk one can see over the back wall of the pier (about ten feet high) and right across the surrounding countryside and sea.

There are some weather-bleached furnishings lying around the pier floor: fragments of fishing nets, pieces of lobster pots, broken fish boxes. Some rusty bollards and rings. A drift of sand in the top right-hand corner. Stones once used as weights inside lobster pots. A listing and rotting wooden stand, cruciform in shape, on which hangs the remnant of a lifebelt.

People can enter and exit only stage left.

Wonderful Tennessee was first produced, by Noel Pearson, at the Abbey Theatre, Dublin, on 30 June 1993, with the following cast:

ANGELA	Catherine Byrne
TRISH	Marion O'Dwyer
BERNA	Ingrid Craigie
TERRY	Donal McCann
FRANK	John Kavanagh
GEORGE	Robert Black

Directed by	Patrick Mason
Stage Direction by	Michael Higgins
Assistant Stage Direction by	Catriona Behan
Set and Costume Design by	Joe Vanek
Lighting Design by	Mick Hughes
Sound by	David Nolan

for D E S Maxwell

ACT ONE

Scene One

A very warm day in August. Early afternoon. Silence and complete stillness.

Then, after a time, we become aware that there are natural sounds: the gentle heave of the sea; a passing seagull; the slap and sigh of water against the stone steps. This lasts until we have established both a place and an environment of deep tranquillity and peace.

Now we hear another sound from a long distance away — an approaching minibus — and almost as soon as we identify the sound, discrepant and abusive in this idyllic setting, fade in the sound of people singing 'Happy Days Are Here Again'. Boisterous singing, raucous singing, slightly tiddly, day-excursion singing that is accompanied on the piano accordion.

TRISH sings a solo line and this is greeted with laughter, mockery, cheers, encouragement. Then everybody joins in again.

Now the minibus has arrived and stops at the end of the pier (i.e. stage left, off) and the idyllic atmosphere is completely shattered: doors banging; shouting; laughter; a sense of excitement and anticipation; animated, overlapping chatter.

    TRISH Help! We're lost!
    BERNA Where are we?
    TERRY This is it.
    TRISH You're lost, Terry; admit it; we're lost.
    FRANK It — is — wonderful!
  ANGELA This can't be it, is it?
    TERRY Believe me — this is it.
    TRISH Help!

> FRANK, *off, sings the title of 'Happy Days Are Here Again'.*

ANGELA Where's this wonderful island? I see no island.

TRISH We're lost — we're lost — we're lost! Help!

TERRY This is where we get the boat, Trish.

TRISH Oh my God — lost!

FRANK Anybody seen my camera?

TRISH Lost — lost!

TERRY Isn't it wonderful?

FRANK Sober up, everybody, please.

ANGELA You're joking, Terry, aren't you?

TRISH Lost, I'm telling you. This is the back of nowhere.

TERRY This is it — believe me.

> GEORGE *plays: 'O Mother, I could weep for mirth /
> Joy fills my heart so fast'.* TRISH *sings '* — weep for
> mirth — ' *and says:*

TRISH So could I, George.

> *And* FRANK *simultaneously sings the line, 'Joy fills my
> heart so fast' to* GEORGE's *accompaniment.*

BERNA Mind the step.

ANGELA Admit it, Terry: you're lost.

BERNA Here's your camera, Frank.

TRISH Let me out of here. Help!

FRANK Thanks, Berna.

TRISH I'm going straight back with you, Charlie.

ANGELA What in God's name are we doing here?

TERRY Admit it — isn't it wonderful?

TRISH Wonderful, he says! Help!

TERRY Yes, I think it's wonderful.

FRANK There's not a house within a hundred miles.

BERNA Let's all go back with Charlie.

TRISH Heeeeeeeelp!

> *Now* GEORGE *begins to play 'I Want to Be Happy'.
> Cheers and mocking laughter at the choice. Through
> his playing:*

166

ANGELA Right, George! So do I!

TRISH Happy — here?

ANGELA Yeah-yeah-yeah-yeah! Why not?

BERNA Happy, happy, happy, happy.

FRANK Yes, George, yes.

> *And they join in the song and continue talking through it.*

BERNA Whose sleeping bag is this?

TRISH Mine, Berna. Thank you.

ANGELA At least we'll get a bit of sun.

TRISH Hand me that blanket, Berna.

FRANK We're the first people ever to set foot here.

BERNA Here's your sun hat, Angela.

FRANK Careful. I'm closing this door.

TRISH Help!

> TERRY *enters, animated, laughing, excited. Like all the others he is dressed in colourful summer clothes. He has a sleeping bag slung over his shoulder and carries two large expensive hampers filled with food and drink. As he enters* TRISH *calls:*

(*Off*) Is this your idea of a joke, Terry?

> GEORGE *stops playing.*

TERRY (*On*) What's that?

TRISH (*Off*) Is this some kind of practical joke?

TERRY Believe me — it's everything you ever dreamed of.

FRANK (*Off*) Wonderful!

TERRY Believe me.

> *And immediately* GEORGE *strikes up 'I Want to Be Happy' again.*

Quite right, George! (*Sings*) ' — but I won't be happy / Till I make you happy too — '

GEORGE *continues with the song; and some of the people off join in the singing. But* TERRY's *laughter suddenly stops. Eagerly, with a hint of anxiety, he searches out the island (at the back of the auditorium, right) and at the same time in a low, barely audible voice, he mumbles/speaks the words of the song the others are singing, off.*

Now he has found the island. He drops the hampers. He slips the straw hat off his head, holds it against his chest and gazes out to sea. After a few seconds FRANK *enters. Like* TERRY *he is dressed in bright summer clothes.*

FRANK The minibus is about to —

      TERRY *is so intent on the island that he does not hear him.*

      Terry, your minibus is about to head home and Charlie wants to know — (*Calls impatiently*) Please, Angela!
TERRY Look, Frank.
FRANK Turn it down, Angela, would you?
TERRY There it is.
FRANK That's a crowd of lunatics you have there. So what time tomorrow is Charlie to come back for us?
TERRY Whenever it's bright.
FRANK It'll be sort of bright all night, I hope. Let's say — what? Seven? Seven-thirty?
TERRY That's fine.
FRANK Seven-thirty OK with you?
TERRY (*Indifferently*) Fine — fine.

      Burst of laughter, off.

FRANK Surely to God they can't keep that pace up all night!

      As he turns to leave BERNA *enters. Dressed for the outing and carrying a holdall, various bags, a sleeping bag, etc.*

BERNA (*Singing earnestly*) 'When skies are grey and you say you are blue — '

FRANK Certainly am, Berna.

> *He swings her round in a dance and sings along with her.*

DUET 'I'll send the sun shining through — '

FRANK Wow-wow-wow-wow! Hey, Terry: some mover that lady of yours! (*Exiting*) Right, Charlie. All settled. Seven-thirty tomorrow morning.

> *The moment* FRANK *exits* BERNA's *brittle-bright face is transformed with anxiety. She goes quickly to* TERRY's *side and speaks in a low, urgent voice.* GEORGE *suddenly stops playing 'I Want to Be Happy' in mid-phrase and plays 'Jesu, Joy of Man's Desiring'.*

TRISH Lovely, George.

> *She sings with* GEORGE.

BERNA I want to go home.

TERRY There it is, Berna. Look.

BERNA Take me home, Terry — please.

TERRY Wonderful, isn't it?

BERNA Please, Terry.

TERRY Just for tonight, Berna — just one night. Believe me — you'll love it.

BERNA Have you any idea how desperately unhappy I am?

TERRY Berna, I —

BERNA I don't think I can carry on, Terry.

TERRY Of course you can carry on. The doctor says you're a lot better. (*He reaches out to touch her*) Did you remember to take your pills this morning?

> *The music stops.*

BERNA (*Quietly, almost with pity*) For God's sake . . .

She moves quickly away from him and busies herself with her belongings. The moment she says 'For God's sake' the engine starts up. Again the overlapping voices, off.

TRISH He's going.
ANGELA See you tomorrow morning.
TRISH Help!
FRANK Don't go, Charlie! Don't abandon us!
ANGELA Thank you, Charlie.
TRISH Stop him. Don't let him go!

GEORGE *begins to play 'Aloha', and this is greeted with laughter and groans and singing.*

FRANK Perfect, George!

FRANK *sings a phrase of the song.*

TRISH Come back, Charlie! Help! Come back!
ANGELA 'Bye, lovely world!

FRANK *continues singing.*

TRISH 'Bye, civilization.
ANGELA 'Bye, Charlie.
TRISH Don't forget us, Charlie.
ALL 'Bye . . . 'bye . . . 'bye . . .

TERRY *and* BERNA *stand in silence, motionless, watching the departing bus.*

BERNA (*Softly*) 'Bye, Charlie . . . 'bye . . .

The music, the singing, the shouting all stop. The sound of the departing bus fades away. Silence. Once again the landscape is still and totally silent. Then ANGELA, *unaccompanied and at half the song's usual tempo, belts out the defiant line:*

ANGELA (*Sings*) 'I want to be happy — '
TRISH Damn right, Angela!
ANGELA (*Sings*) 'But I won't be happy — '
TRISH Why not?
ANGELA (*Sings*) 'Till I make you happy too.'

> *And at this point she is joined first by* GEORGE *on the accordion, then by* TRISH, *and then very privately, almost inaudibly, by* BERNA.
>
> *After* ANGELA's *first line, 'I want to be happy', slowly accelerate the tempo to normal.*
>
> *Now enter — immediately after the line 'Till I make you happy too — '* GEORGE, ANGELA, FRANK *and* TRISH *(in that order); each holding on to the waist of the person in front; all (except* GEORGE*) singing lustily; all doing a clownish, parodic conga dance, heads rolling, arms flying — a hint of the maenadic. All are dressed in bright summer clothes and each carries some gaudy summer equipment — straw bags, sun hats, sleeping bags, sun umbrellas, cameras, binoculars, etc., etc.*
>
> *Suddenly the pier becomes a fairground.*
>
> GEORGE *is the accordionist. His neck is swathed in a white bandage. On those rare occasions when he speaks his voice is husky and barely audible.* TRISH *has a plastic cup (wine) in one hand.* ANGELA *swings an empty wine bottle by the neck. The moment they come on stage* TERRY's *face lights up and happily, extravagantly he joins in the singing and the dance.*

ALL 'Life's really worth living — '
TRISH Come on, Berna! Party time!

> *And after a moment's hesitation* BERNA *joins in the parade and the singing with earnest, deliberate enthusiasm.*

ALL '— when we are mirth-giving / Why can't I give some to you?'

FRANK *now stands aside and takes a series of rapid photographs. Now only* TERRY *and* ANGELA *sing to* GEORGE'*s accompaniment.*

DUET 'When skies are grey — '
TRISH Terrific, Angela!
DUET ' — and you say you are blue — '
TERRY Your wife's a star, Frank.
FRANK Blessed, amn't I?
ANGELA (*Solo*) 'I'll send the sun smiling through — ' Give me your hand, Berna! So —

Now back to the very slow tempo and the exaggerated steps. ANGELA *and* BERNA, *hand in hand, dance / promenade across the pier.*

ANGELA ⎫
BERNA ⎬ 'I want to be happy — '
FRANK The wonderful sisters!
ANGELA ⎫
BERNA ⎬ 'But I won't be happy / Till I make you happy too.'

ANGELA *suddenly stops and holds her head.*

ANGELA Oh God!

The music stops.

The head's beginning to reel!
FRANK (*Sings*) 'In the good old summer time — '

GEORGE *drowns* FRANK'*s singing with a very formal 'Amen' cadence.*

TERRY Thank you, George.

General laughter. TERRY *holds his hands up.*

And now, my children — please.

TRISH Quiet, everybody!

TERRY Your attention, please.

FRANK Please!

TERRY I bid you all welcome.

FRANK Thank you, Terence.

TRISH Where are we, Terry?

FRANK Arcadia.

TERRY Ballybeg pier — where the boat picks us up.

TRISH County what?

TERRY County Donegal.

TRISH God. Bloody Indian territory.

FRANK Where does the boatman live?

TERRY Back there. At the end of the sand dunes.

TRISH (*To* GEORGE) Ballybeg, George. In County Donegal.

> GEORGE *nods and smiles.*

TERRY Right. So — stage one complete. Welcome again.

ANGELA Sounds proprietorial, doesn't he?

TERRY I'm only the sherpa.

TRISH Only what? (*To* BERNA) What's a sherpa?

FRANK (*Up on catwalk*) Next parish Boston, folks!

TERRY (*Privately*) Are you all right?

ANGELA A little too much wine.

TERRY And you've changed your hair.

ANGELA For the big occasion! Of course!

TERRY Lovely.

> *She touches his shoulder quickly, lightly, and moves away. They deposit their belongings at various places along the pier — that place becomes that person's 'territory' for the rest of the night.*
>
> *Now they all move around slowly, silently, assessing the pier itself and its furnishings and the surrounding sea and countryside.* TERRY *watches them. He is anxious to have their approval.*

Well?

FRANK (*In approval*) Well-well-well-well.

TERRY So far so good?
FRANK So far wonderful, Terry.
TERRY (*To all*) Isn't it?
FRANK Wonderful.

> FRANK *comes down from the catwalk.*

TERRY Some place, George?
GEORGE Yes. Yes.
TRISH Sorry, Terry — where is this again?
FRANK (*To* TERRY) Permanently lost, that sister of yours.
TERRY Ballybeg pier.
TRISH In County — ?
FRANK Wasting your time, Terry.
TERRY Donegal. This is where the boat picks us up.
TRISH You've told me that three times. (*To* GEORGE) The boat picks us up here.

> GEORGE *nods and smiles. Pause.*
> *Again they gaze around, touching the furnishings, sitting on the bollards. As they move around* GEORGE *plays 'Jesu, Joy of Man's Desiring'.* ANGELA *busies herself with her belongings, deliberately ignoring the surroundings.*

A long time since this has been used.
TERRY Not for fifty years.
FRANK More, I'd say.
TERRY Well?
FRANK Listen! Not a sound.
TERRY Trish?
TRISH Very . . . remote, isn't it?
TERRY But worth four hours in that minibus?
TRISH (*Not quite certain*) Oh yes . . .
FRANK The bus was fine. It's Charlie's terrible jokes I can't take. If he were my driver, Terry, I'd muzzle him.
TERRY (*To* ANGELA) Some place, isn't it?
TRISH Wonderful, Terry. Isn't it, Berna?
BERNA Yes.

FRANK These (*rings*) were made to last.

TERRY And that stone — all cut by hand. (*Again attempting to include* ANGELA) What do you call that mossy stuff — lichen?

TRISH And that view! Look!

FRANK What were these stones for?

TERRY Weights for lobster pots.

FRANK Amazing. Another world altogether.

TRISH Heavenly.

TERRY Yes.

TRISH You'd think you could see *beyond* the horizon. It really is wonderful. Oh my goodness . . . (*To* GEORGE) Ballybeg pier. In County Donegal.

GEORGE I know, Trish!

TERRY (*To* ANGELA) What do you think of it?

ANGELA 'Wonderful.' I know another happy song, George.

> ANGELA *sings the first line of the refrain of 'I Don't Know Why I'm Happy'.* GEORGE *picks it up immediately.*

Yes! He's a genius!

> *She sings the second line of the refrain.*

TERRY Your wonderful wife — off again.

FRANK (*Spreading his hands*) Your wonderful sister-in-law.

> TERRY *sings the third and fourth lines with* ANGELA.

TERRY Once more!

> *And accompanied by* GEORGE *and with* TRISH *clapping in time they sing the whole refrain again.*

Remember Father singing that every Christmas?

TRISH Don't remember that. Did he?

ANGELA Your George is a genius, Trish.

TRISH I know.

ANGELA Give me a kiss, George.

She kisses him.

You should be wearing a toga and playing a lyre and gorging yourself with black grapes.

She picks up a wreath of dried seaweed and places it on his head.

There! Dionysus!

TRISH I have a suggestion, Terry: let's have the party here.

FRANK (*Holding up a fragment of the lifebelt*) Anybody drowning?

TERRY We have a boat coming for us, Trish.

TRISH We don't have to take it, do we?

TERRY Yes, we do.

TRISH Why?

FRANK Because it's all arranged.

TRISH Berna, what do you say?

BERNA I don't care. Here's fine. Here's wonderful.

TRISH Angela?

ANGELA I know another happy song!

FRANK (*Icily*) Angela, we're all trying to —

TERRY (*Sings*) 'Here we are again — '

ANGELA That's it!

GEORGE *picks up the melody. (Sings) 'Happy as can be — '*

TRISH I know that!

TRISH, TERRY *and* ANGELA *all sing together.*

TRIO 'All good pals and jolly good company.'

ANGELA *now continues alone. She hoists up her skirts and does a parodic dance up and down the pier as she sings.* TERRY *and* TRISH *clap hands.* ANGELA*'s perform-*

ance *is full and exuberant but at the same time there*
is a hint of underlying panic.

ANGELA (*Singing and dancing*) 'A kiss for Bernadette,
My darling sister, B.
I think I need a very strong cup of tea.'
FRANK (*Icily*) Not at all! You're wonderful!
ANGELA 'I may be slightly drunk
As teachers oughtn't be.
But Frank, my husband,
Tra-la-la-la-la-la-lee — '
Oh, God . . .

She flops on to a bollard.

FRANK Thank you very much. Now — what about this boat,
Terry?
TRISH I vote we stay here. Berna?
FRANK Terry's day, Trish.
TRISH Aren't we all happy enough here?
ANGELA (*Sings to same air*) 'Today is Terry's day — '
FRANK (*To* TERRY) What do you say?
TERRY You think this is great? Believe me, my children, you
ain't seen nuthin' yet.
ANGELA One final happy song —
FRANK For Christ's sake!
ANGELA And despite my husband's encouragement the last
happy song I'll sing.
TRISH Yes, Angela, sing! Let's have a song!
ANGELA And this last happy song is for our host, Terry
Martin.
TRISH My wonderful brother.
FRANK Mister Terence Martin!
TERRY Terence Mary Martin.
ANGELA Concert promoter.
TERRY She means showman.
ANGELA Turf accountant.
FRANK Yeah!
TERRY She means bookie.

ANGELA Gambler.

TERRY She means eejit.

ANGELA And a man of infinite generosity and kindness.

Overlapping voices:

GEORGE Yes!

FRANK Hear — hear!

ANGELA Yeah-yeah-yeah!

TRISH Perfectly true!

FRANK Yes!

TERRY (*Embarrassed*) That sho' is me, folks.

ANGELA (*Raising a bottle*) To Terence Mary.

TRISH To Terry and Berna.

ANGELA Friend, brother-in-law, most generous of —

GEORGE *plays another 'Amen' chord that drowns out
the rest of her speech.*

Behave yourself, you!

TERRY Wait-wait-wait-wait-wait. Give me a hand here, Frank.

TERRY *throws open a hamper and produces bottles.*

FRANK We're not having the party here, are we?

ANGELA I want to sing another cheap song.

TERRY There are more cups in that bag.

ANGELA You sing, Berna!

BERNA Later, maybe.

TRISH It's not champagne, is it?

TERRY That's what the man sold me.

ANGELA George! A cheap song!

GEORGE We'll drink first.

TRISH Oh God, Terry!

FRANK Anybody need a cup?

TRISH A bit mad this, isn't it? What time of day is it? (*To*
BERNA) Maybe we're all mad, are we?

BERNA Maybe.

FRANK May concerts and gambling and bookmaking always

prosper.

TRISH Oh God, Terry, something wrong with this, isn't there?

TERRY Why?

ANGELA (*Sings*) 'Oh, Terry Martin, what can I do — '

TERRY (*Sings*) 'I took a bus to Ballybeg and I found myself with you.' Berna? (*Drink*)

BERNA Up to the top, please.

TERRY (*Softly*) You OK?

BERNA (*Loudly*) That's not the top.

TERRY Shouldn't you go easy on — ?

BERNA That's sufficient, thank you.

ANGELA (*To* FRANK) Both (*cups*) up to the brim, please.

FRANK You'll get your share.

ANGELA Jesus, how I love a prodigal man! To cheap songs!

TERRY George? (*Drink*)

GEORGE Please.

TRISH Just a little, Terry.

But GEORGE *tilts the bottle and fills his cup to over-flowing.*

GEORGE Lovely. Thanks.

TERRY Good idea this, isn't it?

TRISH We're blessed in the weather. He's (*George*) looking well, isn't he?

TERRY Great. To the old band, George.

GEORGE The Dude Ranchers.

TERRY The Dude Ranchers. The best band ever to tour Ireland. How many years were we on the road?

TRISH Twenty-one.

TERRY Were we?

GEORGE A lifetime.

TRISH A lifetime, he says.

GEORGE And we'll do it again.

TRISH You were told not to speak.

TERRY Yes, we'll do it again! And this time we'll tour the world!

GEORGE *smiles, spreads his hands and moves away.*

BERNA I'll have some more champagne, Frank.

FRANK On the way.

ANGELA (*To* BERNA) Shouldn't you go easy on that, love?

FRANK Don't spare it. Loads more in that hamper.

BERNA Thank you, Frank.

TRISH *and* TERRY *are alone.*

TERRY How is he? (*George*)

TRISH He plays all day long. As if he were afraid to stop.

TERRY He's looking great.

TRISH You've got to stop sending that huge cheque every week, Terry.

TERRY Nothing. It's —

TRISH We can manage fine.

TERRY It's only —

TRISH We don't need it. Honestly.

TERRY How was the check-up last week?

TRISH Three months at most.

TERRY Oh, Christ. Does he know?

TRISH He's very brave about it.

TERRY Is there anything — ?

TRISH (*Aloud*) Quiet, please! The brother is going to make a speech!

TERRY The brother is — !

FRANK Speech! Silence! Speech!

TERRY The brother is going to do nothing —

FRANK Glasses all full?

Overlapping talk.

Any more champagne?

TRISH Listen to the brother.

ANGELA Good man, Terry.

TRISH Go ahead.

FRANK Please! Quiet!

TRISH And make it short, Terry.

ANGELA Terence Mary Martin!

FRANK But first — first — may I say something? To Terry, for

whom we all have the utmost respect and affection,
and to his lovely Berna, both of whom have made all
our lives —

ANGELA (*Quickly, lightly*) Happy birthday.

FRANK A very happy —

And the rest is drowned by GEORGE *playing 'Happy
Birthday to You'. And everybody joins in the singing.*
    TERRY *covers his face in exaggerated but genuine
embarrassment and pretends to hide behind the lifebelt stand while they sing to him. When the chorus
ends he sings the first two lines of the refrain of 'I'm
Twenty-one Today'. General laughter.*

TRISH All right, Terry. One very short speech.

TERRY No-no-no-no-no. No speeches. May I have your attention, please? Berna? George?

FRANK Attention, please.

TERRY OK?

They all fall silent. TERRY *points out to sea. They line
up around him —* FRANK, TRISH, BERNA, GEORGE.
ANGELA *moves off and stands alone.*

Straight out there. That island. That's where we're
going.

FRANK Yes . . .

TRISH I'm lost — where? — Is it — ?

FRANK Wonderful . . .

TERRY (*To* TRISH) Directly in front of you.

FRANK Further left, Trish.

TERRY (*To* BERNA) Straight out there.

BERNA I see it, Terry.

FRANK (*To* TRISH) Got it?

TRISH Think so . . .

TERRY George?

GEORGE See it.

TERRY See it, Angela?

She does not answer.

FRANK That's no distance out, Terry.

TERRY I suppose not.

TRISH It's shaped like a ukulele, is it?

FRANK That's a perfect circle for God's sake.

TERRY So. There we are. See it, Angela? Our destination.

ANGELA (*Softly; toasting*) Our 'destination'.

TRISH I do see it. Yes.

TERRY Wonderful, isn't it?

BERNA It's not circular, Frank. That's a rectangle.

TRISH God, that's miles away, Terry.

TERRY Is it?

TRISH Miles. And that's in County Sligo too, isn't it?

FRANK Jesus.

TERRY Donegal.

TRISH Ah.

TERRY Wonderful, isn't it?

ANGELA (*Softly; toasting*) A destination of wonder.

FRANK (*Coldly*) Aren't you going to join us, Angela?

TRISH (*To* GEORGE) Not Sligo, George. Still Donegal.

> ANGELA *stands beside the lifebelt stand, leans against it, and sings in Marlene Dietrich style the first line of 'Falling in Love Again'.*

FRANK Angela, please —

> GEORGE *accompanies her now. She sings the next two lines and breaks off suddenly.* GEORGE *finishes the verse and then stops.*
> Silence again as they all — *except* ANGELA — *gaze out at the island, each with his/her thoughts.*
> ANGELA *takes off her sun hat and hangs it on the arm of the lifebelt stand.*

TRISH You never said it was a big island, Terry.

TERRY It's not big, is it?

TRISH That's a huge island.

TERRY Is it?

FRANK Hard to know what size it is — it keeps shimmering.

> *Now for the first time* ANGELA *joins them and looks out to sea.*

ANGELA Has it a name, our destination?

TERRY *Oileán Draíochta.* What does that mean, all you educated people?

TRISH That rules me out. Where's our barrister? (*Berna*)

BERNA Island of Otherness; Island of Mystery.

TRISH God, it's not spooky, Terry, is it?

BERNA Not that kind of mystery. The wonderful — the sacred — the mysterious — that kind of mystery.

FRANK Good girl, Berna!

TRISH All the same, it's beautiful. (*To* GEORGE) Isn't it?

GEORGE Yes.

TRISH Dammit, I've lost it again. (*To* TERRY) You're sure it's not a mirage?

> FRANK *catches her head and turns it.*

FRANK You're looking away beyond it.

TRISH Am I?

TERRY There *is* a legend that it was once a spectral, floating island that appeared out of the fog every seven years and that fishermen who sighted it saw a beautiful country of hills and valleys, with sheep browsing on the slopes, and cattle in green pastures, and clothes drying on the hedges. And they say they saw leaves of apple and oak, and heard a bell and the song of coloured birds. Then, as they watched it, the fog devoured it and nothing was seen but the foam swirling on the billow and the tumbling of the dolphins.

TRISH Will we see dolphins? God, I love dolphins.

ANGELA You know that by heart.

TERRY (*Embarrassed*) Do I?

BERNA When did it stop being spectral?

TERRY On one of its seven year appearances fishermen landed on it and lit a fire.

FRANK What was wrong with that?

TERRY Fire dispels the enchantment — according to the legend. (*To* ANGELA) You're right. From a pamphlet about the place my father had.

FRANK Maybe it is a bit like a ukulele.

TERRY Nearly forgot — shoes off, everybody!

FRANK What?

TERRY We're supposed to be barefoot.

FRANK You're joking, Terry!

TRISH Why barefoot?

TERRY Don't ask me. That's the custom. That's what people used to do long ago.

> *They slip out of their shoes. And again they gaze out to sea.*

BERNA There are bushes on it.

FRANK Come on, Berna! And clothes drying on the hedges?

BERNA Whins, I think. Yes; they're whins. And a small hill away to the left.

TRISH God, you've all powerful eyes.

FRANK Looks more like clouds to me.

BERNA A low hill. At the end of that side.

ANGELA (*To* TERRY) You're our expert. Is there a hill there?

TERRY Expert! I was there just once with my father. I was only seven at the time.

TRISH I never heard that story.

TERRY We fasted from the night before, I remember. And for the night you were on the island you were given only bread and water. (*To* GEORGE) Like some of our digs when we were on the road!

> GEORGE *nods and smiles.* FRANK *now takes a series of photographs — of the others, of the island, of the furnishings of the pier.*

TRISH And what did you do out there?

TERRY I don't remember a lot. There were three beds — you

know, mounds of stone — and every time you went round a bed you said certain prayers and then picked up a stone from the bottom of the mound and placed it on the top.

FRANK   Trish! (*Photograph*)

TRISH   Oh, Frank!

TERRY   And I remember a holy well, and my father filling a bottle with holy water and stuffing the neck with grass — you know, to cork it. And I remember a whin bush beside the well —

TRISH   There! Good for you, Berna!

TERRY   And there were crutches and walking sticks hanging on the bush; and bits of cloth — *bratóga*, my father called them — a handkerchief, a piece of a shawl bleached and turning green from exposure. Votive offerings — isn't that the English word? And there's the ruins of a Middle Age church dedicated to Saint Conall. (*To* FRANK) Isn't that the period you're writing your book about?

FRANK   Something like that. Close enough.

TRISH   But it's not a pilgrimage island now?

TERRY   No, no; that all ended years and years ago.

TRISH   Why?

FRANK   People stopped believing, didn't they?

TERRY   Nobody does that sort of thing nowadays, do they? And when the countryside around here was populated, apparently they made *poitín* out there — that wouldn't have helped the pilgrimage business. There were even stories of drunken orgies.

ANGELA   (*Salute*) Saint Dionysus.

TRISH   But years ago people went there to be cured?

BERNA   To remember again — to be reminded.

TRISH   To remember what?

FRANK   George! (*Photograph*)

BERNA   To be in touch again — to attest.

FRANK   Angela! (*Photograph*)

TERRY   People went there just to make a pilgrimage, Trish.

FRANK   And to see apparitions. Patricia! (*Photograph*)

TRISH   But you saw crutches on that bush. So people must

have been cured there.

FRANK Apparitions were commonplace in the Middle Ages. Saint Conall must have seen hundreds of apparitions in his day. Terry! (*Photograph*)

TRISH Don't be so cheap, Frank.

FRANK Thousands maybe.

TRISH (*To* TERRY) Do you believe people were cured there?

TERRY All I know is that at seven years of age just to get sitting up all night was adventure enough for me. The first time I ever saw the dawn. I remember my head was giddy from want of sleep.

TRISH And Father?

FRANK Berna! (*Photograph*)

TRISH Why did Father go out there? He believed in nothing.

FRANK You're beautiful.

TRISH Why did Father go out there?

FRANK For God's sake, Trish! That was another age. To pray — to do penance —

BERNA To acknowledge — to make acknowledgement.

TERRY You had another word, Berna — to attest!

GEORGE *makes a sound.*

What's that, George?

TRISH To attest to the mystery, he says.

TERRY And why not! (*Laughs*) I'm a bookie, for God's sake. All I know is: that's where we'll have our party tonight. OK?

ANGELA Once when the Greek god, Dionysus, was going to the island of Naxos he was captured by pirates who took him to be a wealthy prince —

FRANK You'd never guess. My wife teaches Classics.

ANGELA But suddenly his chains fell away, and vines and ivy sprouted all over the pirate ship, and the sailors were so frightened they jumped into the sea and turned into dolphins.

TRISH Will we really see dolphins? God, I love dolphins.

FRANK *is now up on the catwalk.*

FRANK   Where does our boat come from?

TERRY   A house just across there. (*To* ANGELA) You know *that*
by heart.

FRANK   No house. No boat. Nothing from here to Boston
except a derelict church — without a roof.

TRISH   I'm sure it's very beautiful out there. But I'd be happy
to settle for this. But if you all . . .

> *Silence as they gaze out again. Then suddenly* ANGELA
> *leaps on top of a bollard, flings her hands above her
> head and proclaims in the style of an American evan-
> gelist.*

ANGELA   There it is, friends — *Oileán Draíochta*, our destination! Wonderful — other — mysterious! Alleluia! So I
ask you to join with me in that most beautiful song,
'Heavenly Sunshine'. Brother George?

> *As* GEORGE *plays a brief introduction:*

Now — open your minds, your lungs, your arms,
your hearts. All together, brothers and sisters. (*Sings*)
'Heavenly sunshine, heavenly sunshine — 'Can't hear
you, friends. 'Flooding my soul with glory divine — '

> TERRY *now joins her.*

DUET   'Heavenly sunshine, heavenly sunshine,
Alleluia, Jesus is mine.'

ANGELA   And one more time! Sister Tricia, Sister Berna — ?

> TERRY, TRISH, BERNA *and* ANGELA *all together:*

ALL   'Heavenly sunshine, heavenly sunshine,
Flooding my soul with glory divine,
Heavenly sunshine, heavenly sunshine,
Alleluia, Jesus is mine.'

ANGELA   And one more time, Brother George —

> *But instead of a reprise — and without a break in his playing —* GEORGE *goes straight into 'Knees Up, Mother Brown'. This is greeted with laughter, cheers, derision — voices overlapping.*

George!

FRANK Wonderful!

TRISH Good man, George!

TERRY Sing it, Angela!

BERNA I know that one!

> *And they all — except* GEORGE *— dance around the pier and sing the chorus at the top of their voices. When they get to the end of the chorus:*

TERRY One more time!

> *And again they sing the chorus. Just before it ends* FRANK *shouts:*

FRANK Quiet, please! Shut up, will you?

> *They fall silent.*

We have a problem, good brethren. I'm telling you — there is no boat.

ANGELA Who's for a quick drink?

> TRISH *nods: Yes.*

FRANK And not only is there no boat, there isn't a house within a hundred miles of us.

ANGELA (*To* TRISH) Champagne?

> TRISH *nods.*

TRISH (*To* FRANK) Use these (*binoculars*).

TERRY Yes, there is, Frank. Just beyond the sand dunes.

ANGELA *sings to the air of 'Abide With Me'.*

ANGELA 'Beyond the sand dunes / You will find our boat — '
FRANK Nothing but bogland from here to the mountains. And not a boat from here to the horizon.
TERRY A thatched cottage — further to your left.
FRANK Sorry.
TRISH You're the one with the eyes, Berna.
TERRY As far as I remember it's down at the very edge of the water.
FRANK Hold on . . . yes . . . is that not a byre?
TERRY They're the people who do the ferrying.
FRANK Deserted, Terry. And there's grass growing out of the thatch.
TERRY Carlin's the name. Been there for generations.
ANGELA (*Holding up a bottle*) Berna?

BERNA *signals: No.*

FRANK Hold on . . . wait . . . Yes, you're right! There's smoke coming out of the chimney! God, that's a hovel! (*He comes down*) Right, I'll go and get Carlin. Are we all set to leave?
TERRY Think so. Aren't we?
FRANK And he picks us up on the island tomorrow morning — when? About seven?
TERRY That's the plan.
FRANK Right.
ANGELA (*Sings air of 'Abide With Me'*) 'That is the place / That shapes our destiny — '

As FRANK *passes behind her:*

FRANK (*Privately*) You're making a nuisance of yourself.

ANGELA *sings the title of the song 'I Don't Know Why I'm Happy'.*

What if Carlin isn't at home?

189

TRISH   Or refuses to ferry bowsies.

ANGELA   Or is dead.

FRANK   Seriously. What if — ?

TERRY   Someone from the house will take us, Frank. They've been ferrying people for thousands of years.

FRANK   I'm sure they have. All I'm asking is: supposing there is nobody free now to —

TERRY   (*Sharply, impatiently*) Tell him the new owner of the island sent you for him!

He stops short; tries to laugh.

I didn't mean to . . .

'Let that out' is unsaid. Pause.

TRISH   Well, aren't you a close one, Terry Martin!

TERRY   I'm sorry. I —

TRISH   You kept that a big secret.

FRANK   You've actually bought *Oileán Draíochta*?

TERRY   Four months ago. Sight unseen. Ridiculous, isn't it?

ANGELA   So it's your island we're going to?

TERRY   Stupid, I know. Heard by accident it was on the market. (*To* ANGELA) Miles from anywhere — good for nothing, isn't it?

ANGELA *spreads her hands.*

ANGELA   Challenge for a sherpa.

TERRY   I know it's ridiculous. I know it sounds —

FRANK   This is no mystery tour he's taking us on — he's taking us home! Wonderful, Terry!

TRISH   And I wish you luck with it. Congratulations. (*To* BERNA) So you own your own island, Mrs Martin. Very posh.

BERNA   It's news to me.

TERRY   I was going to tell you all out there tonight — tomorrow morning — whenever. Anyhow . . . (*To* FRANK) Will you get Carlin for us?

FRANK   I'm away. Well done. Terrific!

FRANK *goes off.* TERRY *feels that some further explanation is necessary.*

TERRY Haven't seen it for over thirty years . . . and I was always curious to have another look at it . . . obsessed in a kind of way . . . and the fact that it came on the market . . .

TRISH Good. Great.

They drift apart and attend to their belongings. TERRY *goes to* TRISH.

All I can say is — you have money to burn.

TERRY Not true at all, I'm afraid.

TRISH Berna seems in better form.

TERRY Do you think so?

TRISH Plenty of chat out of her in the minibus.

TERRY She's really most content when she's in the nursing home.

TRISH (*Very softly*) Mother was right, you know: if you didn't spoil her so much.

TERRY Trish! (*To* GEORGE) Met an old friend of yours in London last week — Michael Robinson.

TRISH You never did! (*To* GEORGE) He met Michael Robinson in London, George. (*To* TERRY) And how was he?

TERRY Great . . . fine . . . well, not so good. Bumped into him in a pub. Didn't recognize him — not that I ever knew him well. Actually I thought he was a down-and-out touching me.

TRISH Michael?

TERRY I know — awful. Asking very warmly for you (*George*). Talked for over an hour about you and him at college together . . . doing your degree . . . and the duets you used to play —

TRISH Sonatas.

TERRY That's it — sonatas.

TRISH Beethoven sonatas.

TERRY Talked for over an hour. Couldn't shut him up. Eventually I gave him some money and just . . . walked away.

GEORGE *moves away and sits on a bollard.*

TRISH That's all they did for three whole years at college —
play piano and violin sonatas — day and night. The
Aeolians — that's what they called themselves.

TERRY He said you talked about going professional.

GEORGE Maybe . . .

TRISH They were the stars of the college. Oh such stars they
were. Michael was going to be Ireland's first great
concert violinist. He could have been, too. And there
was absolutely no doubt that George was the new
Rachmaninoff — no doubt at all about that. And
together they were so brilliant, especially in the
Beethoven sonatas. Oh I can't tell you how brilliant
they were . . . Michael Robinson . . . oh my goodness . . .

Pause. BERNA *hums the line 'O Mother, I could weep
for mirth' and stops suddenly.*

TERRY (*To* ANGELA) I know you think it's crass.

ANGELA What's that?

TERRY Bookie Buys Island Sight Unseen.

ANGELA But an island remembered, however vaguely.

TERRY I did it on impulse. In memory of my father, maybe.

ANGELA A new venue for rock concerts, wrestling matches?

TERRY Why not? Bullfights, revivalist meetings. I was afraid
you mightn't come this morning.

ANGELA Terry Martin Productions! Dionysian Nights On *Oileán
Draíochta*!

TERRY If you hadn't come I'd have called it off.

ANGELA Celebrate The Passions That Refuse To Be Domesti-
cated!

TERRY I would have —

ANGELA Nature Over Culture! Instinct Over Management!

TERRY Angela —

ANGELA A Hymn To The Forces That Defy Civilization!

TERRY Oh God, Angela —

ANGELA (*Passionately, urgently*) Please, Terry — for Christ's sake
— please, not now — not now!

BERNA *stands on a fishbox and proclaims:*

BERNA Lord, it is good for us to be here!
ANGELA Amen to that, sister!
TERRY Careful, Berna. That box is rotten.
BERNA I want to sing a hymn.
ANGELA Yes! Sing your hymn, Berna!

BERNA *now sings, her face frozen in a fixed and desperate smile.*

BERNA 'O Mother, I could weep for mirth — '
TERRY Berna —
BERNA 'Joy fills my heart so fast — ' Help me, George!
ANGELA Help her, George.
BERNA I'll start again. Give me a note.

GEORGE *gives her a chord.*

Thank you. 'O Mother, I could weep for mirth / Joy fills my heart so fast — '

ANGELA *now sings with her.*

DUET 'My soul today is heaven on earth, / O could the transport last.'
TRISH Good girl, Berna!

Now TRISH *joins them.*

TRIO 'I think of thee and what thou art — '

Now TERRY *joins them.*

QUARTET 'Thy majesty, thy state.
And I keep singing in my heart,
Immaculate! Immaculate!'

End of Scene One.

ACT ONE

Scene Two

Before the lights come up we hear GEORGE *playing the entire first verse of 'Oft in the Stilly Night'.*

About twelve hours later — the early hours of the following morning. The pier is lit by a midsummer night glow that illuminates with an icy, surreal clarity. The boisterous, day-excursion spirit has long ago evaporated. Waiting for the boat has made them weary and a bit irritable. Each has retreated into his/her own privacy and does not wish to be intruded on.

ANGELA *is sitting on a bollard, gazing without interest through the binoculars in the general direction of the island.* TRISH *is sitting with her back to the pier wall, her arms round her legs, her face on her knees.*

FRANK *is on the catwalk and looking towards Carlin's house.* BERNA *is sitting on the edge of the pier (stage right), her legs hanging over the edge of the pier floor.* GEORGE *is sitting on a fishbox, head back, eyes closed, body erect and tense, playing the last bars of the song.* TERRY *looks casually through the hampers, examining the contents, tidying up, killing time.*

The music ends.

TERRY Anybody for a slice of melting birthday cake?

No answer. He continues tidying. Pause.

Glass of flat champagne?

No answer. He continues tidying. Pause.

Venison and Apricot Compôte? Honey Gateau? Ever hear of Honey Gateau?

TRISH Give our heads peace, Terry, would you?

TERRY Maybe I should bring this cake over to Carlin. Might soften his bark.

FRANK Hey-hey-hey-hey-hey! Look at that! There's smoke coming from the chimney again!

TRISH (*Wearily*) Wonderful.

FRANK He lets the fire die at midnight and then three hours later he lights it up again. What the hell is Mr Carlin up to?

TRISH We could do with a fire. It's got chilly.

FRANK What sort of a game is he playing with us?

TERRY Time has no meaning for a man like that. (*He holds up a small box*) Cherry and Mandarin Chartreuse — ? (*To* TRISH) Sorry.

> Pause. GEORGE *now plays the full chorus of 'Down by the Cane-brake'. He plays very softly and more slowly than the song is scored. His arrangement with its harmonium-style chords endows the song with the tone and dignity of a hymn. It sounds almost sacred.*
> *Immediately after he plays 'Down by the cane-brake, close by the mill'* ANGELA *looks at him.*

ANGELA 'Down by the Cane-brake.'

GEORGE Know it?

ANGELA Haven't heard it in years.

TERRY What's a cane-brake?

ANGELA Shelterbelt of canes, I suppose. Protection against the elements.

TERRY Ah.

FRANK If he's not playing some sort of bizarre game with us then explain why he lights his fire at three in the morning.

ANGELA He just loves tormenting us.

TRISH The poor man's cold, Frank.

FRANK Not that man. That man has no human feelings.

ANGELA Maybe he wants to dispel the enchantment.

TERRY Marrons Glacés — whatever they are. George?

GEORGE No, thanks.

FRANK He has betrayed us, the bastard.

TERRY He'll come, Frank. Believe me.

TRISH We could do with a cane-brake here.

FRANK If he never had any intention of ferrying us across —
fine! Say that straight out! 'Sorry, bowsies, no ferrying today.'

TERRY He'll come.

TRISH Couldn't we rent his boat from him and row ourselves out?

FRANK Where's the boat? Has he got a boat?

TERRY (*To* TRISH) He'd never allow that.

TRISH Why not?

TERRY That's his job.

TRISH Too late to go out now anyway.

TERRY It's only ten-to-three. We'll still make it — believe me.

TRISH Of course when I proposed we spend the night here
I was shouted down. Perverse — that's what you are.

FRANK 'Give me a while at the turf, sir. That's all I need.' And
four hours later, 'A mouthful of tea and I'll be over
behind you.'

TRISH Maybe he's past ferrying people. Is he very old?

FRANK Ancient; and filthy; and toothless. And bloody smiling all the time.

ANGELA Forget Mr Carlin, my darlings. Put Mr Carlin out of
your thoughts.

FRANK God, I always hated peasants.

TRISH And bloody Sligo peasants are the worst, I'm sure.

TERRY He'll come. Believe me. He'll come.

ANGELA 'Believe me — believe me — ' I suppose it's enviable
in a way. Is it?

TERRY What is?

She does not answer. She goes to BERNA *at the end of
the pier.*

ANGELA What's the water like?

BERNA Warm. Warmish.

ANGELA Wouldn't mind a swim. Brighten us all up.

She hugs BERNA *quickly.*

And how's the baby sister?

BERNA *shrugs.*

You're looking much stronger.

BERNA Am I?

ANGELA Terry says you'll be back in the practice in a month.

BERNA That's not true. Who's looking after the children to-night?

ANGELA The McGuires next door.

BERNA The whole brood?

ANGELA I know. Hearts of gold.

BERNA I have a birthday present for young Frankie. I'll drop it in at the weekend.

ANGELA You have that godson of yours spoiled.

BERNA No, I'll get Terry to leave it in. The godson has got very . . . tentative with me recently.

ANGELA You couldn't make that —

BERNA I make him uneasy. You know how intuitive children are. I think maybe I frighten him.

ANGELA Frankie's dying about you, Berna.

BERNA 'Frighten' is too strong. When I reach out to touch him he shrinks away from me. I . . . disquiet him. Anyhow. Do you really think I look stronger?

ANGELA I know you are.

BERNA Terry thinks the reason for my trouble is that we couldn't have a child. That's what he tells the doctors. And that never worried me all that much. But it's an obsession with him. He's even more neurotic than Trish about not having children. A Martin neurosis, I tell him.

ANGELA Shhh.

BERNA And he would have been so good with children. Married the wrong sister, didn't he?

ANGELA Berna —

BERNA Oh, yes; oh, yes. When you married Frank a little por-tion of him atrophied. Then he turned to me. I'm the surrogate.

ANGELA You've got to —

BERNA Are you happy, Angela?

ANGELA (*Hums*) 'Happy days are here again.'

BERNA There are times when I feel I'm . . . about to be happy. That's not bad, is it? Are you laughing at me?

ANGELA Of course I'm not laughing at you.

BERNA Maybe that's how most people manage to carry on — 'about to be happy'; the real thing *almost* within grasp, just a step away. Maybe that's the norm. But then there are periods — occasions — when just being alive is . . . unbearable.

TERRY Marinated Quail and Quince Jelly. God!

TRISH The delights of the world — you have them all there.

ANGELA There are times when all of us —

BERNA He has no happiness with me — Terry. Not even 'about to be' happiness. He should leave me. I wouldn't mind if he did. I don't think I'd mind at all. Because in a way I feel I've moved beyond all that.

She stands up.

But then what would he do, where would he go?

She moves away. ANGELA *picks up the binoculars.*

TERRY Six months ago there was a horse called Quince Fruit running at Cheltenham. Worst mistake of my whole life. Practically cleaned me out. Quince Fruit almost ruined me.

Pause. Now BERNA *begins singing the verse of 'Down by the Cane-brake'. Immediately* GEORGE *accompanies her. She sings in the mood* GEORGE *established earlier, softly, quietly, but not quite as slowly as* GEORGE *played the chorus. She tells the story of the song with intimacy and precision, as do the others when they sing or join in, each singing in the same quiet, internal, personal way.*

BERNA 'Down by the cane-brake, close by the mill
There lived a blue-eyed girl by the name of Nancy
Dill — '

TERRY (*To* TRISH) Mother's song.

She nods.

BERNA 'I told her that I loved her, I loved her very long,
I'm going to serenade her and this will be my
song — '

TRISH *now sings the chorus with* BERNA.

DUET 'Come, my love, come, my boat lies low,
She lies high and dry on the O-hi-o.
Come, my love, come, and come along with me
And I'll take you back to Tennessee.'

A very brief bridging passage by GEORGE. *Then* TERRY
sings alone.

TERRY 'Down by the cane-brake some happy day
You'll hear a wedding-bell a-ringing mighty gay.
I'm going to build a cabin and in a trundle bed
There'll be a blue-eyed baby and all because you
said — '

Chorus sung by FRANK, BERNA, TRISH *and* TERRY.
Then TRISH *alone:*

TRISH 'Down by the cane-brake, that's where I'll stay,
Longside of Nancy Dill till we are laid away.
And when we get to heaven and Peter lets us in
I'll start my wings a-flappin' and sing to her again — '

Chorus sung by FRANK, BERNA, TRISH, TERRY *and*
ANGELA. *Then a final cadence from* GEORGE. *Brief pause.*

What time is it?

TERRY Just after three.

TRISH 'Night, everybody. See you in the morning. 'Bye.

> *Again they all retreat into their privacies.* ANGELA *looks through the binoculars.* TERRY *passes behind her. As he does:*

TERRY Tennessee still there?

ANGELA Lost it again.

TERRY Still there. 'Believe me.'

> *She shrugs and smiles.* TERRY *looks around at them all. Then he addresses them:*

I know — I'm sorry — it's a mess. And when we were planning it, it seemed a wonderful idea. It still is a wonderful idea. And there's still a good chance we'll make it — a very good chance. Carlin *will* come. I honestly . . . Anyhow . . . sorry, sorry . . .

> *Pause.*

TRISH (*Sits up*) I know when I was in Sligo before! Seventeen years ago — at a bridge congress.

TERRY Donegal, Trish.

TRISH No, Sligo. At the old Great Southern Hotel. My partner was a man —

FRANK Here he comes! There he is! Look! Look!

TRISH What? — Who? —

FRANK The boatman! Carlin! With his boat! He's here! He's bloody here!

> *Suddenly everybody is excited, agitated. They all talk at the same time.*

TRISH Who's here?

TERRY Carlin.

BERNA Oh God.

TERRY Where is he?

TRISH Who's Carlin?

ANGELA I don't believe it.

TERRY Great — terrific! Are you sure, Frank?

BERNA (*Anxious, agitated*) Oh God! — Oh my God!

ANGELA The bastard — where is he?

TRISH Where, Frank? Where?

ANGELA I don't believe it.

BERNA Oh my God!

TERRY Is he alone? Quiet, please!

BERNA Oh my God, Angela —

TERRY Where is he, Frank?

TRISH Can you see him?

ANGELA I don't believe it.

TERRY Where is he, Frank?

FRANK 'Wolf!' cried the naughty boy. 'Wolf.'

TRISH What? Where is he?

FRANK 'Wolf — wolf.'

BERNA He's not there at all?

FRANK 'Fraid not. Woke you up all the same, didn't it?

TERRY (*Quiet fury*) That is not funny, for Christ's sake.

TRISH Oh, Frank, how could you?

FRANK Joke.

ANGELA (*Calmly*) Damn you, Frank.

FRANK A joke — that's all.

TERRY Not funny at all, Frank.

FRANK Sorry.

TRISH Oh, Frank, that was cruel.

FRANK Sorry — sorry — sorry. For God's sake, what's eating you all?

> *Again they retreat into themselves. And as they do*
> GEORGE *plays 'Regina caeli, laetari, alleluia; quia quem meruisti portare — ' He breaks off mid-phrase. Silence.*

ANGELA (*Suddenly, with great energy*) All right, everybody! Story time! So we're stuck here! We're going nowhere! We'll pass the night with stories.

TRISH Good for you, Angela. Yeah-yeah-yeah-yeah!

ANGELA 'Once upon a time — ' Who goes first? Terry!

TERRY I don't know any stories.

TRISH Yes, you do. He's a wonderful story teller.

ANGELA We'll get him later. You start off, Trish.

TRISH Let someone else start. I'll go second. Berna, tell us one of your law stories.

BERNA All right. Let me think of one.

TRISH A clean law story! We'll come back to you. Frank — 'Once upon a time.'

FRANK Pass.

TERRY Get it over with, Frank.

TRISH Come on, Frank. Be a sport. It's only a bit of fun.

FRANK Later. After Berna.

ANGELA I think George wants to go first.

FRANK What about yourself, Terry?

TERRY Couldn't tell a story to save my life.

ANGELA Have you a story to tell, George?

TRISH What's wrong with you all? You go first, Angela. Then a clean law story. Then Frank. Then —

ANGELA George?

GEORGE Yes?

TRISH Then me. Then Terry —

ANGELA George will go first. Tell us your story, George.

TRISH Right — I'll kick off.

ANGELA (*To* GEORGE) 'Once upon a time — '

FRANK Stop bullying, Angela.

GEORGE *moves into the centre of the group.*

TRISH This woman had ten children, one after the other, and —

ANGELA Right, George?

TERRY Angela —

ANGELA (*To* GEORGE) Ready?

TRISH And the ten children all had red hair like the —

ANGELA (*To* TRISH) Please. (*To* GEORGE) 'Once upon a time — '

Silence. GEORGE *looks at each of them in turn. Then he plays the first fifteen seconds of the Third Movement (Presto) of Beethoven's Sonata No. 14 (Moonlight).*

He plays with astonishing virtuosity, very rapidly, much faster than the piece is scored, and with an internal fury; so that his performance, as well as being dazzlingly dexterous and skilful and fast — because of its dazzling dexterity and skill and speed — seems close to parody. And then, in the middle of a phrase, he suddenly stops. He bows to them all very formally as if he had given a recital in a concert hall.

GEORGE Thank you. Thank you very much.

He now removes the accordion and puts it in the case. Pause.

TRISH (*Almost shouting, very emotional, close to tears*) Are you satisfied now? Happy now, are you? Do you see you all? Not one of you is fit to clean his boots!

GEORGE now spreads out a sleeping bag and lies on top of it. TRISH spreads a rug over him. Pause.

BERNA I'm going for a swim. Anybody coming?
TERRY Please, Berna; not now.
BERNA Angela?
TERRY That water could be dangerous, Berna.
ANGELA Wait until daybreak. I'll go with you then. I'd love a swim, too. As soon as it's daylight.

FRANK comes down from the catwalk. He goes to TERRY.

FRANK Waiting — just waiting — waiting for anything makes you a bit edgy, doesn't it? Sorry about that 'wolf' thing.

TERRY makes a gesture of dismissal and continues looking through the hampers.

It wasn't meant cruelly. Just stupid.

TERRY Brandied Peaches and Romanian Truffles. Christ. I order two hampers of good food and they fill them with stuff nobody can eat. (*He holds up a bottle*) Drop of brandy?

FRANK If you had some whiskey.

TERRY Should have.

FRANK Can't take it neat though.

TERRY (*Searching hamper*) Of course — everything except water.

> *He points to a shallow hollow on the floor of the pier where water has gathered.*

Is that rainwater or saltwater?

> FRANK *dips a finger and tastes it.*

FRANK We're in business.

> FRANK *scoops some water into a paper cup and makes a drink.*

(*Toasts*) Happy birthday, Terry.

TERRY That was yesterday.

FRANK Was it? All the same.

TERRY How's the book coming on?

FRANK The finishing post is in sight . . . at last. Time for it, says you, after three-and-a-half years.

TERRY Great.

FRANK I know I shouldn't say this but I hope — Goddamn it, I pray — this is going to be the breakthrough for me. And some instinct tells me it will. Well . . . maybe . . . touch wood.

TERRY You've told me a dozen times — I'm sorry — clock-making through the ages — is that it?

FRANK Terence!

TERRY Sorry.

FRANK *The Measurement of Time and Its Effect on European Civilization.*

TERRY Ah.

FRANK   I know. But they assure me there is a market for it —
              not large but worldwide. It *is* fascinating stuff. I never
              seem to thank you for all your help, Terry.
TERRY   Nothing — nothing. Another splash?

        He pours more whiskey into the cup.

FRANK   How can I thank you adequately? Only for you I'd
              still be sitting in that estate-agent's office. Instead of
              which — ta-ra! — the thrilling life of a journeyman
              writer, scrounging commissions. Angela going back
              to lecturing after all these years — that was a huge
              help, too, of course. And the poor girl hates it, hates
              it. But your support, Terry, every bloody week —
              magnanimous! I hope some day I'll —
TERRY   Don't talk about it. Please.
FRANK   A new Medici.
TERRY   Is that a horse?
FRANK   You know very well —
TERRY   I'd put money on that myself!
FRANK   Thanks. That's all I can say. Thank you.

        He finishes his drink rapidly and makes another. TRISH
        puts a pillow under GEORGE's *head.*

TRISH   Lift your head. Good. Are you warm enough? That's
              better.
FRANK   I annoyed Trish a while ago. She said I was cheap,
              joking about apparitions out there.
TERRY   She has her hands full.
FRANK   Tough life. Courageous lady.
TERRY   Yes. So — the clock book — when is it going to appear?
FRANK   Another apparition. This time next year, we hope.
              Actually I was thinking of doing a chapter on appari-
              tions — well, visions, hallucinations, whatever.
TERRY   In a book about clocks?
FRANK   Time measurement, Terry! Did you know that the accu-
              rate measurement of time changed monastic practices
              in the Middle Ages, when Saint Conall and company

flourished out there? See? You never knew that! Before that monks prayed a few times during the day — a casual discipline that depended on nature — maybe at cockcrow, at high noon, when it got too dark to work in the fields. But Saint Benedict wanted ·more than that from his monks: he wanted continuous prayer. And with the invention of clocks that became possible.

TERRY But there weren't clocks then, were there?

FRANK No, no; crude timepieces; sophisticated egg timers. But with these new instruments you could break the twenty-four hours into exact sections. And once you could do that, once you could waken your monks up at *fixed* hours two or three times a night, suddenly — (*he claps his hands*) — continuous prayer!

TERRY What has that to do with apparitions?

FRANK Think about it. At the stroke of midnight — at 2.00 a.m. — at 4.00 a.m. — at 6.00 a.m. you chase your monks out of their warm beds. Into a freezing chapel. Fasting. Deprived of sleep. Repeating the same chant over and over again. And because they're hungry and dis-oriented and giddy for want of sleep and repeating the same droning chant over and over again, of course they hallucinate — see apparitions — whatever. Wouldn't you?

TERRY (*Laughs*) Frank!

FRANK Honestly! Medieval monks were always seeing apparitions. Read their books. And all because of the invention of timepieces. A word of warning, Terry. Be careful at matins — that's just before dawn. That's when you're most susceptible.

TERRY Is that going to be in your book!

FRANK Maybe. Why not? Anything to explain away the wonderful, the mystery.

TERRY But you don't believe a word of that, do you?

FRANK How would I know? But there must be some explanation, mustn't there? The mystery offends — so the mystery has to be extracted. (*He points to the island*) They had their own way of dealing with it: they embraced it all — everything. Yes, yes, yes, they said;

why bloody not? A rage for the absolute, Terry —
that's what they had. And because their acceptance
was so comprehensive, so open, so generous, maybe
they *were* put in touch — what do you think? — so
intimately in touch that maybe, maybe they actually
did see.

TERRY In touch with what? See what?

FRANK Whatever it is we desire but can't express. What is
beyond language. The inexpressible. The ineffable.

TERRY To spend their lives out there in the Atlantic, I suppose they must have been on to something.

FRANK And even if they were in touch, even if they actually
did see, they couldn't have told us, could they, unless they had the speech of angels? Because there is
no vocabulary for the experience. Because language
stands baffled before all that and says of what it has
attempted to say, 'No, no! That's not it at all! No, not
at all!' (*He drinks rapidly*) Or maybe they did write it
all down — without benefit of words! That's the only
way it could be written, isn't it? A book without words!

TERRY You've lost me, Frank.

FRANK And if they accomplished that, they'd have written
the last book ever written — and the most wonderful!
And then, Terry, then maybe life would cease!

> *He laughs. Brief pause.*

Or maybe we've got it all wrong as usual, Terry.
Maybe Saint Conall stood on the shores of the island
there and gazed across here at Ballybeg and said to
his monks, 'Oh, lads, lads, *there* is the end of desire.
Whoever lives there lives at the still core of it all.
Happy, happy, lucky people.' What do you think?

> FRANK *is now very animated. He laughs again. He
> drinks again.*

TERRY That's us — happy people.

FRANK (*Calls*) Come and join us, Conall! It's all in place here!

(*To* TERRY) Well — why not?

TERRY Indeed.

FRANK (*Laughs*) Despite appearances.

TERRY Why not?

TERRY fills the outstretched cup again.

FRANK Can't drink it without water.

TERRY Any left in the holy well?

FRANK Enough.

Again he scoops up water and makes a drink.

Aren't you joining me?

TERRY Pass this time. To the book.

FRANK No, no, not to the book. The book's nothing, nothing at all; a silly game of blind-man's buff. No, to the other, to the mystery itself, Terry. To the goddamn wonderful, maddening, necessary mystery.

He shudders as if with cold.

TERRY You're cold in that shirt. Here. Put this on.

TERRY takes off his jacket and puts it round FRANK's shoulders.

That's definitely your colour.

FRANK And to my goddamn wonderful wife. Is it profane to talk about her in the same breath as the sacred?

TERRY Is it?

FRANK Look at her. Now there's an apparition. She's . . . miraculous in that light, isn't she? Fourteen years married and the blood still thunders in my head when I look at her . . . Have you any idea, Terry, have you any idea at all of the turmoil, the panic people like me live in — the journeymen, the clerks of the world? No, no, the goddamn failures, for Christ's sake.

TERRY Frank, you —

FRANK Of course I am. Husband — father — provider — worthless.

TERRY Your book will —

FRANK The great book! (*He makes a huge gesture of dismissal*) She pretends to believe in it, too. But she's such a bright woman — she knows, she knows. You both know. Oh Jesus, Terry, if only you knew, have you any idea at all just how fragile it all is . . . ? (*Calls*) Maybe you should stay where you are, lads. It's not quite all in place here yet . . . Damn good whiskey. What is it? Coleraine 1922! That's very special. May I help myself? (*Proclaims*) Lord, it *is* good for us to be here! Isn't it . . . ?

He moves away. Pause.

ANGELA (*Softly, tentatively*) Oh my God . . .

TERRY What is it?

ANGELA Oh God, is it . . . ?

TRISH What's the matter, Angela?

ANGELA I think — oh God — I think —

TRISH Angela, are you sick?

ANGELA There's our boat.

BERNA Where?

TRISH Stop that, Angela.

FRANK Where? Where is it?

GEORGE *sits up.*

BERNA I see no boat.

TERRY Where is it, Angela?

FRANK Are you sure?

TRISH Where? — Show me — where? (*To* GEORGE) The boat's here, she says.

ANGELA (*Points*) There. It is, Terry, isn't it?

TRISH Is it, Terry?

BERNA There is no boat.

ANGELA Oh God, Terry, that's our boat — isn't it?

TRISH Point to it.

ANGELA   Maybe it's only — can you see nothing? — That patch of light on the water — just beyond that I thought I saw —

FRANK   Nothing. There's nothing.

TRISH   Where's the patch of light?

BERNA   There's no patch of light.

TERRY   Is it anywhere near that mist?

FRANK   Nothing. All in her head.

ANGELA   He's right . . . sorry . . . nothing . . . for a minute I was certain . . . sorry . . .

BERNA   You shouldn't do that, Angela.

ANGELA   Sorry.

BERNA   You really shouldn't do that.

ANGELA   I'm very sorry. I really am.

TERRY   There *is* a patch of light there; if you stare at it long enough it seems to make shapes . . . Anyhow, no harm done.

Pause.

(*Privately to* ANGELA) I ordered your favourite chocolate mints. Somebody must have eaten them. I suspect Charlie.

ANGELA   The boatman?

TERRY   My driver. Minibus Charlie. How could you forget Charlie? And the boatman's name is Carlin.

ANGELA   Give me a drink, Terry, would you?

TERRY   Wine? — Gin? — Vodka?

ANGELA   Anything at all. Just a drop.

BERNA *suddenly stands up and proclaims:*

BERNA   All right! I'll tell my story now!

TRISH   Good girl, Berna.

BERNA   I had a different psychiatrist in the clinic last week, a very intense young Englishman called Walsingham. He told me this story.

ANGELA   (*Accepting drink from* TERRY) Thanks.

TERRY   Anybody else?

FRANK Quiet.

TRISH Attention, please. (*To* BERNA) 'Once upon a time . . . '

BERNA Not once upon a time, Trish. I can give you the exact date: 1294. And in the year 1294, in the village of Nazareth, in the land that is now called Israel, a very wonderful thing happened. There was in the village a small, whitewashed house built of rough stone, just like these; and for over a thousand years the villagers looked on that house as their most wonderful possession; because that house had been the home of Mary and Joseph and their baby, Jesus.

And then in the year 1294, on the seventh day of March, an amazing thing happened. That small, whitewashed house rose straight up into the air, right away up into the sky. It hung there for a few seconds as if it was a bird finding its bearings. Then it floated — flew — over the Mediterranean Sea, high up over the Island of Crete, across the Aegean Sea, until it came to the coast of Italy. It crossed that coast and came to a stop directly above a small town called Loreto in the centre of Italy. Then it began to descend, slowly down and down and down, until it came to rest in the centre of the town. And there it sits to this day. And it is known as the Holy House of Loreto — a place of pilgrimage, revered and attested to by hundreds of thousands of pilgrims every year. The Holy House of Loreto.

Nobody knows how to respond. Pause.

TRISH A flying house? . . . And it's there now? . . . Well, heavens above, isn't that a —

BERNA And because it took off and flew across the sea and landed safely again, all over the world Our Lady of Loreto is known as the Patron Saint of Aviation.

Another brief pause.

FRANK There you are . . .

TRISH   (*Breezily*) Good girl, Berna.

FRANK   Never knew that . . .

TRISH   Live and learn.

FRANK   Indeed . . . live and learn . . .

TERRY   Wonderful story, Berna. Well done.

FRANK   Terry says this is my colour. What do you think?

BERNA   In our second year we had a lecturer in Equity, a Scotsman called — I've forgotten his name. We called him Offence to Reason because he used that phrase in every single lecture. We used to wait for it to come. 'Does that constitute an offence to reason?' (*Laughs*) He was in awe of reason. He really believed reason was the key to 'truth', the 'big verities'.

TERRY   The sun's trying to come up, is it?

BERNA   No, it's not a wonderful story, Trish. It's a stupid story. And crude. And pig-headed. A flying house is an offence to reason, isn't it? It marches up to reason and belts it across the gob and says to it, 'Fuck you, reason. I'm as good as you any day. You haven't all the fucking answers — not by any means.' That's what Dr Walsingham's story says. And that's why I like it.

> *She begins to cry quietly.* TERRY *moves towards her. But* TRISH *holds up her hand and he stops. Then* TRISH *goes to her and holds her.*

TRISH   Shhh, love, shhh . . .

BERNA   (*Into* TRISH's *face*) It's defiance, Trish — that's what I like about it.

TRISH   I know . . . I know . . .

BERNA   It's stupid, futile defiance.

TRISH   Shhh . . .

> *She moves away from* TRISH *and goes to the end of the pier. Her narrative has charged the atmosphere with unease, with anxiety.*

FRANK   (*Breezily*) You're right, Terry; the sun is trying to come up.

TERRY Yes?

> FRANK *begins singing the chorus of 'The World is Waiting for the Sunrise'.* TERRY *joins him. They sing two lines.*

FRANK You and I could do a neat dance to that, Berna. George?

> GEORGE *does not play.*

TRISH George is tired. He (*Frank*) knows the words of everything. What sort of a head have you got?
FRANK (*Brightly*) Full of rubbish. And panic.
ANGELA Did you bring a swimsuit, Berna?

> *No answer.* BERNA *now moves up to the catwalk.*

TRISH (*To* BERNA) I brought mine. You can have mine.
FRANK Or better still, Berna — I say, I say, I say — you may have mine!
ANGELA We're all too tired, Frank.
FRANK Are we?

> *He sings the first two lines of the refrain of 'Lazy River'. Brief pause.*

Right, Trish — all set?
TRISH What?
FRANK You're next!
TRISH What's he talking about?
FRANK For a story!
TERRY Yes, Trish!
TRISH I don't know any —
TERRY You're a wonderful story teller. Isn't she, Berna?
TRISH Ah, come on, Terry. You know very well —
ANGELA Go on, Trish!
FRANK Any kind of fiction will do us.
ANGELA Myth — fantasy —

TERRY A funny story —

ANGELA A good lie —

FRANK Even a bad lie. Look at us for God's sake — we'll accept anything! Right, Berna?

Now TRISH *understands that their purpose is to engage* BERNA *again.*

TRISH You want a story? Right!

She jumps to her feet and launches into her performance with great theatricality and brio.

So I'm on then? All right-all right-all right!

FRANK Certainly are.

TRISH (*Stalling, improvizing*) You want a story?

ANGELA We need a story.

TERRY Come down and hear this, Berna.

BERNA *looks over the wall.*

TRISH A story. Absolutely. Yes. Once upon a time and a very long time ago —

TERRY She's bluffing.

ANGELA Terry!

TERRY Look at her eyes.

FRANK What do her eyes say, George?

ANGELA (*To* TRISH) Pay no attention to him (*Terry*). Once upon a time . . . ?

TRISH May I proceed?

FRANK Let the lady speak.

TERRY That's no lady — that-sa ma sista.

ANGELA Terry!

TRISH Once upon a time and a very long time ago —

FRANK *sings the first line of 'Just a Song at Twilight'.*

ANGELA Please, Frank.

214

Suddenly TRISH *knows what her story is.*

TRISH The morning we got married, George! OK?
GEORGE OK.
FRANK Good one. Yeah.
ANGELA What story's that?
TRISH May I, George?
GEORGE Go ahead.
ANGELA I've forgotten that story.
TERRY That's a boring story, Trish.
FRANK Is it? Great! Boring is soothing.
ANGELA Do I know the story?
FRANK Boring reassures.
TERRY Course you do.
FRANK I'm all for boring. Sedate us, Trish.
TRISH If I may continue . . . ?
FRANK And it came to pass —
TRISH Twenty-two years ago. St Theresa's church.
FRANK Parish of Drumragh.
TRISH Ten o'clock Mass.
TERRY Best man. (*He bows*)
TRISH And little Patricia, all a-quiver in gold tiara, cream chiffon dress and pale blue shoes with three-quarter heels, has left her home for the last time and —
FRANK (*Sings*) 'There was I — ' George?

> GEORGE *picks up his accordion.*

TERRY You were bridesmaid, Berna. Remember?
ANGELA (*Remembering*) It's the story of the missing — !
FRANK Don't! (*Interrupt*)
TRISH May I? She arrives at the door of St Theresa's. And now her little heart starts to flutter because just as she enters the church on her Daddy's arm, Miss Quirk begins to play the harmonium —

> *She is suddenly drowned out by* GEORGE *playing the first line of 'There was I' — which is immediately picked up by* FRANK.

FRANK (*Sings*) '— waiting at the church — ' That's it! 'Waiting at the church — ' Terry!

> TERRY *and* FRANK *do a dance/march routine and sing together:*

DUET 'Waiting at the church / When I found — '
FRANK What?
TERRY ' — he'd left me in the lurch — ' Angela!
ANGELA (*Sings*) 'Oh how it did upset me — '

> TERRY *and* FRANK *sing* 'Tra-la-la-la-la'.

Sorry, Trish.
TRISH (*Pretended anger*) Fine — fine —
ANGELA Behave yourselves, you two!
TRISH Have your own fun.
FRANK Please, Trish —
TRISH No point, is there?
FRANK Go on, Patricia. 'The flutter bride was all a-chiffon — '
TRISH See?
TERRY Anyhow we all know how the story ends, don't we?
FRANK So what? All we want of a story is to hear it again and again and again and again and again.
ANGELA Are you going to let the girl finish?
FRANK And so it came to pass . . .

> GEORGE *now plays Wagner's 'Wedding March' very softly, with a reverence close to mockery.*

TRISH Thank you, George. (*She blows him a kiss*) The church is full to overflowing. My modest eyes are still on the ground. Daddy's gaze is manfully direct. We walk up that aisle together with quiet dignity until we come to the altar —
FRANK She's a natural!
TRISH And then for the first time I raise those modest eyes so that I can feast them on my handsome groom-to-be, my belovèd George.

FRANK Yes?

TRISH But lo —

FRANK Go on!

TRISH Who steps out to receive me — ?

FRANK But —

TERRY The anxious bookie — the groomsman!

FRANK Groomsman? Where's the groom?

TRISH No groom. No George.

Howls of dismay.

ANGELA Shame, George, shame!

FRANK Where can he be?

TERRY (*Calls*) George!

FRANK (*Calls*) We need you, George!

TERRY (*Calls*) Where are you, George?

FRANK (*Calls*) Heeelp!

FRANK }
TERRY } (*Call*) Heeelp!

ANGELA Will you let the girl finish her story?

TRISH Haven't seen him for over a week. Last heard from him two days ago from Limerick —

TERRY Cork.

TRISH — where the Aeolians — Michael Robinson and himself — they've been giving Beethoven recitals in schools and colleges there.

TERRY Knew she'd get it wrong.

FRANK (*To* TERRY) Please.

TRISH But these concerts, I know, are finished. Why isn't he here?

TERRY Playing with the Dude Ranchers.

TRISH Why isn't he here for his wedding?

TERRY Finishing a tour in County Cork.

TRISH Terry, the Aeolians were in Limerick doing a series of —

TERRY The Aeolians had broken up three months before you got married.

TRISH Don't you think I might — ?

TERRY George was working fulltime with the Ranchers when

you and he got married.

TRISH Terry —

FRANK Those details don't —

TERRY That's why George packed in the Aeolians — to make some money — so that you and he could get married. Right, George?

ANGELA So what? The point of Trish's story is —

TERRY (*To* TRISH) You asked me to take George on. Don't you remember?

TRISH So that when we — ?

TERRY And that's when the Ranchers really took off. When he packed in the Aeolians and joined the Ranchers. He made the Ranchers. We would never have come to anything without George.

TRISH *is totally bewildered.*

TRISH But how could I? . . . God . . . And when did — ?

TERRY You've forgotten — that's all. (*He hugs her quickly*) I'd signed George up three months before your wedding.

ANGELA And all this has nothing to do with the story. The point is that he did turn up at St Theresa's — and only ten minutes late. Well done, George.

TERRY (*To* TRISH) I didn't mean to —

TRISH But how could I have — ?

FRANK Certainly did turn up. On a motorbike — right? Soaked through and purple with cold.

ANGELA With the wedding suit in a rucksack on his back.

FRANK Changed in the organ loft — remember?

TRISH Oh my God, how could that have happened?

ANGELA That was a good day.

FRANK Great day.

TERRY (*To* TRISH) Sorry.

FRANK A wonderful day . . . God . . . what a day that was . . .

ANGELA Well done, Trish. A great story. The best story yet. Very well done.

Silence. Again they withdraw into themselves. BERNA now climbs from the catwalk up to the top wall. As *she does she hums 'O, Mother, I Could Weep'. She walks along the top of the wall.* TERRY *now sees her.*

TERRY Berna, please come down from there.
FRANK Berna!
TERRY That is dangerous, Berna.
TRISH (*To* TERRY) For God's sake, bring her down!
ANGELA Berna, love —
TERRY (*Command*) Come down, Berna! At once!

BERNA, *still humming, is now at the end of the wall. Without looking at anybody she jumps into the sea.*

FRANK Berna!
TERRY Jesus!
ANGELA Berna!
TERRY Oh Jesus Christ . . . !

End of Act One.

ACT TWO

Before the lights go up we hear GEORGE *playing 'All things bright and beautiful, all creatures great and small, / All things wise and wonderful, the Lord God made them all'.*

At that point lights up. A new day has opened. A high sky. A pristine and brilliant morning sunlight that enfolds the pier like an aureole and renovates everything it touches.

BERNA, *a cardigan round her shoulders, is in different clothes — her Act One clothes are drying across a bollard.* TRISH *is brushing and combing* BERNA'S *hair.* TERRY *is up on the catwalk, looking casually across the landscape, occasionally using binoculars.* ANGELA *is playing a game she has invented. From a distance of about five feet she pitches stones (lobster-pot weights) at an empty bottle placed close to the lifebelt stand. (When the game ends there is a small mound of stones.) On the lifebelt stand now hangs — as well as Angela's sun hat from Act One — the silk scarf Berna wore in Act One.* GEORGE *continues playing: 'Each little flower that opens, each little bird that sings, / He made their glowing colours, he made their tiny wings. / All things bright and beautiful, all creatures great and small — '*

Now ANGELA *sings to the music:*

ANGELA 'All things wise and wonderful, the Lord God makes them all.' You are 'wise and wonderful', George: you're the only one of us that slept all night.

GEORGE Did I?

ANGELA For an hour. And you snore.

GEORGE Sorry. (*He beckons her to him*) If I ever decide to go I want your children to have this (*accordion*).

ANGELA You are going —

GEORGE One of them might take it up.

ANGELA George, that's —

GEORGE Bit battered but it's working all right.

ANGELA That's a lovely thought. (*She kisses him*) Thank you.

GEORGE *If* I ever decide to go.

TERRY Where did Frank say he was going?

ANGELA To take photographs, he said. Probably to beat the head off poor old Carlin.

Pause.

TERRY Listen to those birds.

ANGELA Larks, are they?

TERRY 'And they heard the song of coloured birds.' You wouldn't believe me.

ANGELA They're larks, Terry. Ordinary larks.

GEORGE *begins to play 'Skylark' very softly.*

Exactly, George.

TERRY Has it a name, that game?

ANGELA It's called: how close can you get without touching it. Anybody got the time?

TERRY Just after seven.

BERNA (*Looks at her watch*) Stopped. Saltwater finished it.

ANGELA When does the minibus come for us?

TERRY Half-an-hour or so.

BERNA *takes off her watch, shakes it and holds it to her ear.*

BERNA That's that.

She casually tosses it into the sea. Only TRISH *sees this.*

TERRY There must be hundreds of them (*birds*). And they *are* coloured.

TRISH (*Quietly*) You put the heart across us, Berna, jumping into the sea like that.

BERNA Are you nearly finished? (*Hairdressing*)

TRISH You shouldn't have done that.

BERNA I wanted a swim.

TRISH It was a naughty thing to do. It was a cruel thing to do.

BERNA I told you — I wanted a swim.

TRISH Particularly cruel to Terry.

BERNA Oh poor Terry. (*She stands up abruptly*) That's fine, Trish. Thank you. (*To* ANGELA) May I play?

ANGELA Of course.

TERRY Well, would you look at that! Carlin has lit his fire again! (*Laughs*) What a strange man.

ANGELA (*To* BERNA) There are stones over there.

TERRY Maybe he'll come for us after he's had his breakfast. What do you think?

TRISH (*Wearily*) Terry.

ANGELA (*To* TRISH) Going to play?

TRISH Yes.

TERRY We still have time for a quick dart out and straight back. We'd do it in less than an hour.

TRISH D'you know what I would love? A cup of strong tea!

TERRY There's still a chance. Why not? I'm offering five-to-one against. Three-to-one. Any takers?

> GEORGE *has come to the last line of 'Skylark'.* TRISH *sings the line. The music stops.*

TRISH Now tell us what to do.

ANGELA The aim is to get as close as possible to that bottle. But every time you touch it you lose a point.

TRISH You *lose* a point? What sort of a makey-up game is that!

TERRY Looks wonderful in this light (*the island*). I'm not giving up. Two-to-one against. Even money.

TRISH We should all be exhausted, shouldn't we? But I feel . . . exhilarated. Play something exhilarating, George.

> GEORGE *plays 'Regina Caeli' right through. Immediately he begins:*

That's not exhilarating, is it?

ANGELA (*To* TRISH) Your throw.

BERNA Is there a chill in the air?

TRISH (*Preparing to throw*) Right.

> BERNA *reaches out to take her scarf from the lifebelt stand.*

ANGELA (*Quickly*) No; take mine. It's warmer. Like a hall-stand, isn't it? Good one, Trish. You have the hang of it.

> BERNA *drapes Angela's scarf around her shoulders.* FRANK *enters.*

FRANK Well — well — well! What Eden is this? And what happy people have we here, besporting themselves in the sunlight?

TERRY (*Coming down*) We thought we had lost you.

FRANK For you, George. Found it in the sand dunes back there.

> *Music stops.*

GEORGE Yes?

FRANK Interesting, isn't it? Polished flint-stone. The head of an axe, I think.

GEORGE Thank you.

FRANK That's the hole for the handle. Beautifully shaped, isn't it?

GEORGE Lovely.

TERRY Where did you find it?

FRANK Just behind the pier. Probably buried in the sand at one time. Then the sand shifted.

TERRY May I see it?

GEORGE Thank you, Frank.

FRANK Some weapon. That's a lethal edge there.

TERRY And the weight of it.

FRANK We'll make a handle for it; and on your next tour, if audiences aren't appreciative enough —

> *He mimes striking with the axe.*

TERRY That *is* sharp.

FRANK Meant for business, that weapon.

TERRY Did you get some good pictures?

FRANK Don't talk to me about pictures! Tell you all in a moment.

He goes to BERNA *and presents her with a bunch of wild flowers.*

For you, my lady. (*He kisses her*)

BERNA Oh, Frank.

ANGELA Aren't they pretty? Look at that blue.

TRISH You got them around here?

FRANK Just over the sand dunes.

TRISH (*To* GEORGE) He's a *real* gentleman.

FRANK (*To* BERNA) And d'you know what? — I could eat you in that dress.

BERNA They're beautiful, Frank. Thank you.

FRANK Welcome.

ANGELA Now — Berna. (*The game*)

TRISH You want to know how it's really done, girls? Just watch this.

They continue playing.

TERRY Lovely flowers. Thank you.

FRANK The place is full of them.

TERRY We thought maybe you'd gone to chastise Mr Carlin.

FRANK Just before daybreak there was a white mist suspended above the island; like a white silk canopy. And as the sun got up you could see the mist dissolve and vanish. So of course I thought: *Oileán Draíochta* emerging from behind its veil — capture this for posterity!

TERRY Did you get it?

FRANK Two bloody spools of it. Wasted all my film.

ANGELA (*To* TRISH) Not bad. Not bad.

TRISH Not bad? Wonderful!

BERNA Very close, Trish. Good one.

TRISH I think this could well be my game. Want to play, Frank?

FRANK (*To* ALL) Listen to this. You won't believe what I saw out there, Trish.

TRISH What?

Brief pause.

BERNA What did you see, Frank?

> FRANK *looks at them. He is not sure if he will tell his story.*

FRANK Just as the last wisp of the veil was melting away, suddenly — as if it had been waiting for a sign — suddenly a dolphin rose up out of the sea. And for thirty seconds, maybe a minute, it danced for me. Like a faun, a satyr; with its manic, leering face. Danced with a deliberate, controlled, exquisite abandon. Leaping, twisting, tumbling, gyrating in wild and intricate contortions. And for that thirty seconds, maybe a minute, I could swear it never once touched the water — was free of it — had nothing to do with water. A performance — that's what it was. A performance so considered, so aware, that you knew it knew it was being witnessed, wanted to be witnessed. Thrilling; and wonderful; and at the same time — I don't know why — at the same time . . . with that manic, leering face . . . somehow very disturbing.

BERNA Did you get pictures of it?

FRANK Nothing. You'd almost think it waited until my last shot was used up before it appeared. Thirty seconds, maybe a minute . . . Unbelievable. (*Embarrassed laugh*) Another apparition, Terry.

TERRY Maybe.

> *Pause.* FRANK *is now embarrassed at his own intensity and because the others are all staring at him. He laughs again.*

FRANK So I saw a porpoise or a dolphin or something leap

out of the water and dance about a bit. Wonderful!

TRISH I love dolphins. I think they are terrific. (*Briskly*) Right. Who's next?

ANGELA, TRISH *and* BERNA *play their game.*

FRANK Left them speechless, didn't it? My Ballybeg epiphany.

TERRY Sorry I missed that.

FRANK (*To* GEORGE) Upset me, that damn thing, for some reason.

GEORGE *nods and smiles.*

TERRY Drink?

FRANK (*Gestures: No*) Could have done with one back there. It really was a ceremonial dance, Terry — honest to God. And they look so damned knowing — don't they? — with those almost human faces . . . I'm getting to like this (*jacket*).

TERRY Well, what are our chances?

FRANK Chances?

TERRY *indicates Carlin's house.*

Forget him. Next time we'll bring our own boat.

TERRY Sorry. Not allowed.

FRANK Maybe you're right. Maybe he still will come. Who's to say?

TERRY *moves to the end of the pier where he sits by himself.*

ANGELA That hit the bottle. Point lost, Trish.

TRISH Didn't hit it, did it?

ANGELA Sorry. Point down. Berna?

BERNA, *her flowers still in her hand, picks up a stone close to* FRANK. *At the same time she puts one of her flowers in her hair and blows a kiss to him. As she does this* GEORGE *plays 'Bring Flowers of the Rarest'.*

GEORGE   'Bring flowers of the rarest, bring blossoms the fairest
From garden and woodland and hillside and dale,
Our full hearts are swelling, our glad voices telling
The praise of the loveliest flower of the vale.'

> *Immediately after he plays the first line 'Bring flowers
> . . . fairest' and as he continues playing:*

TRISH   I know that song, don't I?

FRANK   So do I.

BERNA   It's a hymn — is it?

GEORGE   Guess.

FRANK   It *is* a hymn — isn't it?

BERNA   Play the chorus, George.

TRISH   I do know it, whatever it is.

FRANK   I do, too.

> GEORGE *now begins the chorus, 'O Mary we crown
> thee with blossoms today — '*

TRISH   Yes! (*Sings*) — 'Queen of the angels and queen of the
May — '

FRANK   Haven't heard that since I was a child.

TRISH⎱ (*Sing*) 'O Mary we crown thee with blossoms today,
BERNA⎰ Queen of the angels and queen of the May.'

BERNA   (*To* GEORGE) Thank you.

FRANK   Not since I was a child.

> *Brief pause. And immediately* ANGELA *plunges into
> 'Oh Dem Golden Slippers'. And as she sings* GEORGE
> *accompanies her. She picks up Frank's shoes and,
> singing loudly, raucously, defiantly, and waving the
> shoes above her head, she parades/dances around the
> pier. She sings the entire chorus. She stops suddenly.
> The performance is over.*
>
> *Pause. Now she sings very softly the first two lines
> of the chorus of 'I Don't Know Why I'm Happy'. She
> tails off listlessly. She looks at the shoes and tosses them
> over to where* FRANK *is sitting. She looks at them all.*

ANGELA What a goddamn, useless, endless, unhappy outing this has been! (*Pause*) I'm sorry, Terry . . .

Pause.

FRANK (*To* TERRY) May I? (*Drink*)

FRANK *pours a drink and scoops up water.*

Should do a rain dance. Well's almost dry.

TERRY *now rises and joins them.*

TERRY I just remembered — I do have a story.
TRISH Too late, Terry. Story time's over.
FRANK No, it's not. It's always story time. Right, Berna?
BERNA Is it?
FRANK Certainly is.
TRISH All right. But make it short, Terry. Short and funny. I need a laugh.
FRANK Terence . . . ?
TERRY Yes. Well. The solicitor who is handling the sale of *Oileán Draíochta* — he told me this story. We were having lunch together. No; we had finished eating. He was having coffee and I was having tea and we both —
TRISH The story, Terry.
TERRY (*Almost reluctantly*) Yes — yes — the story. Well, the story he told me was this. Many years ago a young man was killed out there.
BERNA Killed how?
TERRY I suppose . . . murdered.
FRANK God.
TERRY His name was Sean O'Boyle. He was seventeen years of age. If you were to believe my solicitor friend he was . . . ritually killed.
TRISH What do you mean?
TERRY A group of young people — he was one of them — seven young men and seven young women. It wasn't

228

a disagreement, a fight; nothing like that. They were all close friends.

ANGELA And what happened?

TERRY The evidence suggests some sort of ritual, during which young O'Boyle was . . . (*He shrugs*)

TRISH Oh my God.

BERNA What evidence?

TERRY Burned-out fires — empty wine bottles — clothes left behind — blood smeared on rocks. It's thought there was some sort of orgy. Anyhow, at some point they dismembered him. That's accurate enough — from the pieces they found.

FRANK Jesus Christ, Terry . . . Oh Jesus Christ . . .

ANGELA When did this happen?

TERRY 1932. On the night of June 26th.

ANGELA These young people — they were from here?

TERRY Part of a group from this parish who had just returned from Dublin from the Eucharistic Congress. The older people went straight to their homes. The young group — our fourteen — apparently they had been drinking all the way home from Dublin — they stole a half-decker — from this pier, actually — and headed out for *Oileán Draíochta*. Some people say they had *poitín* stashed out there and that one of the girls was a great fiddler and that they just went out to have a dance. My friend has his own theory. These people were peasants, from a very remote part of the country. And he believes they were still in a state of intoxication after the Congress — it was the most spectacular, the most incredible thing they had ever witnessed. And that ferment and the wine and the music and the dancing . . .

TRISH I don't know what you're saying, Terry.

TERRY That young O'Boyle was . . . sacrificed.

FRANK Jesus Christ.

BERNA The other thirteen — they were charged?

TERRY No charges were ever brought.

TRISH Why not?

ANGELA The police weren't brought in?

TERRY Oh, yes. But by then the situation was away beyond their control. The parish was in uproar. Passions were at boiling point. Families were physically attacking one another. The police were helpless. The only person who could control the situation was the bishop of the time. He had led the group that had just made the pilgrimage to the Eucharistic Congress. And every year on August 15th he organized a pilgrimage out to the island.

TRISH So?

TERRY So the thirteen were summoned to the bishop's palace. All that is known is that they made a solemn pledge never to divulge what happened that night on the island; that they had to leave the country immediately and forever; and that before the end of the week they had all left for Australia.

TRISH Oh my God.

BERNA So nobody was ever charged?

TERRY Nobody. O'Boyle was an only child. Both his parents were dead within the year.

ANGELA *Oileán Draíochta* — wonderful.

TERRY Then the war came. Times were bad. People moved away. Within ten years the area was depopulated — that's your derelict church back there, Frank. The local belief was that the whole affair brought a curse on the parish and that nothing would ever prosper here again.

FRANK Jesus Christ, what a story! Jesus Christ, we don't know half of what goes on in the world!

TERRY (*To* TRISH) I'm sure that's the real reason why the pilgrimage out there really petered out. Couldn't have survived that.

TRISH Damn you, Terry Martin, how could you have brought us out to a place like that?

TERRY Trish, it is just an —

TRISH And how could you have bought an evil place like that?

TERRY The place is not evil, Trish.

TRISH I hate that story. That's a hateful story. You shouldn't have told us that story.

> *She moves quickly away and busies herself with her belongings. Silence.*

BERNA (*To* FRANK) These grew (*her flowers*).

FRANK What's that?

BERNA He said nothing ever grew again. These did.

FRANK True . . . that's true . . . . Going to be another warm day.

TERRY Think so.

FRANK Yes. Very warm. Wonderful.

> *They all drift apart.*

TRISH Shouldn't we tidy the place up a bit? Carlin could arrive any time.

BERNA You mean Charlie, don't you?

TRISH Do I? Whatever.

> *They begin tidying up, each attending to his/her own belongings. First they put on their shoes. Then* TERRY *puts bottles, flasks, etc. back into the hampers.* TRISH *folds up sleeping bags and packs her other belongings.* BERNA *folds her now dry clothes and puts them away.* FRANK *looks after his cameras, binoculars, etc.* ANGELA *makes a pile of the paper napkins, plastic cups, etc. scattered around the pier.* GEORGE *watches the others at their tasks. While all this tidying up is taking place the following episodes happen:* BERNA *takes her scarf off the lifebelt stand and puts it round her neck. Then she sees Angela's hat.*

BERNA Isn't this your hat, Angela?

ANGELA Thanks.

BERNA Do you want it?

ANGELA My good hat, for God's sake! Why wouldn't I want it? Thank you. The only sun hat I have.

> BERNA *hands the hat to* ANGELA. *A moment's hesitation. Then she removes the scarf from her neck and*

knots it on one of the arms of the stand. FRANK *witnesses this episode.*

TRISH (*To* GEORGE) I'll take that (*accordion*).
GEORGE Why?
TRISH What d'you mean why? I'll put it in the case for you.
GEORGE Why?
TRISH Because we're about to — Fine — fine! Suit yourself!
GEORGE Yes.

> TRISH *moves away from him.* FRANK *goes to the stand, takes off his belt and buckles it round the upright. Now he sees* TERRY *watching him.*

FRANK (*Breezily*) Maybe that's a bit reckless, is it? D'you think they'll stay up by themselves?
TERRY I'm all for a gamble.
FRANK Pot belly. Safe enough.

> TRISH *witnesses this episode. She looks at the mound of stones.*

TRISH Should we put these back where we found them?
BERNA I wouldn't bother. They were scattered all over the place when we got here.

> TRISH *goes to the stand. She takes off her bracelet and hangs it on one of the arms, balancing Berna's scarf. Then she goes back to* GEORGE *who is standing immobile beside their belongings.*

TRISH Give me your handkerchief.

> *He does not move.* TRISH *takes the handkerchief out of his breast pocket, returns to the stand, and knots the handkerchief beside her bracelet.*

ANGELA (*To* TERRY) Did you say you had honey cake?
TERRY Yes. Are you hungry?

He produces the cake from the hamper. A sealed tin.

How do you open this thing?
ANGELA No, no; don't open it. I'll leave it here, I think.

She places the tin on top of a bollard.

TERRY What are you doing?
ANGELA For Carlin. You don't mind, do you? He's sure to come snooping around after we've gone. A present.
TERRY Will you ever come back here?
ANGELA Just to keep him sweet.
BERNA Is this yours, Frank (*camera case*)?
FRANK Just looking for that. Thank you.
ANGELA (*To* TERRY) Sorry for that outburst a while ago.
TERRY Please . . .
ANGELA It was a lovely birthday.
TERRY We'll not talk about that. Interesting place, though.
ANGELA Pretty.
TERRY Wonderful, isn't it?
ANGELA (*Gesturing to island*) I can live without all that stuff, Terry. Honestly. Housework — the kids — teaching — bills — Frank — doctors — more bills — just getting through every day is about as much as I can handle; more than I can handle at times. (*Remembering that the island is his*) I really wish you luck with it. Yes — yes — yes, of course it's wonderful — beautiful and wonderful.
TERRY When will I see you?
ANGELA Terry —
TERRY Next Sunday?
ANGELA No. Please.

She spreads her hands as if to say 'What's the point? Can't you see there's no point?' Then very quickly she takes his hands in hers, squeezes them, and then swiftly moves away from him.
FRANK *has found a small bottle. He holds it up.*

FRANK Anybody mind if I pour this out? (*Reads*) Cherry Brandy.

He empties it out.

God, that's a sin, isn't it?

Now he picks up a plastic cup, scoops whatever water is left in the 'well', and pours it into the brandy bottle. Now he is aware that TERRY *and* ANGELA *are watching him. He laughs.*

For a quick shot on the way home. In case Charlie's jokes get too bad. Hardly any (*water*) left . . .

He corks the bottle with paper tissues. TRISH *goes to the small pile of rubbish (paper tissues, plastic cups, etc) that* ANGELA *gathered. She strikes a match. Just as she is about to set fire to the refuse* ANGELA *rushes to her and stamps the fire out with her foot.*

ANGELA For God's sake, woman!
TRISH What have I — ?
ANGELA You can't light a fire here! (*Calm again*) We can take this away with us, can't we? That would be simpler, wouldn't it?

She begins piling the rubbish into a plastic bag.

TRISH (*Excessive astonishment*) Oh good Lord, we're suddenly very house proud, aren't we?

ANGELA *puts her hand on* TRISH's *elbow.*

ANGELA Sorry, Trish. Could do with some sleep.

She moves away to the end of the pier and looks around. The various tasks have been completed.

FRANK Now, Terry. Yourself.

TERRY What's that?

FRANK You're going to leave a visiting card, aren't you?

TERRY A visiting — ?

FRANK On the stand. 'Terry Martin Was Here.'

TERRY (*Laughs*) Nothing to leave. (*Produces coins*) Is money any good?

TRISH Useless, Terry.

TERRY What else can I give you?

FRANK What else can he give us? What about that shirt?

Suddenly everybody is listening, watching.

BERNA Yes, Terry. The shirt.

FRANK Is the shirt what we want?

TRISH The shirt will do.

BERNA We want the shirt!

TRISH Hand it over, Terry.

TERRY Ah, come on now —

FRANK We all want the shirt, don't we?

GEORGE Yes — yes — yes!

Now TRISH sings rapidly — and keeps singing again and again, 'I want the shirt — I want the shirt', to the air of 'Here Comes the Bride'.

FRANK We'll take it now, Terry.

BERNA We want it now, Terry, now.

TERRY Here — I'll give you a penknife — matches —

FRANK No good. The shirt, Terry. Hand it over.

TERRY tries to back away from them. They encircle him. They sing with TRISH:

ALL 'We want the shirt — we want the shirt — '

TERRY My shoes! My shoes and socks —

BERNA The shirt, Terry.

TRISH The shirt — the shirt!

FRANK The shirt — the shirt — the shirt!

ALL *sing again, 'We want the shirt — we want the shirt — '* GEORGE *plays 'Here Comes the Bride' and continues playing until after* FRANK's *'Pull — pull — pull!'*

TERRY For God's sake, this is the only shirt I have here!
FRANK Grab him!
TERRY Frank — !

And suddenly they all grab him (all except ANGELA *who is by herself at the end of the pier — but watching).* TERRY *falls to the ground. They pull at his shirt. As they do, overlapping:*

BERNA We have him!
FRANK Hold his feet!
TERRY For God's sake!
TRISH Give it to us!
FRANK Hold him — hold him!
TRISH We want it — we want it!
TERRY Help!
BERNA Want it — want it — want it!
FRANK Want it, Terry — want it!
BERNA Pull — pull — pull!
TRISH I've got it!
BERNA Rip it off!
TERRY Angela, help — !
FRANK Hold his hands!
BERNA Need it — need it!
TRISH Got it! Yes!
TERRY Please — !
FRANK Pull — pull — pull!

Now FRANK *stands up in triumph, a portion of* TERRY's *shirt held aloft.*

There!
TRISH Well done, Frank.
BERNA Now hang it up, Terry. (*To* ALL) Yes?

GEORGE Yes — yes!

TRISH Hang it up there, Terry. Come on — be a sport!

TERRY gets to his feet and pulls the remnant of his shirt together.

TERRY Happy now, are you?

FRANK On the lifebelt stand. Has to be done in person.

TERRY You're a shower of bastards — you know that?

He takes the piece of the shirt and hangs it up. They applaud.

BERNA 'Terry Martin Was Here.'

TERRY Satisfied?

TRISH Wonderful!

TERRY OK?

FRANK You'll be remembered here forever, Terry.

TERRY Happy now? I hope you're all happy now.

BERNA Don't be such a crank.

FRANK Bit of fun, Terry. That's all.

TERRY (*Relenting*) Not a button left.

FRANK Just passing the time — killing time.

TERRY And I could have split my head on those stones!

FRANK Just a bit of fun.

FRANK goes to one of his bags and produces a shirt.

TRISH You look wonderful, Terry. Doesn't he?

FRANK This should fit you.

TERRY raises his hand in a pretended gesture of striking him.

And it's your colour.

TERRY I like this now. I'm not going to part with it. Bastards . . .

The moment has passed. They finish tidying up. They

look around the pier, now restored to what it was when they arrived.

TRISH So . . .
BERNA So . . .

They look like people at a station — some standing, some sitting — just waiting patiently to get away.

TRISH Lovely harvest day, isn't it?
BERNA What time is it now?
FRANK Coming up to seven-thirty.

Brief pause. FRANK *sees two stones a few feet away from the mound of stones. He picks one up and places it on top of the mound.*

Simple domestic instincts . . .

He now picks up the second stone and places it on top of the mound.

(*To* TERRY) At seven-thirty in the morning the rage for the absolute isn't quite so consuming . . . The acceptance of what *is* . . .

Brief pause.

ANGELA He's out there somewhere, just below the surface.
TERRY Who's that?
ANGELA His dancing porpoise.
FRANK Damn right. Waiting for an audience.
TERRY Not many audiences around here.
FRANK Or maybe just searching for the other thirteen. Who's to say?

Short pause.

TRISH Is he punctual?

TERRY *(Laughs)* Carlin?

TRISH *(Wearily)* God! Your driver — Charlie!

TERRY He'll be on time. He's always on bloody time.

> *Short pause.*

TRISH *(To* GEORGE*)* Are you not going to put that into the case?

GEORGE No.

TRISH What's got into you?

GEORGE I'm not finished playing.

> *Short pause.* ANGELA *is still by herself at the end of the pier.*

ANGELA There was a city called Eleusis in Attica in ancient Greece; and every year at the end of summer religious ceremonies were held there in honour of Demeter, the goddess of the harvest — what we would call a harvest festival. And they were known as the Eleusinian Mysteries.

FRANK Off again!

TRISH No more stories, Angela. Let's get back to real life.

ANGELA All we know about the ceremonies is that they began with a period of fasting; that there was a ritual purification in the sea; and that young people went through a ceremony of initiation. And there was music and dancing and drinking. And we know, too, that sacrifice was offered. And that's about all we know. Because the people who took part in the ceremonies vowed never to speak of what happened there. So that when that civilization came to an end it took the secrets of the Eleusinian Mysteries with it.

FRANK What's your point — that they had bishops too? I'll tell you something: it's going to be another roaster of a day.

> *Brief pause.*

BERNA Play something for us, George.
GEORGE What?
BERNA Whatever gives you pleasure.
GEORGE My pleasure . . . right . . .

He strikes a few chords as he wonders what he will play. Then suddenly:

TRISH Shhh! Listen! Listen!
BERNA What is it?
TRISH Stop! Quiet! Stop!
FRANK Is it — ?
TRISH The minibus! Isn't it? Listen!
FRANK I don't hear —
BERNA It is! She's right!
TRISH At last! At last!
TERRY Told you he was bloody punctual.

They are all suddenly animated, excited, joyous. They pick up their belongings. They all talk at the same time.

FRANK Good old Charlie!
TERRY Whose is this?
TRISH What new jokes will he have?
ANGELA Don't forget your sleeping bag.
BERNA We'll be home by lunchtime.
ANGELA Can you manage all that?
FRANK You're sunburned.
GEORGE Am I?
FRANK Your forehead.
TRISH The moment I get home — straight to bed!
FRANK You're very lucky to have Charlie.

And gradually as the minibus gets closer their chatter and their excitement dies away. Now the minibus has arrived. The engine is switched off. FRANK *goes to the exit.*

Good man, Charlie. With you in a moment.

He now sees the tin of honey cake and picks it up.

What's this?

TERRY That's for Carlin.

FRANK Like hell. I'm taking —

TERRY Leave it, Frank.

FRANK Sorry . . .

Nobody moves. They look around. Nobody speaks. Finally:

TRISH Nice place all the same . . . Isn't it?

FRANK Lovely.

TRISH It really is, Terry.

BERNA So peaceful.

TRISH Lovely.

FRANK Really peaceful.

TRISH Wonderful.

FRANK Wonderful.

TRISH (*To* GEORGE) Isn't it wonderful?

GEORGE Yes.

TERRY Angela's right: it was a mess, the whole thing.

FRANK Terry —

TERRY The least said . . . I just feel I've let you all down.

FRANK Don't say another word. It was a great birthday party. We had a wonderful time.

TRISH He's right, Terry. Terrific.

FRANK Thank you. And we'll do it again some time. (*To* ALL) Agreed? (*To* GEORGE) Right, George?

GEORGE *spreads his hands and smiles.*

Only this time I'll take Mr Carlin in hand and he'll do what he's supposed to do.

TRISH And even though we don't make it out there —

FRANK Of course we'll make it! Why wouldn't we make it?

TRISH Well at least now we know . . . it's there.

FRANK (*Calls*) 'Bye, Conall!

TRISH (*Calls*) 'Bye, Conall!

FRANK *sings, 'Aloha'.*

TERRY I should tell you —
TRISH (*Calls*) Be good, Conall!
TERRY I should have said —
FRANK Trish, my love, you're looking nowhere near it.
TRISH What do you — ?

FRANK *turns her head to the right.*

FRANK Got it now?
TRISH Ah.
FRANK Still County Sligo.
TRISH I know it's County Sligo, Frank.
FRANK (*To* ALL) See? Nothing changes.
ANGELA (*To* TERRY) You should have told us what?
TERRY Nothing.
ANGELA What should you have told us?
TERRY (*Reluctantly*) What I said yesterday afternoon — this morning — I'm confused — when was it? — Anyhow, when I told you I owned the island, that *is* true — well partially true. I *have* taken an option on it. That option expires in a month. And I'm not going to pick it up.
TRISH Now that's the best news I've heard all day! The moment you told that story about —

TERRY *holds up his hand to silence her.*

TERRY I want to pick it up. Oh, yes. Trouble is — I haven't the money. The bookie business — concert promotion — the last few years have been disastrous. And I'm afraid — (*laughs*) — not to put a tooth in it — I'm broke.
TRISH But, Terry, you —
TERRY Things will pick up. The tide will turn. I'll rise again. Oh, yes, I'll rise again. (*To* BERNA) That's why I didn't tell you I'd optioned it. Knew I'd lose it. (*To* ALL) Actually I didn't mean to tell anybody . . . Look at those solemn

faces! (*Laughs*) To own *Oileán Draíochta* for four whole months — wasn't that wonderful enough? Wasn't that a terrific secret to have? Anyway . . . One small thing. I'd be glad if you kept it to yourselves — that I'm broke. Don't want a hundred creditors descending on me.

BERNA I'm sorry, Terry.

TERRY So we'll come back again, will we? What d'you say?

TRISH But, Terry, how can you — ?

TERRY When will we come back?

FRANK Good God, Terry, how can you?

TERRY Next year? What about next year?

FRANK If I'd known — if any of us had any idea you were —

TERRY My birthday next year — right?

FRANK And you've been doling out — day after day — month after —

ANGELA (*Triumphantly*) Yes, we will! Next year — and the year after — and the year after that! Because we want to! Not out of need — out of desire! Not in expectation — but to attest, to affirm, to acknowledge — to shout Yes, Yes, Yes! Damn right we will, Terry! Yes — yes — yes!

FRANK Twelve months' time — agreed?

TRISH Agreed!

FRANK Berna?

BERNA Yes!

FRANK George?

GEORGE Agreed!

FRANK No more talk! Settled! (*Calls*) 'Bye, Conall! 'Bye, lads. They're waving to us! Wave back to them!

FRANK *waves vigorously.* TRISH, GEORGE *and* BERNA *make smaller gestures.*

TRISH 'Bye!

FRANK (*Calls*) Terry's birthday next year! And for a whole night!

They all join in, overlapping.

TRISH 'Bye, sheep!
GEORGE 'Bye.
TRISH 'Bye, cattle.
TERRY 'Bye, coloured birds.
BERNA 'Bye, whin bush.
FRANK 'Bye, bell.
TERRY 'Bye, clothes on bushes.
ANGELA 'Bye, low hill.
GEORGE 'Bye.
TRISH 'Bye, oak trees.
ANGELA 'Bye, apple trees.
TERRY 'Bye, Conall.
ALL 'Bye . . . 'bye . . . 'bye . . .
FRANK 'Bye, dancing dolphin . . . 'bye . . . 'bye . . .

> *Still nobody moves. Now* GEORGE *plays in his 'sacred' style 'Come, my love, come, my boat lies low, / She lies high and dry on the O-hi-o, / Come, my love, come, and come along with me / And I'll take you back to Tennessee'.*

TRISH Charlie's waiting for us. Shouldn't we make a move?

> *But nobody moves. Now* BERNA *begins to hum with the song, beginning with the first verse:*

BERNA 'Down by the cane-brake, close by the mill
There lived a blue-eyed girl and her name was
Nancy Dill — '

> GEORGE *accompanies her. Now* TERRY *hums with her. Together they hum:*

TERRY⎫ 'I told her that I loved her, I loved her very long,
BERNA⎭ I'm going to serenade her and this will be my
song . . . '

> *Now* TRISH *and* FRANK *join in the humming: 'Come, my love, come, my boat lies low, / She lies high and*

244

*dry on the O-hi-o, / Come my love, come, come along
with me, / And I'll take you back to Tennessee — '
They play/hum another verse and this time* ANGELA
*joins them. (And this continues to the end of the
play.)*

TRISH *goes to the mound of stones. She walks around
it once. Then she picks up a stone from the bottom of the
mound and places it on the top. Then she walks around
the mound a second time, and again she places a
stone on top. Then she goes to the lifebelt stand and
lightly touches her votive offering. Then she goes to
her belongings, picks them up, and slowly moves off.*

The moment TRISH *completes her first encircling*
BERNA *joins her. First she places the flowers* FRANK *gave
her at the foot of the stand. Then she does the ritual
that* TRISH *is doing. And this ceremony — encircling,
lifting a stone, encircling, lifting a stone, touching the
votive offering — is repeated by every character.* FRANK
immediately behind BERNA, TERRY *immediately after*
FRANK. *And when they finish they pick up their belongings and — still humming to* GEORGE's *accompaniment — move slowly off. Now only* GEORGE *and* ANGELA
are left. GEORGE *stops playing. He looks at her and gestures towards the mound.*

ANGELA You go ahead, George. I think I'll pass.

*She watches him as he does the ritual. When he has
finished he stands beside her and puts his arm on hers.
They take a last look round.*

GEORGE Nice place.
ANGELA Nice place.

She nods in agreement.

GEORGE You'll come back some day.
ANGELA I don't think —
GEORGE Yes, you will. Some day. And when you do, do it for

me. No, no, I don't mean *for* me — just in memory of
me.

> *She looks at him for a second. Then quickly, impetu-*
> *ously, she catches his head between her hands and*
> *kisses him. Then she breaks away from him, rushes to*
> *the stand, kisses her sun hat and hangs it resolutely*
> *on the very top of the stand.*

ANGELA (*Defiantly*) For you, George! For both of us!

> *She rushes back to him, takes his arm and begins*
> *singing 'Down by the Cane-brake' loudly, joyously,*
> *happily — and he accompanies her with comparable*
> *brio. The others, off, join in.*
>
> GEORGE *and* ANGELA *exit. The engine starts up.*
> *The singing and the engine compete. Both sounds are*
> *encompassed by the silence and complete stillness*
> *and gradually surrender to it.*

MOLLY
SWEENEY

Characters

MOLLY SWEENEY
FRANK SWEENEY
MR RICE

Molly Sweeney was first produced at the Gate Theatre, Dublin, on 9 August 1994, with the following cast:

MOLLY   Catherine Byrne
FRANK   Mark Lambert
MR RICE   T P McKenna

Directed by   Brian Friel

I am particularly indebted to Oliver Sacks' case history 'To See and Not See' and the long, strange tradition of such case histories.

— BF

Tell all the Truth but tell it slant —
Success in Circuit lies
Too bright for our infirm Delight
The Truth's superb surprise
As Lightning to the Children eased
With explanation kind
The Truth must dazzle gradually
Or every man be blind —

— Emily Dickinson

Learning to see is not like learning a new language. It's like learning language for the first time.

— Denis Diderot

for Megan

ACT ONE

When the lights go up we discover the three characters — MOLLY
SWEENEY, MR RICE, FRANK SWEENEY — on stage. All three stay on
stage for the entire play.

   I suggest that each character inhabits his/her own special acting area
— MR RICE stage left, MOLLY SWEENEY centre stage, FRANK SWEENEY
stage right (left and right from the point of view of the audience).

   MOLLY SWEENEY *and* FRANK *are in their late thirties/early forties.*
MR RICE *is older.*

   Most people with impaired vision look and behave like fully sighted
people. The only evidence of their disability is usually a certain
vacancy in the eyes or the way the head is held. MOLLY *should indicate*
her disability in some such subtle way. No canes, no groping, no dark
glasses, etc.

MOLLY By the time I was five years of age my father had
     taught me the names of dozens of flowers and herbs
     and shrubs and trees. He was a judge and his work
     took him all over the county. And every evening when
     he got home, after he'd had a few quick drinks, he'd
     pick me up in his arms and carry me out to the walled
     garden.
       'Tell me now,' he'd ask. 'Where precisely are we?'
       'We're in your garden.'
       'Oh, you're such a clever little missy!' And he'd pre-
     tend to smack me.
       'Exactly what part of my garden?'
       'We're beside the stream.'
       'Stream? Do you hear a stream? I don't. Try again.'
       'We're under the lime tree.'
       'I smell no lime tree. Sorry. Try again.'
       'We're beside the sundial.'
       'You're guessing. But you're right. And at the bottom

of the pedestal there is a circle of petunias. There are about twenty of them all huddled together in one bed. They are — what? — seven inches tall. Some of them are blue-and-white, and some of them are pink, and a few have big, red, cheeky faces. Touch them.'

And he would bend over, holding me almost upside down, and I would have to count them and smell them and feel their velvet leaves and their sticky stems. Then he'd test me.

'Now, Molly. Tell me what you saw.'

'Petunias.'

'How many petunias did you see?'

'Twenty.'

'Colour?'

'Blue-and-white and pink and red.'

'Good. And what shape is their bed?'

'It's a circle.'

'Splendid. Passed with flying colours. You *are* a clever lady.'

And to have got it right for him and to hear the delight in his voice gave me such pleasure.

Then we'd move on to his herb bed and to his rose bed and to his ageratum and his irises and his azaleas and his sedum. And when we'd come to his nemophila, he always said the same thing.

'Nemophila are sometimes called Baby Blue Eyes. I know you can't see them but they have beautiful blue eyes. Just like you. You're my nemophila.'

And then we'd move on to the shrubs and the trees and we'd perform the same ritual of naming and counting and touching and smelling. Then, when our tour was ended, he'd kiss my right cheek and then my left cheek with that old-world formality with which he did everything; and I loved that because his whiskey breath made my head giddy for a second.

'Excellent!' he'd say. 'Excellent testimony! We'll adjourn until tomorrow.'

Then, if Mother were away in hospital with her nerves, he and I would make our own meal. But if she

were at home she'd appear at the front door — always
in her headscarf and wellingtons — and she'd shout,
'Molly! Daddy! Dinner!' I never heard her call him anything but Daddy and the word always seemed to have
a mocking edge. And he'd say to me, 'Even scholars
must eat. Let us join your mother.'

And sometimes, just before we'd go into that huge,
echoing house, sometimes he'd hug me to him and
press his mouth against my ear and whisper with fierce
urgency, 'I promise you, my darling, you aren't missing a lot; not a lot at all. Trust me.'

Of course I trusted him; completely. But late at night,
listening to Mother and himself fighting their weary
war downstairs and then hearing him grope his way
unsteadily to bed, I'd wonder what he meant. And it
was only when I was about the same age as he was
then, it was only then that I thought — I thought perhaps I was beginning to understand what he meant.
But that was many, many years later. And by then
Mother and he were long dead and the old echoing
house was gone. And I had been married to Frank for
over two years. And by then, too, I had had the operation on the first eye.

MR RICE The day he brought her to my house — the first time I
saw them together — my immediate thought was: what
an unlikely couple!

I had met him once before about a week earlier; by
himself. He had called to ask would I see her, just to
give an opinion, if only to confirm that nothing could
be done for her. I suggested he phone the hospital and
make an appointment in the usual way. But of course
he didn't. And within two hours he was back at my
door again with an enormous folder of material that
had to do with her case and that he had compiled over
the years and he'd be happy to go through it with me
there and then because not only were the documents
and reports and photographs interesting in themselves
but they would be essential reading for someone like

myself who was going to take her case on.

Yes, an ebullient fellow; full of energy and enquiry and the indiscriminate enthusiasms of the self-taught. And convinced, as they usually are, that his own life story was of compelling interest. He had worked for some charitable organization in Nigeria. Kept goats on an island off the Mayo coast and made cheese. Sold storage batteries for those windmill things that produce electricity. Endured three winters in Norway to ensure the well-being of whales. That sort of thing. Worthy pursuits, no doubt. And he was an agreeable fellow; oh, yes; perfectly agreeable. Frank. That was his name. She was Molly. Reminded me instantly of my wife, Maria. Perhaps the way she held her head. A superficial resemblance. Anyhow. Molly and Frank Sweeney.

I liked her. I liked her calm and her independence; the confident way she shook my hand and found a seat for herself with her white cane. And when she spoke of her disability there was no self-pity, no hint of resignation. Yes, I liked her.

Her life, she insisted, was uneventful compared with his. An only child. Father a judge. Mother in and out of institutions all her days with nervous trouble. Brought up by various housekeepers. For some reason she had never been sent to a blind school. Said she didn't know why; perhaps because her father thought he could handle the situation best at home.

She had been blind since she was ten months old. She wasn't totally sightless: she could distinguish between light and dark; she could see the direction from which light came; she could detect the shadow of Frank's hand moving in front of her face. But for all practical purposes she had no useful sight. Other ophthalmologists she had been to over the years had all agreed that surgery would not help. She had a full life and never felt at all deprived. She was now forty-one, married just over two years, and working as a massage therapist in a local health club. Frank and she had met there and had married within a month. They were fortunate they had her earnings to live on because he was out of work at the moment.

She offered this information matter-of-factly. And as she talked he kept interrupting. 'She knows when I pass my hand in front of her face. So there is some vision, isn't there? So there is hope, isn't there, isn't there?' Perhaps, I said. 'And if there is a chance, any chance, that she might be able to see, we must take it, mustn't we? How can we not take it? She has nothing to lose, has she? What has she to lose? — Nothing! Nothing!'

And she would wait without a trace of impatience until he had finished and then she would go on. Yes, I liked her at once.

His 'essential' folder. Across it he had written, typically, *Researched and Compiled by Frank C Sweeney*. The 'C' stood for Constantine, I discovered. And it did have some interest, the folder. Photographs of her cycling by herself across a deserted beach. Results of tests she had undergone years ago. A certificate for coming first in her physiotherapy exams. Pictures of them on their honeymoon in Stratford-on-Avon — his idea of self-improvement, no doubt. Letters from two specialists she had been to in her late teens. An article he had cut out of a magazine about miraculous ophthalmological techniques once practised in Tibet — or was it Mongolia? Diplomas she had won in provincial swimming championships. And remarkably — in his own furious handwriting — remarkably, extracts from essays by various philosophers on the relationship between vision and knowledge, between seeing and understanding. A strange fellow, indeed.

And when I talked to them on that first occasion I saw them together in my house, I knew that she was there at Frank's insistence, to please him, and not with any expectation that I could help. And as I watched her sitting there, erect in her seat and staring straight ahead, two thoughts flitted across my mind. That her blindness was his latest cause and that it would absorb him just as long as his passion lasted. And then, I wondered, what then? But perhaps that was too stern a judgement.

And the second and much less worthy thought I had was this. No, not a thought; a phantom desire, a fantasy in my head; absurd, bizarre, because I knew only the barest outlines of her case, hadn't even examined her yet; the thought, the bizarre thought that perhaps, perhaps — up here in Donegal — not in Paris or Dallas or Vienna or Milan — but perhaps up here in remote Ballybeg was I about to be given — what is the vulgar parlance? — the chance of a lifetime, the one-in-a-thousand opportunity that can rescue a career — no, no, transform a career — dare I say it, restore a reputation? And if that opportunity were being offered to me and if after all these years I could pull myself together and measure up to it, and if, oh my God, if by some miracle pull it off perhaps . . . (*He laughs in self-mockery*)

Yes, I'm afraid so. People who live alone frequently enjoy an opulent fantasy life.

FRANK One of the most fascinating discoveries I made when I was in the cheese business — well, perhaps not fascinating, but interesting, definitely interesting — one of the more interesting discoveries I made — this was long before I met Molly — for three-and-a-half years I had a small goat farm on the island of Inis Beag off the Mayo coast — no, no, not a farm for small goats — a farm for ordinary goats — well, extraordinary goats as a matter of fact because I imported two piebald Iranian goats — and I can't tell you how complicated and expensive that whole process was; and the reason I wanted them, the reason I wanted Iranians, was that in all the research I had done and according to all the experts they were reputed to give the highest milk yield — untrue as it turned out — and because their pelts were in great demand as wall coverings in

California — equally untrue, I'm afraid; and although they bred very successfully — eventually I had a herd of fourteen — they couldn't endure the Mayo winters with the result that I had to keep them indoors and feed them for six months of the year — in Mayo the winter lasts for six months for God's sake — at least it did on Inis Beag. And of course that threw my whole financial planning into disarray. As you can imagine. And yes, as a matter of interest, they are small animals, Iranian goats. And, as I say, from Iran which, as you know, is an ancient civilization in South West . . . Asia . . .

But I was telling you about — what? The interesting discovery! Yes! Well, perhaps not an interesting discovery in any general sense but certainly of great interest to anybody who hopes to make cheese from the milk of imported Iranian goats, not that there are thousands of those people up and down the country! Anyhow — anyhow — what I discovered was this. I had those goats for three-and-a-half years, and even after all that time their metabolism, their internal clock, stayed Iranian; never adjusted to Irish time. Their system never made the transition. They lived in a kind of perpetual jet lag.

So what, you may ask. So for three-and-a-half years I had to get up to feed them at three in the morning my time because that was 7.00 a.m. their time, their breakfast time! And worse — worse — they couldn't be kept awake and consequently couldn't be milked after eight in the evening because that was midnight their time — and they were lying there, dead out, snoring! Bizarre! Some imprint in the genes remained indelible and immutable. I read a brilliant article once by a professor in an American magazine and he called this imprint an engram, from the Greek word meaning something that is etched, inscribed, on something. He said it accounts for the mind's strange ability to recognize instantly somebody we haven't seen for maybe thirty years. Then he appears. The sight of him connects with the imprint, the engram. And bingo — instant recognition!

Interesting word — engram. The only other time I heard it used was by Mr Rice, Molly's ophthalmologist. In that swanky accent of his — 'engram'. And he was born in the village of Kilmeedy in County Limerick for God's sake! I really never did warm to that man. No wonder his wife cleared off with another man. No, no, no, I don't mean that; I really don't mean that; that's a rotten thing to say; sorry; I shouldn't have said that. But I was talking about the word engram and how he pronounced it. That was before any of the operations, and he was explaining to Molly that if by some wonderful, miraculous good fortune her sight were restored, even partially restored, she would still have to learn to see and that would be an enormous and very difficult undertaking.

The way he explained it was this. She knew dozens of flowers; not to see; not by sight. She knew them only if she could touch them and smell them because those tactile engrams were implanted in her brain since she was a child. But if she weren't allowed to touch, to smell, she wouldn't know one flower from another; she wouldn't know a flower from a football. How could she?

And interestingly, interestingly this very same problem was debated three hundred years ago by two philosophers, William Molyneux and his friend, John Locke. I came across this discussion in a Do-It-Yourself magazine of all places! Fascinating stuff, philosophy — absolutely fascinating. Anyhow — anyhow. If you are blind, said Molyneux — he was an Irishman by the way and in fact his wife was blind — if you are blind you can learn to distinguish between a cube and a sphere just by touching them, by feeling them. Right? Right. Now, supposing your vision is suddenly restored, will you be able — by sight alone, without touching, without feeling — will you be able to tell which object is the cube and which the sphere? Sorry, friend, said Locke — incidentally he went to West-minster School where he was flogged regularly — sorry, friend, you will not be able to tell which is which.

Then who comes along to join in the debate but another philosopher, George Berkeley, with his essay entitled 'An Essay Towards a New Theory of Vision'. Another Irishman incidentally; Bishop Berkeley. And actually when I say along came the Bishop, his 'Essay' didn't appear until seventeen years after the discussion I told you about between Locke and Molyneux. Anyhow — anyhow. When the problem was put to the Lord Bishop, he came to the same conclusion as his friends. But he went even further. He said that there was no necessary connection *at all* between the tactile world — the world of touch — and the world of sight; and that any connection between the two could be established only by living, only by experience, only by learning the connection.

Which, indeed, is really what Rice said to Molly three hundred years later. That most of us are born with all five senses; and, with all the information they give us, we build up a sight world from the day we are born — a world of objects and ideas and meanings. We aren't given that world, he said. We make it ourselves — through our experience, by our memory, by making categories, by interconnections. Now Molly had only ten months of sight and what she had seen in that time was probably forgotten. So, if her sight were restored, everything would have to be learned anew: she would have to *learn* to see. She would have to build up a whole repertory of visual engrams and then, then she would have to establish connections between these new imprints and the tactile engrams she already possessed. Put it another way: she would have to create a whole new world of her own.

How in God's name did I get into all that? The goats! Engrams! Three o'clock every bloody morning! I'll tell you something: three-and-a-half years on that damned island and I lost four stone weight. And not an ounce of cheese — ever!

Not that it mattered, I suppose. I didn't go to Inis Beag to make my fortune. God knows why I went. God knows why I've spent my life at dozens of mad schemes. Crazy . . . Billy Hughes — Billy's an old pal of mine — Billy says I'm haunted for God's sake, always looking for . . . whatever . . .

Anyhow — anyhow. To go back for a second to our friend who knew what a cube was by touching it but couldn't identify it by sight alone. Rice talked a lot to Molly about all that stuff. He said neurologists had a word for people in that condition — seeing but not knowing, not recognizing, what it is they see. A word first used in this context by Freud, apparently. He said that people in that condition are called agnostic. Yes. Agnostic. Strange; because I always thought that word had to do with believing or not believing.

MOLLY I didn't like Mr Rice when I first met him. But I got to like him. I suppose because I trusted him. Frank never warmed to him. He was put off by his manner and the way he spoke. But I thought that for all his assurance there was something . . . unassured about him.

He was said to have been one of the most brilliant ophthalmologists ever in the country. Worked in the top eye hospitals all over the world — America, Japan, Germany. Married a Swiss girl. They had two daughters. Then she left him — according to the gossip; went off with a colleague of his from New York. The daughters lived with her parents in Geneva. For years after that there are gaps in his story. Nobody seems to know what became of him. They say that he had a breakdown; that he worked as a labourer in Bolivia; that he ran a pub in Glasgow. Anyhow he turned up here in Ballybeg and got a job in the hospital and took a rented bungalow at the outskirts of the town. He looked after himself in a sort of way. Walked a bit. Did a lot of fly-fishing during the season — Frank said he was beautiful to watch. People thought him a bit prickly, a bit uppity, but that was probably because he didn't mix much. I'm sure a brilliant man like that never thought he'd end up in a Regional Hospital in the north-west of Donegal. When I wondered what he looked like I imagined a face with an expression of some bewilderment.

Maybe I liked him because of all the doctors who examined me over the years he was the only one who never quizzed me about what it felt like to be blind — I suppose because he knew everything about it. The others kept asking me what the idea of colour meant to me, or the idea of space, or the notion of distance. You live in a world of touch, a tactile world, they'd say. You depend almost entirely on tactile perceptions, on knowing things by feeling their shape. Tell us: how do you think your world compares with the world the rest of us know, the world you would share with us if you had visual perception as well?

He never asked me questions like that. He did ask me once did the idea, the possibility, of seeing excite me or frighten me. It certainly excited Frank, I said. But why should it be frightening? A stupid question, I know, he said. Very stupid.

Why indeed should it be frightening? And how could I answer all those other questions? I knew only my own world. I didn't think of it as a deprived world. Disadvantaged in some ways; of course it was. But at that stage I never thought of it as deprived. And Mr Rice knew that.

And how could I have told those other doctors how much pleasure my world offered me? From my work, from the radio, from walking, from music, from cycling. But especially from swimming. Oh I can't tell you the joy I got from swimming. I used to think — and I know this sounds silly — but I really did believe I got more pleasure, more delight, from swimming than sighted people can ever get. Just offering yourself to the experience — every pore open and eager for that world of pure sensation, of sensation alone —

sensation that could not have been enhanced by sight — experience that existed only by touch and feel; and moving swiftly and rhythmically through that enfolding world; and the sense of such assurance, such liberation, such concordance with it . . . Oh I can't tell you the joy swimming gave me. I used to think that the other people in the pool with me, the sighted people, that in some way their pleasure was actually diminished because they could see, because seeing in some way qualified the sensation; and that if they only knew how full, how total my pleasure was, I used to tell myself that they must, they really must envy me.

Silly I suppose. Of course it was. I tried to explain how I felt to Mr Rice.

'I know what you mean,' he said.

And I think he did know.

Yes, maybe he was a bit pompous. And he could be sarcastic at times. And Frank said he didn't look at all bewildered; ever. But although I never saw my father's face I imagine it never revealed any bewilderment either.

MR RICE   In the present state of medicine nothing can be done for people who are born blind, the clinically blind. Their retinas are totally insensitive to light and so are nonfunctional. There are no recorded cases of recovery from clinical blindness.

Molly Sweeney wasn't born blind. She was functionally blind and lived in a blind world for forty years. But she wasn't clinically blind: her retinas weren't totally insensitive to light. For God's sake, how often did the husband, Mr Autodidact, tell me that she was aware of the shadow of his hand in front of her face?

So in theory, perhaps — purely theoretically — her case wasn't exactly hopeless. But I did make a point of giving her and her husband the only statistic available to us; and a dispiriting statistic it is. The number of cases known to us — of people who became blind shortly after birth and had their sight restored many years later — the number of cases over the past ten centuries is not more than twenty. Twenty people in a thousand years.

I know she believed me. I wasn't at all sure Frank Constantine did.

Anyhow, as a result of that first cursory examination in my home I decided to bring her into the clinic for tests.

FRANK Well of course the moment Rice said in that uppity voice of his, 'In theory — in theory — in theory — perhaps in theory — perhaps — perhaps' — the first time Molly met him — after a few general questions, a very quick examination — ten o'clock in the morning in his house — I'll never forget it — the front room in the rented bungalow — no fire — the remains of last night's supper on a tray in the fireplace — teapot, crusts, cracked mug — well of course, goddammit, of course the head exploded! Just *ex*-ploded!

Molly was going to see! I knew it! For all his perhapses! Absolutely no doubt about it! A new world — a new life! A new life for both of us!

Miracle of Molly Sweeney. Gift of sight restored to middle-aged woman. 'I've been given a new world,' says Mrs Sweeney.

Unemployed husband cries openly.

And why not?

Oh my God . . .

Sight . . .

I saw an Austrian psychiatrist on the television one night. Brilliant man. Brilliant lecture. He said that when the mind is confronted by a situation of overwhelming intensity — a moment of terror or ecstasy or tragedy — to protect itself from overload, from overcharge, it switches off and focusses on some trivial detail associated with the experience.

And he was right. I know he was. Because that morning in that front room in the chilly bungalow — immediately after that moment of certainty, that explosion in the head — my mind went numb; fused; and all I could think of was that there was a smell of fresh whiskey off Rice's breath. And at ten o'clock in the morning that seemed the most astonishing thing in the world and I could barely stop myself from saying to Molly, 'Do you not smell the whiskey off his breath? The man's reeking of whiskey!'

Ridiculous . . .

MR RICE Tests revealed that she had thick cataracts on both eyes. But that wasn't the main problem. She also had retinitis pigmentosa; as the name suggests, a discoloration of the retina. She seemed to have no useful retinal function. It wasn't at all surprising that other doctors had been put off.

There were scars of old disease, too. But what was encouraging — to put it at its very best — was that there was no current, no active disease process. So that if I were to decide to operate and if the operation were even partially successful, her vision, however impaired, ought to be stable for the rest of her life.

So in theory perhaps . . .

FRANK On the morning of Tuesday, October 7th, he operated on the right eye to remove a cataract and implant a new lens.

I was told not to visit her until the following day because the eye would be bandaged for twenty-four hours and she had to have as much rest and quiet as possible. Naturally, of course . . .

And a wonderful thing happened that night when I was at home by myself. I got a call from London; from a friend I knew in Nigeria in the old days. Chap called Winterman, Dick Winterman. Inviting me to set up and supervise a food convoy to Ethiopia. Was I interested?

Of course I was interested. The first job I'd been offered in months. But not now. How could I go now for God's sake? Molly was on the verge of a new life. I had to be with her now. Anyhow, as I told Dick, those rambling days were over.

All the same it was nice to be remembered. And to be remembered on that night — I thought that was a good omen.

MR RICE I'm ashamed to say that within a week I crossed the frontier into the fantasy life again. The moment I decided I was going to operate on Molly I had an impulse — a dizzying, exuberant, overmastering, intoxicating instinct to phone Roger Bloomstein in New York and Hans Girder in Berlin and Hiroko Matoba in Kyoto — even old Murnahan in Dublin — and tell them what I was about to do. Yes, yes, especially old Murnahan in Dublin; and say to him, 'Paddy Rice here, Professor. Of course you remember him! You called him a rogue star once — oh, yes, that caused a titter. Well, he works in a rundown hospital in Donegal now. And I suspect, I think, I believe for no good reason at all that Paddy Rice is on the trembling verge, Professor. He has a patient who has been blind for forty years. And do you know what? He is going to give her vision — the twenty-first recorded case in over a thousand years! And for the first time in her life — how does Saint Mark put it in the gospel? — for the first time in her life she will 'see men walking as if like trees'.

Delirium . . . hubris . . . the rogue star's token insurrection . . . a final, ridiculous flourish. For God's sake, a routine cataract operation?

Of course I made no calls. Instead I wrote to my daughters, Aisling and Helga, in Geneva, and enclosed what money I could afford. Then to Maria, my ex-wife, in New York; yet another open-heart letter, full of candour and dreary honesty. I told her I was busy and in good spirits and involved in a new case that was unusual in some respects.

Then I made supper; had a few drinks; fell asleep in the armchair. I woke again at 4.00 a.m., my usual hour, and sat there waiting for a new day, and said to myself over and over again: why the agitation over this case? You remove cataracts every day of the week, don't you? And isn't the self-taught husband right? (*Angrily*) What has she to lose for Christ's sake? Nothing! Nothing at all!

MOLLY What a party we had the night before the operation! Three o'clock in the morning before we got the house cleared. Oh, God! And I had to be in the hospital for ten — fasting. Frank wanted to get a taxi but I said we should walk to get all that alcohol out of the system.

And it wasn't that we had organized anything that night. A few neighbours just dropped in to wish me luck; and then a few more; and then Frank said, 'Come on! This is beginning to feel like a wake!' and away he went to the off-licence and came back with a load of stuff.

Who was there? Tony and Betty from this side; with Molly, their baby; they called her after me; she was just a toddler then. And the Quinns from that side; Jack and Mary. Jack wasn't drinking for some reason and Mary certainly was; so that was a delicate situation. And old Mr O'Neill from across the street; first time outside his house since his wife, Louise, died three months before; and Frank just took him by the arm and said he would fall into a decline if he didn't pull himself together. Anyhow, after two or three beers, what does Mr O'Neill do? Up on top of the table and begins reciting 'A bunch of the boys were whooping it up in the Malamute saloon' — or whatever the right name is! Yes! Little timid Mr O'Neill, the mourning widower! And he acted it out so seriously. And of course we all began to snigger. And the more we sniggered the more melo-dramatic he became. So that by the time he got to 'The woman that kissed him and pinched his poke was the lady that's known as Lou' — he always called Louise, his dead wife, Lou —well of course by that time we were falling about. Oh, he was furious. Sulked in the comer for ages. God!

Who else? Billy Hughes was there; an old bachelor friend of Frank. Years ago Frank and he borrowed money from the bank and bought forty beehives; but I gather that didn't work out. And Dorothy and Joyce; they're physiotherapists in the hospital. And Tom McLaughlin, another of Frank's bachelor friends. He's a great fiddler, Tom. And that was it. And of course Rita, Rita Cairns, my oldest, my closest friend. She managed the health club I was working in. Rita probably knows me better than anybody.

There was a lot of joking that there were thirteen of us if you counted the baby. And Billy Hughes, who was already well tanked by the time he arrived, he suggested that maybe Jack — from that side — maybe Jack would do the decent and volunteer to leave since he was in a bad mood and wasn't drinking anyway. And Mary, Jack's wife, she said that was the brightest idea all evening. So that was an even trickier situation.

And at some point in the night — it must have been about two — I'm afraid I had a brainwave. Here we are, all friends together, having a great time; so shouldn't I phone Mr Rice and ask him to join us? Wasn't he a friend, too? And I made for the phone and dialled the number. But Frank, thank God, Frank pulled the phone out of my hand before he answered. Imagine the embarrassment that would have been!

Anyway, we chatted and we played tapes and we sang and we drank. And Tony and Betty from this side, Molly's parents, they sang 'Anything You Can Do I Can Do Better' and there was so much tension between them you knew they weren't performing at all. And Dorothy and Joyce did their usual Laurel and Hardy imitation. And Billy Hughes, the bee-man, told some of his jokes that only Frank and he find funny. And as usual Rita, Rita Cairns, sang 'Oft in the Stilly Night', her party piece. That was my father's song, too. She has a sweet voice, really a child's voice, and she sings it beautifully. And as usual, when she had finished, so she tells me, she nodded her head and smiled and cried all at the same time. That's what she — 'The Shooting of Dan McGrew'! That's the title of Mr O'Neill's poem! Poor old Mr O'Neill. Somebody told me recently that he's in a hospice now.

And shortly after midnight — long before I had the brainwave to phone Mr Rice — Tom McLaughlin, Tom the fiddler, played 'The Lament for Limerick'! He played it softly, delicately. And suddenly, suddenly I felt utterly desolate. Maybe it was Rita singing 'Oft in the Stilly Night' earlier. Or maybe it was because all that night nobody once mentioned the next day or how they thought the operation might go; and because nothing was said, maybe that made the occasion a bit unreal, a bit frantic. Or maybe it was because I was afraid that if things turned out as Frank and Mr Rice hoped, I was afraid that I would never again know these people as I knew them now, with my own special knowledge of each of them, the distinctive sense each of them exuded for me; and knowing them differently, experiencing them differently, I wondered — I wondered would I ever be as close to them as I was now.

And then with sudden anger I thought: why am I going for this operation? None of this is my choosing. Then why is this happening to me? I am being used. Of course I trust Frank. Of course I trust Mr Rice. But how can they know what they are taking away from me? How do they know what they are offering me? They don't. They can't. And have I anything to gain? Anything? Anything?

And then I knew, suddenly I knew why I was so desolate. It was the dread of exile, of being sent away. It was the desolation of homesickness.

And then a strange thing happened. As soon as Tom played the last note of 'The Lament for Limerick' I found myself on my feet in the middle of the sitting room and calling, 'A hornpipe, Tom! A mad, fast hornpipe!' And the moment he began to play I shouted — screamed, 'Now watch me! Just you watch me!' And in a rage of anger and defiance I danced a wild and furious dance round and round that room; then out to the hall; then round the kitchen; then back to the room again and round it a third time. Mad and wild and frenzied. But so adroit, so efficient. No timidity, no hesitations, no falterings. Not a glass overturned, not a shoulder brushed. Weaving between all those people, darting between chairs and stools and cushions and bottles and glasses with complete assurance, with absolute confidence. Until Frank said something to Tom and stopped him playing.

God knows how I didn't kill myself or injure somebody. Or indeed how long it lasted. But it must have been terrifying to watch because, when I stopped, the room was hushed.

Frank whispered something to me. I don't know what he said — I was suddenly lost and anxious and frightened. I remember calling, 'Rita? Where are you, Rita?'

'Here at the window,' she said. And I stumbled, groped my way to her and sat beside her. 'Come on, sweetie,' she said. 'We'll have none of that. You're not allowed to cry. I'm the only one that's allowed to give a performance and then cry.'

MR RICE   The night before I operated on Molly Sweeney I thought about that high summer in my thirty-second year. Cairo. Another lecture; another conference; another posh hotel. As usual we all met up: Roger Bloomstein from New York, Hans Girder from Berlin, Hiroko Matoba from Kyoto, myself. The meteors. The young turks. The four horsemen. Oslo last month. Helsinki next week. Paris the week after. That luminous, resplendent life. Those glowing, soaring careers.

Maria left the children with her parents in Geneva and flew down to join us. Still wan and translucent after the birth of Helga. And so beautiful; my God, so beautiful. We had a dinner party for her the night she arrived. Roger was master-of-ceremonies. Toasted her with his usual elegance. Said she was our Venus — no, our Galatea. She smiled her secret smile and said each

273

of us was her Icarus.

Insatiable years. Work. Airports. Dinners. Laughter. Operating theatres. Conferences. Gossip. Publications. The professional jealousies and the necessary vigilance. The relentless, devouring excitement. But above all, above all the hunger to accomplish, the greed for achievement.

Shards of those memories came back to me on the night before I operated on Molly Sweeney on Tuesday, October 7th. I had had a few drinks. I had had a lot of drinks. The fire was dead. I was drifting in and out of sleep.

Then the phone rang; an anxious sound at two in the morning. By the time I had pulled myself together and got to it, it had stopped. Wrong number probably.

I had another drink and sat beside the dead fire and relived for the hundredth time that other phone call. The small hours of the morning, too. In Cairo. That high summer of my thirty-second year.

It was Roger Bloomstein. Brilliant Roger. Treacherous Icarus. To tell me that Maria and he were at the airport and about to step on a plane for New York. They were deeply in love. They would be in touch in a few days. He was very sorry to have to tell me this. He hoped that in time I would see the situation from their point of view and come to understand it. And he hung up.

The mind was instantly paralyzed. All I could think was: he's confusing seeing with understanding. Come on, Bloomstein. What's the matter with you? Seeing isn't understanding.

You know that! Don't talk rubbish, man!

And then . . . and then . . . oh, Jesus, Maria . . .

FRANK Just as I was about to step into bed that night — that same Tuesday night that Dick Winterman phoned — the night of the operation — I was on the point of stepping into bed when suddenly, suddenly I remembered: Ethiopia is Abyssinia! Abyssinia is Ethiopia! They're the same place! Ethiopia is the new name for the old

Abyssinia! For God's sake, only last year the *National Geographic* magazine had a brilliant article on it with all these stunning photographs. For God's sake, I could write a book about Ethiopia! Absolutely the most interesting country in the world! Let me give you one fascinating fact about the name, the name Abyssinia. The name Abyssinia is derived from the word 'habesh'; and the word 'habesh' means mixed — on account of the varied nature of its peoples. But interestingly, interestingly the people themselves always called themselves Ethiopians, never Abyssinians, because they considered the word Abyssinia and Abyssinians as derogatory — they didn't want to be thought of as mixed! So now the place is officially what the people themselves always called it — Ethiopia. Fascinating!

But of course I had to say no to Dick. As I said. Those rambling days were over. Molly was about to inherit a new world; and I had a sense — stupid, I know — I had a sense that maybe I was, too.

Pity to miss Abyssinia all the same — the one place in the whole world I've always dreamed of visiting; a phantom desire, a fantasy in the head. Pity to miss that.

You shouldn't have dangled it in front of me, Dick Winterman. Bloody, bloody heartbreaking.

MOLLY I remember so well the first day Frank came to the health club. That was the first time I'd met him. I was on a coffee break. A Friday afternoon.

I had known of him for years of course. Rita Cairns and his friend Billy Hughes used to go out occasionally and I'd hear his name mentioned. She never said anything bad about him; but when his name came up you got the feeling he was a bit . . . different.

Anyhow that Friday he came into the club and Rita introduced us and we chatted. And for the whole ten minutes of my coffee break he gave me a talk about a feasibility study he was doing on the blueback salmon, known in Oregon as sockeye and in Alaska as redfish, and of his plan to introduce it to Irish salmon farmers because it has the lowest wastage rate in all canning factories where it is used.

When he left I said to Rita that I'd never met a more enthusiastic man in my life. And Rita said in her laconic way, 'Sweetie, who wants their enthusiasm focussed on bluebacks, for God's sake?'

Anyhow, ten minutes after he left, the phone rang. Could we meet that evening? Saturday? Sunday? What about a walk, a meal, a concert? Just a chat?

I asked him to call me the following Friday.

I thought a lot about him that week. I suppose he was the first man I really knew — apart from my father. And I liked his energy. I liked his enthusiasm. I liked his passion. Maybe what I really liked about him was that he was everything my father wasn't.

FRANK I spent a week in the library — the week after I first met her — one full week immersing myself in books and encyclopedias and magazines and articles — anything, everything I could find about eyes and vision and eye diseases and blindness.

Fascinating. I can't tell you — fascinating. I look out of my bedroom window and at a single glance I see the front garden and the road beyond and cars and buses and the tennis courts on the far side and people playing on them and the hills beyond that.

Everything — all those details and dozens more — all seen in one immediate, comprehensive perception. But Molly's world isn't perceived instantly, comprehensively. She composes a world from a sequence of impressions; one after the other, in time. For example, she knows that this is a carving knife because first she can feel the handle; then she can feel this long blade; then this sharp edge. In sequence. In time. What is this object? These are ears. This is a furry body. Those are paws. That is a long tail. Ah, a cat! In sequence. Sequentially.

Right? Right. Now a personal question. You are going

to ask this blind lady out for an evening. What would be the ideal entertainment for somebody like her? A meal? A concert? A walk? Maybe a swim? Billy Hughes says she's a wonderful swimmer. (*He shakes his head slowly*)

The week in the library pays off. Know the answer instantly. Dancing. Take her dancing. With her disability the perfect, the absolutely perfect relaxation. Forget about space, distance, who's close, who's far, who's approaching. Forget about time. This is not a sequence of events. This is one continuous, delightful event. Nothing leads to nothing else. There is only now. There is nothing subsequent. I am your eyes, your ears, your location, your sense of space. Trust me.

Dancing. Obvious.

Straight into a phone box and asked her would she come with me to the Hikers Club dance the following Saturday. It'll be small, I said; more like a party. What do you say?

Silence.

We'll ask Billy and Rita and we'll make it a foursome and we'll have our own table and our own fun.

Not a word. Please, Molly.

In my heart of hearts I really didn't think she'd say yes. For God's sake, why should she? Middle-aged. No skill. No job. No prospect of a job. Two rooms above Kelly's cake shop. And not exactly Rudolf Valentino. And when she did speak, when she said very politely, 'Thank you, Frank. I'd love to go,' do you know what I said? 'All right then.' Bloody brilliant!

But I vowed to myself in that phone box, I made a vow there and then that at the dance on Saturday night I wouldn't open the big mouth — big? — enormous, for Christ's sake! — I wouldn't open it once all night, all week.

Talking of Valentino, in point of fact Valentino was no Adonis himself. Average height; average looks; mediocre talent. And if he hadn't died so young — in 1926 — he was only 31 — and in those mysterious circumstances that were never fully explained — he would never have become the cult figure the studios worked so hard to . . .

Anyhow . . .

MOLLY As usual Rita was wonderful. She washed my hair, my bloody useless hair — I can do nothing with it — she washed it in this special shampoo she concocted herself. Then she pulled it all away back from my face and piled it up, just here, and held it in place with her mother's silver ornamental comb. And she gave me her black shoes and her new woollen dress she'd just bought for her brother's wedding.

'There's still something not right,' she said. 'You still remind me of my Aunt Madge. Here — try these.' And she whipped off her earrings and put them on me. 'Now we have it,' she said. 'Bloody lethal. Francis Constantine, you're a dead duck!'

FRANK She had the time of her life. Knew she would. We danced every dance. Sang every song at the top of our voices. Ate an enormous supper. Even won a spot prize: a tin of shortbread and a bottle of Albanian wine. The samba, actually. I wasn't bad at the samba once.

Dancing. I knew. I explained the whole thing to her. She had to agree. For God's sake, she didn't have to say a word — she just glowed.

MOLLY It was almost at the end of the night — we were doing an old-time waltz — and suddenly he said to me, 'You are such a beautiful woman, Molly.'

Nobody had ever said anything like that to me before. I was afraid I might cry. And before I could say a word he plunged on: 'Of course I know that the very idea of appearance, of how things look, can't have much meaning for you. I do understand that. And maybe at heart you're a real philosophical sceptic because you question not only the idea of appearance but probably the existence of external reality itself. Do you, Molly?'

Honest to God . . . the second last dance at the Hikers Club . . . a leisurely, old-time waltz . . .

And I knew that night that he would ask me to marry him. Because he liked me — I knew he did. And because of my blindness — oh, yes, that fascinated him. He couldn't resist the different, the strange. I think he believed that some elusive off-beat truth resided in the quirky, the off-beat. I suppose that's what made him such a restless man. Rita of course said it was inevitable he would propose to me. 'All part of the same pattern, sweetie: bees — whales — Iranian goats — Molly Sweeney.'

Maybe she was right.

And I knew, too, after that night in the Hikers Club, that if he did ask me to marry him, for no very good reason at all I would probably say yes.

MR RICE The morning of the operation I stood at the window of my office and watched them walk up the hospital drive. It was a blustery morning, threatening rain.

She didn't have her cane and she didn't hold his arm. But she moved briskly with her usual confidence; her head high; her face alert and eager. In her right hand she carried a grey, overnight bag.

He was on her left. Now in the open air a smaller presence in a shabby raincoat and cap; his hands clasped behind his back; his eyes on the ground; his head bowed slightly against the wind so that he looked . . . passive. Not a trace of the assurance, the ebullience, that relentless energy.

And I thought: are they really such an unlikely couple? And I wondered what hopes moved in them as they came towards me. Were they modest? Reasonable? Outrageous? Of course, of course they were outrageous.

And suddenly and passionately and with utter selflessness I wanted nothing more in the world than that their inordinate hopes would be fulfilled, that I could give them their miracle. And I whispered to Hans Girder

and to Matoba and to Murnahan and to Bloomstein —
yes, to Bloomstein, too! — to gather round me this
morning and steady my unsteady hand and endow
me with all their exquisite skills.

Because as I watched them approach the hospital
that blustery morning, one head alert, one head bowed,
I was suddenly full of anxiety for both of them.
Because I was afraid — even though she was in the
hands of the best team in the whole world to deliver
her miracle, because she was in the hands of the best
team in the whole world — I was fearful, I suddenly
knew that that courageous woman had everything,
everything to lose.

Interval.

ACT TWO

MOLLY The morning the bandages were to be removed a staff nurse spent half-an-hour preparing me for Mr Rice. It wasn't really her job, she told me; but this was my big day and I had to look my best and she was happy to do it.

So she sponged my face and hands. She made me clean my teeth again. She wondered did I use lipstick — maybe just for today? She did the best she could with my hair, God help her. She looked at my finger-nails and suggested that a touch of clear varnish would be nice. She straightened the bow at the front of my nightdress and adjusted the collar of my dressing gown. She put a dab of her own very special perfume on each of my wrists — she got it from a cousin in Paris. Then she stood back and surveyed me and said, 'Now. That's better. You'll find that from now on — if everything goes well of course — you'll find that you'll become very aware of your appearance. They all do for some reason. Don't be nervous. You look just lovely. He'll be here any minute now.'

I asked her where the bathroom was.

'At the end of the corridor. Last door on the right. I'll bring you.'

'No,' I said. 'I'll find it.'

I didn't need to go to the bathroom. I just wanted to take perhaps a last walk; in my own world; by myself.

I don't know what I expected when the bandages would be removed. I think maybe I didn't allow myself any expectations. I knew that in his heart Frank believed that somehow, miraculously, I would be given the perfect vision that sighted people have, even though Mr Rice had told us again and again that my eyes weren't capable of that vision. And I knew what Mr Rice hoped for: that I would have partial sight. 'That would be a total success for me' is what he said. But I'm sure he meant it would be great for all of us.

As for myself, if I had any hope I suppose it was that neither Frank nor Mr Rice would be too disappointed because it had all become so important for them.

No, that's not accurate either. Yes, I did want to see. For God's sake, of course I wanted to see. But that wasn't an expectation, not even a mad hope. If there was a phantom desire, a fantasy in my head, it was this. That perhaps by some means I might be afforded a brief excursion to this land of vision; not to live there — just to visit. And during my stay to devour it again and again and again with greedy, ravenous eyes. To gorge on all those luminous sights and wonderful spectacles until I knew every detail intimately and utterly — every ocean, every leaf, every field, every star, every tiny flower. And then, oh yes, then to return home to my own world with all that rare understanding within me forever. No, that wasn't even a phantom desire. Just a stupid fantasy. And it came into my head again when that poor nurse was trying to prettify me for Mr Rice. And I thought to myself: it's like being back at school — I'm getting dressed up for the annual excursion.

When Mr Rice did arrive, even before he touched me, I knew by his quick, shallow breathing that he was far more nervous than I was. And then as he took off the bandages his hands trembled and fumbled.

'There we are,' he said. 'All off. How does that feel?'

'Fine,' I said. Even though I felt nothing. Were all the bandages off?

'Now, Molly. In your own time. Tell me what you see.'

Nothing. Nothing at all. Then out of the void a blur; a haze; a body of mist; a confusion of light, colour, movement. It had no meaning.

'Well?' he said. 'Anything? Anything at all?'

I thought: don't panic; a voice comes from a face; that blur is his face; look at him.

'Well? Anything?'

Something moving; large; white; the nurse? And lines, black lines, vertical lines. The bed? The door?

'Anything, Molly?' A bright light that hurt. The window maybe?

'I'm holding my hand before your eyes, Molly. Can you see it?'

A reddish blob in front of my face; rotating; liquefying; pulsating. Keep calm. Concentrate.

'Can you see my hand, Molly?'

'I think so . . . I'm not sure . . . '

'Now I'm moving my hand slowly.'

'Yes . . . yes . . . '

'Do you see my hand moving?'

'Yes . . . '

'What way is it moving?'

'Yes . . . I do see it . . . up and down . . . up and down . . . Yes! I see it! I do! Yes! Moving up and down! Yes-yes-yes!'

'Splendid!' he said. 'Absolutely splendid! You are a clever lady!'

And there was such delight in his voice. And my head was suddenly giddy. And I thought for a moment — for a moment I thought I was going to faint.

FRANK There was some mix-up about what time the bandages were to be removed. At least *I* was confused. For some reason I got it into my head that they were to be taken off at eight in the morning, October 8th, the day after the operation. A Wednesday, I remember, because I was doing a crash course in speed reading and I had to switch from the morning to the afternoon class for that day.

So; eight o'clock sharp; there I was sitting in the hospital, all dickied up — the good suit, the shoes polished, the clean shirt, the new tie, and with my bunch of flowers, waiting to be summoned to Molly's ward.

The call finally did come — at a quarter to twelve. Ward 10. Room 17. And of course by then I knew the operation was a disaster.

Knocked. Went in. Rice was there. And a staff nurse, a tiny little woman. And an Indian man — the anaesthetist, I think. The moment I entered he rushed out without saying a word.

And Molly. Sitting very straight in a white chair beside her bed. Her hair pulled away back from her face and piled up just here. Wearing a lime-green dressing gown that Rita Cairns had lent her and the blue slippers I got her for her last birthday.

There was a small bruise mark below her right eye. I thought: how young she looks, and so beautiful, so very beautiful.

'There she is,' said Rice. 'How does she look?'

'She looks well.'

'Well? She looks wonderful! And why not? Everything went brilliantly! A complete success! A dream!'

He was so excited, there was no trace of the posh accent. And he bounced up and down on the balls of his feet. And he took my hand and shook it as if he were congratulating me. And the tiny staff nurse laughed and said 'Brilliant! Brilliant!' and in her excitement knocked the chart off the end of the bed and then laughed even more.

'Speak to her!' said Rice. 'Say something!'

'How are you?' I said to Molly.

'How do I look?'

'You look great.'

'Do you like my black eye?'

'I didn't notice it,' I said.

'I'm feeling great,' she said. 'Really. But what about you?'

'What do you mean?'

'Did you manage all right on your own last night?'

I suppose at that moment and in those circumstances

it did sound a bit funny.

Anyhow, Rice laughed out loud and of course the staff nurse; and then Molly and I had to laugh, too. In relief, I suppose, really . . .

Then Rice said to me,

'Aren't you going to give the lady her flowers?'

'Sorry,' I said. 'I got Rita to choose them. She said they're your favourite.'

Could she see them? I didn't know what to do. Should I take her hand and put the flowers into it?

I held them in front of her. She reached out confidently and took them from me.

'They're lovely,' she said. 'Thank you. Lovely.'

And she held them at arm's length, directly in front of her face, and turned them round. Suddenly Rice said,

'What colour are they, Molly?'

She didn't hesitate at all.

'They're blue,' she said. 'Aren't they blue?'

'They certainly are! And the paper?' Rice asked. 'What colour is the wrapping paper?'

'Is it . . . yellow?'

'Yes! So you know some colours! Excellent! Really excellent!'

And the staff nurse clapped with delight.

'Now — a really hard question, and I'm not sure I know the answer to it myself. What sort of flowers are they?'

She brought them right up to her face. She turned them upside down. She held them at arm's length again. She stared at them — peered at them really — for what seemed an age. I knew how anxious she was by the way her mouth was working.

'Well, Molly? Do you know what they are?'

We waited. Another long silence. Then suddenly she closed her eyes shut tight. She brought the flowers right up against her face and inhaled in quick gulps and at the same time, with her free hand, swiftly, deftly felt the stems and the leaves and the blossoms. Then with her eyes still shut tight she called out desperately, defiantly,

'They're cornflowers! That's what they are! Cornflowers! Blue cornflowers! Centaurea!'

Then for maybe half-a-minute she cried. Sobbed really.

The staff nurse looked uneasily at Rice. He held up his hand.

'Cornflowers, indeed. Splendid,' he said very softly. 'Excellent. It has been a heady day. But we're really on our way now, aren't we?'

I went back to the hospital again that night after my class. She was in buoyant form. I never saw her so animated.

'I can see, Frank!' she kept saying. 'Do you hear me? — I can see!' Mr Rice was a genius! Wasn't it all wonderful? The nurses were angels! Wasn't I thrilled? She loved my red tie — it was red, wasn't it? And everybody was so kind. Dorothy and Joyce brought those chocolates during their lunch break. And old Mr O'Neill sent that 'Get Well' card — there — look — on the window-sill. And didn't the flowers look beautiful in that pink vase? She would have the operation on the left eye just as soon as Mr Rice would agree. And then, Frank, and then and then and then and then — oh, God, what then!

I was so happy, so happy for her. Couldn't have been happier for God's sake.

But just as on that first morning in Rice's bungalow when the only thing my mind could focus on was the smell of fresh whiskey off his breath, now all I could think of was some — some — some absurd scrap of information a Norwegian fisherman told me about the eyes of whales.

Whales, for God's sake!

Stupid information. Useless, off-beat information. Stupid, useless, quirky mind . . .

Molly was still in full flight when a nurse came in and said that visiting time was long over and that Mrs

Sweeney needed all her strength to face tomorrow.

'How do I look?'

'Great,' I said.

'Really, Frank?'

'Honestly. Wonderful.'

'Black eye and all?'

'You wouldn't notice it,' I said.

She caught my hand.

'Do you think . . . ?'

'Do I think what?'

'Do you think I look pretty, Frank?'

'You look beautiful,' I said. 'Just beautiful.'

'Thank you.'

I kissed her on the forehead and, as I said goodnight to her, she gazed intently at my face as if she were trying to read it. Her eyes were bright; unnaturally bright; burnished. And her expression was open and joyous. But as I said goodnight I had a feeling she wasn't as joyous as she looked.

MR RICE When I look back over my working life I suppose I must have done thousands of operations. Sorry — performed. Bloomstein always corrected me on that: 'Come on, you bloody bogman! We're not mechanics. We're artists. We perform.' (*He shrugs his shoulders in dismissal*)

And of those thousands I wonder how many I'll remember.

I'll remember Dubai. An Arab gentleman whose left eye had been almost pecked out by one of his peregrines and who sent his private jet to New York for Hans Girder and myself. The eye was saved, really because Girder was a magician. And we spent a week in a palace of marble and gold and played poker with the crew of the jet and lost every penny of the ransom we had just earned.

And I'll remember a city called Frankfort in Kentucky; and an elderly lady called Busty Butterfly who had been blinded in a gas explosion. Hiroko Matoba and I 'performed' that operation. A tricky one, but he and I always worked well together. And Busty Butterfly was so grateful that she wanted me to have her best racehorse and little Hiroko to marry her.

And I'll remember Ballybeg. Of course I'll remember Ballybeg. And the courageous Molly Sweeney. And I'll remember it not because of the operation — the operation wasn't all that complex; nor because the circumstances were special; nor indeed because a woman who had been blind for over forty years got her sight back. Yes, yes, yes, I'll remember it for all those reasons. Of course I will. But the core, the very heart, of the memory will be something different, something altogether different. Perhaps I should explain that after that high summer of my thirty-second year — that episode in Cairo — the dinner party for Maria — Bloomstein's phone call — all that tawdry drama — my life no longer . . . cohered. I withdrew from medicine, from friendships, from all the consolations of work and the familiar; and for seven years and seven months — sounds like a fairy tale I used to read to Aisling — I subsided into a terrible darkness . . .

But I was talking of Molly's operation and my memory of that. And the core of that memory is this. That for seventy-five minutes in the theatre on that blustery October morning the darkness miraculously lifted, and I performed — I watched myself do it — I performed so assuredly and with such skill, so elegantly, so efficiently, so economically — yes, yes, yes, of course it sounds vain — vanity has nothing to do with it — but suddenly, miraculously all the gifts, all the gifts were mine again, abundantly mine, joyously mine; and on that blustery October morning I had such a feeling of mastery and — how can I put it? — such a sense of playfulness, for God's sake, that I knew I was restored. No, no, no, not fully restored. Never fully restored. But a sense that a practical restoration, perhaps a restoration to something truer — that was possible. Yes, maybe that was possible . . .

Yes, I'll remember Ballybeg. And when I left that dreary little place, that's the memory I took away with me. The place where I restored her sight to Molly Sweeney. Where the terrible darkness lifted. Where the shaft of light glanced off me again.

MOLLY Mr Rice said he couldn't have been more pleased with my progress. He called me his Miracle Molly. I liked him a lot more as the weeks passed.

And as usual Rita was wonderful. She let me off work early every Monday, Wednesday and Friday. And I'd dress up in this new coat I'd bought — a mad splurge to keep the spirits up — brilliant scarlet with a matching beret — Rita said I could be seen from miles away, like a distress signal — anyhow, in all my new style I'd walk to the hospital on those three afternoons — without my cane! — and sometimes that was scary. I can tell you. And Mr Rice would examine me and say, 'Splendid, Molly! Splendid!' And then he'd pass me on to a psychotherapist, Mrs Wallace, a beautiful looking young woman according to Frank, and I'd do all sorts of tests with her. And then she'd pass me on to George, her husband, for more tests — he was a behavioural psychologist, if you don't mind, a real genius apparently — the pair of them were writing a book on me. And then I'd go back to Mr Rice again and he'd say 'Splendid!' again. And then I'd walk home — still no cane! — and have Frank's tea waiting for him when he'd get back from the library.

I can't tell you how kind Frank was to me, how patient he was. As soon as tea was over he'd sit at the top of the table and he'd put me at the bottom and he'd begin my lesson.

He'd put something in front of me — maybe a bowl of fruit — and he'd say,

'What have I got in my hand?'

'A piece of fruit.'

'What sort of fruit?'

'An orange, Frank. I know the colour, don't I?'

'Very clever. Now, what's this?'

'It's a pear.'

'You're guessing.'

'Let me touch it.'

'Not allowed. You already have your tactical engrams. We've got to build up a repertory of visual engrams to connect with them.'

And I'd say, 'For God's sake, stop showing off your posh new words, Frank. It's a banana.'

'Sorry. Try again.'

'It's a peach. Right?'

'Splendid!' he'd say in Mr Rice's accent. 'It certainly is a peach. Now, what's this?'

And he'd move on to knives and forks, or shoes and slippers, or all the bits and pieces on the mantelpiece for maybe another hour or more. Every night. Seven nights a week.

Oh, yes, Frank couldn't have been kinder to me. Rita, too. Even kinder. Even more patient.

And all my customers at the health club, the ones who had massages regularly, they sent me a huge bouquet of pink-and-white tulips. And the club I used to swim with, they sent me a beautiful gardening book. God knows what they thought — that I'd now be able to pick it up and read it? But everyone was great, just great.

Oh, yes, I lived in a very exciting world for those first weeks after the operation. Not at all like that silly world I wanted to visit and devour — none of that nonsense.

No, the world that I now saw — half-saw, peered at really — it was a world of wonder and surprise and delight. Oh, yes; wonderful, surprising, delightful. And joy — such joy, small unexpected joys that came in such profusion and passed so quickly that there was never enough time to savour them.

But it was a very foreign world, too. And disquieting; even alarming. Every colour dazzled. Every light blazed. Every shape an apparition, a spectre that appeared suddenly from nowhere and challenged you. And all that movement — nothing ever still —everything in motion all the time; and every movement unexpected, somehow threatening. Even the sudden sparrows in the garden, they seemed aggressive, dangerous.

So that after a time the mind could absorb no more sensation. Just one more colour — light — movement — ghostly shape — and suddenly the head imploded and the hands shook and the heart melted with panic. And the only escape — the only way to live — was to sit absolutely still; and shut the eyes tight; and immerse yourself in darkness; and wait. Then when the hands were still and the heart quiet, slowly open the eyes again. And emerge. And try to find the courage to face it all once more.

I tried to explain to Frank once how — I suppose how terrifying it all was. But naturally, naturally he was far more concerned with teaching me practical things. And one day when I mentioned to Mr Rice that I didn't think I'd find things as unnerving as I did, he said in a very icy voice,

'And what sort of world did you expect, Mrs Sweeney?'

Yes, it was a strange time. An exciting time, too — oh, yes, exciting. But so strange. And during those weeks after the operation I found myself thinking more and more about my mother and father, but especially about my mother and what it must have been like for her living in that huge, echoing house.

MR RICE I operated on the second eye, the left eye, six weeks after the first operation. I had hoped it might have been a healthier eye. But when the cataract was removed we found a retina much the same as in the right: traces of pigmentosa, scarred macula, areas atrophied. However, with both eyes functioning to some degree, her visual field was larger and she fixated better. She could now see from a medical point of view. From a psychological point of view she was still blind. In other words she now had to learn to see.

FRANK As we got closer to the end of that year it was quite clear that Molly was changing — had changed. And one of the most fascinating insights into the state of her mind at that time was given to me by Jean Wallace, the psychotherapist; very interesting woman; brilliant actually; married to George, a behavioural psychologist, a second-rater if you ask me; and what a bore — what a bore! Do you know what that man did? Lectured me one day for over an hour on cheese-making if you don't mind! Anyhow — anyhow — the two of them — the Wallaces — they were doing this book on Molly; a sort of documentation of her 'case history' from early sight to lifelong blindness to sight restored to . . . whatever. And the way Jean explained Molly's condition to me was this.

All of us live on a swing, she said. And the swing normally moves smoothly and evenly across a narrow range of the usual emotions. Then we have a crisis in our life; so that instead of moving evenly from, say, feeling sort of happy to feeling sort of miserable, we now swing from elation to despair, from unimaginable delight to utter wretchedness.

The word she used was 'delivered' to show how passive we are in this terrifying game: we are delivered into one emotional state — snatched away from it — delivered into the opposite emotional state. And we can't help ourselves. We can't escape. Until eventually we can endure no more abuse — become incapable of experiencing anything, feeling anything at all.

That's how Jean Wallace explained Molly's behaviour to me. Very interesting woman. Brilliant actually. And beautiful, too. Oh, yes, all the gifts. And what she said helped me to understand Molly's extraordinary behaviour — difficult behaviour — yes, goddammit, very difficult behaviour over those weeks leading up to Christmas.

For example — for example. One day, out of the

blue, a Friday evening in December, five o'clock, I'm about to go to the Hikers Club, and she says, 'I feel like a swim, Frank. Let's go for a swim now.'

At this stage I'm beginning to recognize the symptoms: the defiant smile, the excessive enthusiasm, some reckless, dangerous proposal. 'Fine. Fine,' I say. Even though it's pitch dark and raining. So we'll go to the swimming pool? Oh, no. She wants to swim in the sea. And not only swim in the sea on a wet Friday night in December, but she wants to go out to the rocks at the far end of Tramore and she wants to climb up on top of Napoleon Rock as we call it locally — it's the highest rock there, a cliff really — and I'm to tell her if the tide is in or out and how close are the small rocks in the sea below and how deep the water is because she's going to dive — to dive, for God's sake — the eighty feet from the top of Napoleon down into the Atlantic Ocean.

'And why not, Frank? Why not, for God's sake?'

Oh, yes, an enormous change. Something extraordinary about all that.

Then there was the night I watched her through the bedroom door. She was sitting at her dressing table, in front of the mirror, trying her hair in different ways. When she would have it in a certain way she'd lean close to the mirror and peer into it and turn her head from side to side. But you knew she couldn't read her reflection, could scarcely even see it. Then she would try the hair in a different style and she'd lean into the mirror again until her face was almost touching it and again she'd turn first to one side and then the other. And you knew that all she saw was a blur.

Then after about half-a-dozen attempts she stood up and came to the door — it was then I could see she was crying — and she switched off the light. Then she went back to the dressing table and sat down again; in the dark; for maybe an hour; sat there and gazed listlessly at the black mirror.

Yes, she did dive into the Atlantic from the top of Napoleon Rock; first time in her life. Difficult times.

Oh, I can't tell you. Difficult times for all of us.

MR RICE   The dangerous period for Molly came — as it does for all patients — when the first delight and excitement at having vision have died away. The old world with its routines, all the consolations of work and the familiar, is gone forever. A sighted world — a partially sighted world, for that is the best it will ever be — is available. But to compose it, to put it together, demands effort and concentration and patience that are almost super-human.

So the question she had to ask herself was: how much do I want this world? And am I prepared to make that enormous effort to get it?

FRANK   Then there was a new development — as if she hadn't enough troubles already. A frightening new develop-ment. She began getting spells of dizziness when every-thing seemed in a thick fog, all external reality became just a haze. This would hit her for no reason at all — at work, or walking home, or in the house; and it would last for an hour, maybe several hours.

Rice had no explanation for it. But you could see he was concerned.

'It's called "gnosis",' he said. 'How do you spell that?'

'G-n-o-s-i-s.'

'And what is it?'

'It's a condition of impaired vision, Mr Sweeney.' He really was a right little bastard at times.

Anyhow, I looked it up in the library, and interest-ingly, interestingly I could find no reference at all to a medical condition called 'gnosis'. But according to the dictionary the word meant a mystical knowledge, a knowledge of spiritual things! And my first thought was: Good old Molly! Molly's full of mystical know-ledge! God forgive me; I really didn't mean to be so cheap.

I meant to tell Rice about that meaning of the word

the next time I met him — just to bring him down a peg. But it slipped my mind. I suppose because the condition disappeared as suddenly as it appeared. And anyway she had so many troubles at that stage that my skirmishes with Rice didn't matter anymore.

MOLLY Tests — tests — tests — tests — tests! Between Mr Rice and Jean Wallace and George Wallace and indeed Frank himself I must have spent months and months being analyzed and answering questions and identifying drawings and making sketches. And, God, those damned tests with photographs and lights and objects — those endless tricks and illusions and distortions — the Zollner illusion, the Ames distorting room, the Staircase illusion, the Müller-Lyer illusion. And they never told you if you had passed or failed so you always assumed you failed. Such peace — such peace when they were all finished.

I stopped at the florist one evening to get something for Tony and Betty from this side — what was this side; Molly's father and mother. For their wedding anniversary. And I spotted this little pot of flowers, like large buttercups, about six inches tall, with blue petals and what seemed to me a whitish centre. I thought I recognized them but I wasn't quite sure. And I wouldn't allow myself to touch them.

'I'll take these,' I said to the man.

'Pretty, aren't they?' he said. 'Just in from Holland this morning. And do you know what? — I can't remember what they're called. Do you know?'

'They're nemophila.'

'Are they?'

'Yes,' I said. 'Feel the leaves. They should be dry and feathery.'

'You're right,' he said. 'That's what they are. They have another name, haven't they?'

'Baby Blue Eyes,' I said.

'That's it! I'd forgotten that. Getting too old for this job.'

Yes, that gave me some pleasure. One silly little victory. And when I took them home and held them up to my face and looked closely at them they weren't nearly as pretty as buttercups. Weren't pretty at all. Couldn't give that as a present next door.

FRANK It was the clever Jean Wallace who spotted the distress signals first. She said to me: 'We should be seeing a renaissance of personality at this point. Because if that doesn't take place — and it's not — then you can expect a withdrawal.'

And she was right. That's what's happened. Molly just . . . withdrew.

Then in the middle of February she lost her job in the health club. And now Rita was no longer a friend. And that was so unfair — Rita kept making allowances for her long after any other boss would have got rid of her; turning in late; leaving early; maybe not even making an appearance for two or three days. Just sitting alone in her bedroom with her eyes shut, maybe listening to the radio, maybe just sitting there in silence.

I made a last effort on the 1st of March. I took her new scarlet coat out of the wardrobe and I said, 'Come on, girl! Enough of this. We're going for a long walk on Tramore beach. Then we'll have a drink in Moriarity's. Then we'll have dinner in that new Chinese place. Right? Right!' And I left the coat at the foot of her bed.

And that's where it lay for weeks. And weeks. In fact she never wore it out again.

And at that point I had come to the end of my tether. There seemed to be nothing more I could do.

MR RICE In those last few months a new condition appeared. She began showing symptoms of a condition known as blindsight. This is a physiological condition, not psychological. On those occasions she claimed she could see nothing, absolutely nothing at all. And indeed she was telling the truth. But, even as she said this, she behaved as if she could see — reach for her purse, avoid a chair that was in her way, lift a book and hand it to you. She was indeed receiving visual signals and she was indeed responding to them. But because of a malfunction in part of the cerebral cortex none of this perception reached her consciousness. She was totally unconscious of seeing anything at all.

In other words she *had* vision — but a vision that was utterly useless to her.

Blindsight . . . curious word . . .

I remember in Cleveland once Bloomstein and Maria and I were in a restaurant and when Maria left the table Bloomstein said to me, 'Beautiful lady. You *do* know that?'

'I know,' I said.

'Do you really?'

I said of course I did.

'That's not how you behave,' he said. 'You behave like a man with blindsight.'

FRANK We were in the pub this night, Billy Hughes and myself, just sitting and chatting about — yes! I remember what we were talking about! An idea Billy had of recycling old tea leaves and turning them into a substitute for tobacco. We should have followed that up.

Anyhow — anyhow, this man comes up to me in the bar, says he's a journalist from a Dublin paper, asks would I be interested in giving him the full story about Molly.

He seemed a decent man. I talked to him for maybe an hour at most. Of course it was stupid. And I really didn't do it for the bloody money.

Jack from next door spotted the piece and brought it in. *Miracle Cure False Dawn. Molly sulks in darkness. Husband drowns sorrow in pub.*

Of course she heard about it — God knows how. And now I was as bad as all the others: I had let her down, too.

MOLLY   During all those years when my mother was in the
hospital with her nerves my father brought me to visit
her only three times. Maybe that was her choice. Or
his. I never knew.

But I have a vivid memory of each of those three
visits.

One of the voice of a youngish woman. My father
and mother are in her ward, surrounded by a screen,
fighting as usual, and I'm standing outside in the
huge echoey corridor. And I can hear a young woman
sobbing at the far end of the corridor. More lamenting
than sobbing. And even though a lot of people are
passing along that corridor I remember wondering
why nobody paid any attention to her. And for some
reason the sound of that lamentation stayed with me.

And I remember another patient, an old man, leaning
over me and enveloping me in the smell of snuff. He
slipped a coin into my hand and said, 'Go out and buy
us a fancy new car, son, and the two of us will drive
away to beautiful Fethard-on-Sea.' And he laughed. He
had given me a shilling.

And the third memory is of my mother sitting on
the side of her bed, shouting at my father, screaming
at him, 'She should be at a blind school! You know she
should! But you know the real reason you won't send
her? Not because you haven't the money. Because you
want to punish me.'

I didn't tell Mr Rice that story when he first asked
me about my childhood. Out of loyalty to Father, maybe.
Maybe out of loyalty to Mother, too.

Anyhow, those memories came into my head the
other day. I can't have been more than six or seven at
the time.

MR RICE   In those last few months it was hard to recognize the
woman who had first come to my house. The confident way she shook my hand. Her calm and her
independence. The way she held her head.

How self-sufficient she had been then — her home,

her job, her friends, her swimming; so naturally, so easily experiencing her world with her hands alone.

And we had once asked so glibly: what has she to lose?

MOLLY In those last few months I was seeing less and less. I was living in the hospital then, Mother's old hospital. And what was strange was that there were times when I didn't know if the things I did see were real or was I imagining them. I seemed to be living on a borderline between fantasy and reality.

Yes, that was a strange state. Anxious at first; oh, very anxious. Because it meant that I couldn't trust anymore what sight I still had. It was no longer trustworthy.

But as time went on that anxiety receded; seemed to be a silly anxiety. Not that I began trusting my eyes again. Just that trying to discriminate, to distinguish between what might be real and what might be imagined, being guided by what Father used to call 'excellent testimony' — that didn't seem to matter all that much, seemed to matter less and less. And for some reason the less it mattered the more I thought I could see.

MR RICE In those last few months — she was living in the psychiatric hospital at that point — I knew I had lost contact with her. She had moved away from us all. She wasn't in her old blind world — she was exiled from that. And the sighted world, which she had never found hospitable, wasn't available to her anymore.

My sense was that she was trying to compose another life that was neither sighted nor unsighted, somewhere she hoped was beyond disappointment; somewhere, she hoped, without expectation.

FRANK The last time I saw Rice was on the following Easter Sunday; April 7th; six months to the day after the first operation. Fishing on a lake called Lough Anna away up in the hills. Billy Hughes spotted him first.

'Isn't that your friend, Mr Rice? Wave to him, man!'

And what were Billy and I doing up there in the wilds? Embarrassing. But I'll explain.

Ballybeg got its water supply from Lough Anna and in the summer, when the lake was low, from two small adjoining lakes. So to make the supply more efficient it was decided that at the end of April the two small lakes would be emptied into Lough Anna and it would become the sole reservoir for the town. That would raise the water level of Anna by fifteen feet and of course ruin the trout fishing there — not that that worried them. So in fact that Easter Sunday would have been Rice's last time to fish there. But he probably knew that because Anna was his favourite lake; he was up there every chance he got; and he had told me once that he had thought of putting a boat on it. Anyhow — anyhow.

Billy Hughes and his crazy scheme. He had heard that there was a pair of badgers in a sett at the edge of the lake. When Anna was flooded in three weeks' time they would be drowned. They would have to be moved. Would I help him?

Move two badgers! Wonderful! So why did I go with him? Partly to humour the eejit. But really, I suppose, really because that would be our last day together, that Easter Sunday.

And that's how we spent it — digging two bloody badgers out of their sett. Dug for two-and-a-half hours. Then flung old fishing nets over them to immobilize them. Then lifted them into two wheelbarrows. Then hauled those wheelbarrows along a sheep track up the side of the mountain — and each of those brutes weighed at least thirty pounds — so that we were hauling half-a-hundred-weight of bloody badger meat up an almost vertical mountainside. And then — listen to this — the greatest lunacy of all — then tried to force them into an old, abandoned sett halfway up the mountain! Brilliant Billy Hughes!

Because of course the moment we cut them out of

the nets and tried to push them down the new hole, well naturally they went wild; bit Billy's ankle and damn near fractured my arm; and then went careering down the hillside in a mad panic, trailing bits of net behind them. And because they can't see too well in daylight or maybe because they're half blind anyway, stumbling into bushes and banging into rocks and bumping into each other and sliding and rolling and tumbling all over the place. And where did they head for? Of course — of course — straight back to the old sett at the edge of the water — the one we'd destroyed with all our digging!

Well, what could you do but laugh? Hands blistered, bleeding ankle, sore arm, filthy clothes. Flung ourselves on the heather and laughed until our sides hurt. And then Billy turned to me and said very formally, 'Happy Easter, Frank,' and it seemed the funniest thing in the world and off we went again. What an eejit that man was!

Rice joined us when we were putting the wheelbarrows into the back of Billy's van.

'I was watching you from the far side,' he said. 'What in God's name were you doing?'

Billy told him.

'Good heavens!' he said, posh as ever. 'A splendid idea. Always a man for the noble pursuit, Frank.'

The bastard couldn't resist it, I knew. But for some reason he didn't anger me that day; didn't even annoy me. Maybe because his fishing outfit was a couple of sizes too big for him and in those baggy trousers he looked a bit like a circus clown. Maybe because at that moment, after that fiasco with the badgers, standing on that shore that would be gone in a few weeks' time, none of the three of us — Billy, Rice, myself — none of the three of us seemed such big shots at that moment. Or maybe he didn't annoy me that Easter Sunday afternoon because I knew I'd probably never see him again. I was heading off to Ethiopia in the morning.

We left the van outside Billy's flat and he walked

me part of the way home.

When we got to the courthouse I said he'd come far enough: we'd part here. I hoped he'd get work. I hoped he'd meet some decent woman who'd marry him and beat some sense into him. And I'd be back home soon, very soon, the moment I'd sorted out the economy of Ethiopia . . . The usual stuff.

Then we hugged quickly and he walked away and I looked after him and watched his straight back and the quirky way he threw out his left leg as he walked and I thought, my God, I thought how much I'm going to miss that bloody man.

And when he disappeared round the corner of the courthouse, I thought, too — I thought, too —Abyssinia for Christ's sake — or whatever it's called — Ethiopia — Abyssinia — whatever it's called — who cares what it's called — who gives a damn — who in his right mind wants to go there for Christ's sake? Not you. You certainly don't. Then why don't you stay where you are for Christ's sake? What are you looking for?

Oh, Jesus . . .

MR RICE Roger Bloomstein was killed in an air crash on the evening of the 4th of July. He was flying his plane from New York to Cape Cod where Maria and he had rented a house for the summer. An eye witness said the engine stopped suddenly and, for a couple of seconds, the plane seemed to sit suspended in the sky, golden and glittering in the setting sun, and then plummeted into the sea just south of Martha's Vineyard.

The body was never recovered.

I went to New York for the memorial service the following month. Hiroko Matoba couldn't come: he had had a massive heart attack the previous week. So of the four horsemen, the brilliant meteors, there were only the two of us: Hans, now the internationally famous Herr Girder, silver-haired, sleek, smiling; and myself, seedy, I knew, after a bad flight and too much whiskey.

Girder asked about Molly. He had read an article George Wallace had written about 'Mrs M' in the *Journal of Psychology*. The enquiry sounded casual but the smiling eyes couldn't conceal the vigilance. So the vigilance was still necessary despite the success, maybe more necessary because of the success.

'Lucky Paddy Rice,' he said. 'The chance of a lifetime. Fell on your feet again.'

'Not as lucky as you, Hans.'

'But it didn't end happily for the lady?'

''Fraid not,' I said.

'Too bad. No happy endings. So she is totally sightless now?'

'Totally.'

'And mentally?'

'Good days — bad days,' I said.

'But she won't survive?'

'Who's to say?' I said.

'No, no. They don't survive. That's the pattern. But they'll insist on having the operation, won't they? And who's to dissuade them?'

'Let me get you a drink,' I said, and I walked away.

I watched Maria during the service. Her beauty had always been chameleon. She had an instinctive beauty for every occasion. And today with her drained face and her dazed eyes and that fragile body, today she was utterly vulnerable, and at the same time, within her devastation, wholly intact and untouchable. I had never seen her more beautiful.

When the service was over she came to me and thanked me for coming. We talked about Aisling and Helga. They were having a great time with her parents in Geneva; they loved it there and her parents spoiled them; they weren't good at answering letters but they liked getting mine even though they were a bit scrappy. They were happy girls, she said.

Neither of us spoke Roger's name.

Then she took my hand and kissed it and held it briefly against her cheek. It was a loving gesture. But for all its tenderness, because of its tenderness, I knew she was saying a final goodbye to me.

As soon as I got back to Ballybeg I resigned from the hospital and set about gathering whatever belongings I had. The bungalow was rented, never more than a lodging. So the moving out was simple — some clothes, a few books, the fishing rods. Pity to leave the lakes at that time of year. But the lake I enjoyed most — a lake I had grown to love — it had been destroyed by flooding. So it was all no great upheaval.

I called on Molly the night before I left. The nurse said she was very frail. But she could last forever or she could slip away tonight. 'It's up to herself,' she said. 'But a lovely woman. No trouble at all. If they were all as nice and quiet . . . '

She was sleeping and I didn't waken her. Propped up against the pillows; her mouth open; her breathing shallow; a scarlet coat draped around her shoulders; the wayward hair that had given her so much trouble now contained in a net.

And looking down at her I remembered — was it all less than a year ago? — I had a quick memory of the first time I saw her in my house, and the phantom desire, the insane fantasy that crossed my mind that day: was this the chance of a lifetime that might pull my life together, rescue a career, restore a reputation? Dear God, that opulent fantasy life . . .

And looking down at her — the face relaxed, that wayward hair contained in a net — I thought how I had failed her. Of course I had failed her. But at least, at least for a short time she did see men 'walking as if like trees'. And I think, perhaps, yes I think she understood more than any of us what she did see.

MOLLY When I first went to Mr Rice I remember him asking me was I able to distinguish between light and dark and what direction light came from. And I remember thinking: Oh my God, he's asking you profound questions about good and evil and about the source of knowledge and about big mystical issues! Careful! Don't make a fool of yourself! And of course all the poor man wanted to know was how much vision I had. And I could answer him easily now: I can't distinguish between light and dark, nor the direction from which light comes, and I certainly wouldn't see the shadow of Frank's hand in front of my face. Yes, that's all long gone. Even the world of touch has shrunk. No, not that it has shrunk; just that I seem to need much less of it now. And after all that anxiety and drudgery we went through with engrams and the need to establish connections between visual and tactile engrams and synchronizing sensations of touch and sight and composing a whole new world. But I suppose all that had to be attempted.

I like this hospital. The staff are friendly. And I have loads of visitors. Tony and Betty and baby Molly from this side — well, what used to be this side. They light an odd fire in the house, too, to keep it aired for Frank. And Mary from that side. She hasn't told me yet but I'm afraid Jack has cleared off. And Billy Hughes; out of loyalty to Frank; every Sunday in life, God help me; God help him. And Rita. Of course, Rita. We never talk about the row we had. That's all in the past. I love her visits: she has all the gossip from the club. Next time she's here I must ask her to sing 'Oft in the Stilly Night' for me. And no crying at the end!

And old Mr O'Neill! Yes! Dan McGrew himself! And Louise — Lou — his wife! Last Wednesday she appeared in a crazy green cloche hat and deep purple gloves up to here (*elbow*) and eyeshadow halfway down her cheek and a shocking black woollen dress that scarcely covered her bum! Honestly! He was looking just wonderful; not a day over forty. And he stood in the middle of the ward and did the whole thing for me — 'A bunch of the boys were whooping it up in the Malamute saloon'. And Lou gazing at him in admiration and glancing at us as if to say, 'Isn't he just the greatest thing ever?' And he was — he was! Oh, that gave my heart a great lift.

And yesterday I got a letter, twenty-seven pages long.
Frank — who else? It took the nurse an hour to read
it to me. Ethiopia is paradise. The people are heroes.
The climate is hell. The relief workers are completely
dedicated. Never in his life has he felt so committed,
so passionate, so fulfilled. And they have a special bee
out there, the African bee, that produces twice as much
honey as our bees and is immune to all known bee
diseases and even though it has an aggressive nature he
is convinced it would do particularly well in Ireland.
Maybe in Leitrim. And in his very limited spare time
he has taken up philosophy. It is fascinating stuff.
There is a man called Aristotle that he thinks highly
of. I should read him, he says. And he sent a money
order for two pounds and he'll write again soon.

Mother comes in occasionally; in her pale blue headscarf and muddy wellingtons. Nobody pays much
attention to her. She just wanders through the wards.
She spent so much time here herself I suppose she has
an affection for the place. She doesn't talk much — she
never did. But when she sits uneasily on the edge of
my bed, as if she were waiting to be summoned, her
face always frozen in that nervous half-smile, I think I
know her better than I ever knew her and I begin to
love her all over again.

Mr Rice came to see me one night before he went
away.

I was propped up in bed, drifting in and out of
sleep, and he stood swaying at the side of the bed for
maybe five minutes, just gazing at me. I kept my eyes
closed. Then he took both my hands in his and said,
'I'm sorry, Molly Sweeney. I'm so sorry.'

And off he went.

I suppose it was mean of me to pretend I was
asleep. But the smell of whiskey was suffocating; and
the night nurse told me that on his way out the front
door he almost fell down the stone steps.

And sometimes Father drops in on his way from

court. And we do imaginary tours of the walled garden and compete with each other in the number of flowers and shrubs each of us can identify. I asked him once why he had never sent me to a school for the blind. And as soon as I asked him I knew I sounded as if I was angry about it, as if I wanted to catch him out. But he wasn't at all disturbed. The answer was simple, he said. Mother wasn't well; and when she wasn't in hospital she needed my company at home. But, even though I couldn't see the expression on his face, his voice was lying. The truth of the matter was he was always mean with money; he wouldn't pay the blind school fees.

And once — just once — I thought maybe I heard the youngish woman sobbing quietly at the far end of the corridor, more lamenting than sobbing. But I wasn't sure. And when I asked the nurse, she said I must have imagined it; there was nobody like that on our floor. And of course my little old snuff man must be dead years ago — the man who wanted us to drive to beautiful Fethard-on-Sea. He gave me a shilling, I remember; a lot of money in those days.

I think I see nothing at all now. But I'm not absolutely sure of that. Anyhow my borderline country is where I live now. I'm at home there. Well . . . at ease there. It certainly doesn't worry me anymore that what I think I see may be fantasy or indeed what I take to be imagined may very well be real — what's Frank's term? — external reality. Real — imagined — fact — fiction — fantasy — reality — there it seems to be. And it seems to be all right. And why should I question any of it anymore?

GIVE ME YOUR ANSWER, DO!

Characters
(*in order of appearance*)

BRIDGET CONNOLLY
NURSE
TOM CONNOLLY ⎫
DAISY CONNOLLY ⎬ Bridget's parents
DAVID KNIGHT
JACK DONOVAN ⎫
MAGGIE DONOVAN ⎬ Daisy's parents
GARRET FITZMAURICE
GRÁINNE FITZMAURICE

Time and Place

The present. The old manse, Ballybeg, County Donegal, Ireland.

Give Me Your Answer, Do! was first produced at the Abbey Theatre, Dublin, in association with Noel Pearson, on 12 March 1997, with the following cast:

BRIDGET CONNOLLY	Pauline Hutton
NURSE	Kathleen Barrington
TOM CONNOLLY	Tom Hickey
DAISY CONNOLLY	Catherine Byrne
DAVID KNIGHT	Darragh Kelly
JACK DONOVAN	David Kelly
MAGGIE DONOVAN	Aideen O'Kelly
GARRET FITZMAURICE	Des McAleer
GRÁINNE FITZMAURICE	Frances Tomelty

Directed by	Brian Friel
Stage Direction by	Michael Higgins
Set Design by	Frank Flood
Costumes by	Joan O'Clery
Lighting by	Mick Hughes

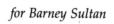

for Barney Sultan

ACT ONE

The stage is in darkness except for a pool of light downstage centre. In the centre of the pool is an iron bed with an uncovered mattress; no sheets, blankets, pillows.

BRIDGET, a woman in her early twenties, is sitting on top of the mattress. Her arms are wrapped around her knees. She is wearing an institutional nightdress and dressing gown. Her mouth is open and her eyes are wide and she stares vacantly in front of her. Slowly and ceaselessly she rocks herself backwards and forwards. One senses quickly that this is how her life is lived. TOM enters left. (Left and right from the point of view of the audience.) He is in his middle-to-late fifties. His dress is casual-to-shabby. He carries an abused briefcase. From a distance he gazes at his daughter for a long time, his face without expression. Then he suddenly and very deliberately animates himself and goes briskly to the bedside.

He talks to BRIDGET with almost excessive enthusiasm. And although she never speaks he pauses occasionally as if he were listening to a response from her and replying to it.

TOM Well! Who is this elegant young woman? What entrancing creature is this 'with forehead of ivory and amethyst eyes and cold, immortal hands'? It's not Miss Bridget Connolly, is it? It most certainly is my Bridget Connolly, beautiful and mysterious as ever. And what's this? Her auburn hair swept back over her *left* ear? Now that's new! And just a little bit saucy! And very, very becoming! The new night nurse did it? Well, the new night nurse has style. We'll make her your official hairdresser from now on. How are you, my darling? Give your father a big kiss.

> *He kisses her on the forehead, sits on the edge of the bed and opens his briefcase.*

313

I like this room — don't you? Nobody can hear a word we say. Now — this week's treasure trove. Clean underclothes. Three oranges. A new facecloth. One very red apple. And a bar of chocolate. Your mother was to have made some scones but — something happened — next week for sure. Yes, of course you want fat, wheaten buns with loads of raisins — I know that! I'll make sure she has them next week.

He leaves the briefcase on the ground.

What news do I have for you today?

First bit of news. Who arrived just as I was stepping out of the house? Grandpa and Grandma! Yes! Haven't seen them for over two years and then they appear out of the blue. *And* they're going to stay the night! Your mother'll give them a blanket and they'll sleep in the potting shed or under the lime tree or somewhere. They won't mind. The weather's good and they're a hardy pair.

And wait till you hear about Grandma. Well, my darling, your grandmother has decided that she has been small for far too long. So every Wednesday evening, when the clock strikes seven, she makes herself grow two inches taller, so that she is now about — what? — she must be eleven feet tall at least. And what a sprinter she has become! D'you know what she tells me? With those extraordinary long legs of hers she can now run from her house down to the old clinic where she used to have her surgery — and back — she can do those six miles in just under two minutes flat. Incredible, I know! But it's true. Grandpa has timed her — twice! And she says that by the time she is fourteen feet tall she'll cut that time by thirty seconds. And she will, too. You know how determined Grandma is. What do you make of that? And they both send you their love, their warmest love. Yes, yes, yes, of course I'll give them yours.

Grandpa? Let me tell you about Grandpa. Only

three months out of jail — the stolen plutonium, the yacht, the helicopter chase, all that fuss — yes, of course you heard all that — anyhow, three months at large and you wouldn't recognize him. Refuses to wash and goes about in green wellingtons and a smelly, brown anorak — even in bed. And guess what he has up the left sleeve of the anorak. A blond ferret! Wasn't half-an-hour out of prison when he slipped into a pet shop and pinched it from its cage. David, he calls it. Is he going to hunt with it? Can't, unfortunately. David's too ill. Grandma diagnosed the condition at once: cirrhosis of the liver. All those ferrets are the same — pickled in alcohol. But maybe it's a good place to die, up the sleeve of a smelly, brown anorak. What do you think? Anyhow, that's your new Grandpa, as God is my judge. Darling, you have totally transformed grandparents.

It's dark in this basement, isn't it? Do you feel it cold? Maybe there's a draught from that little window.

What's that? — Your mother? Great! Wonderful! And of course delighted to have her parents for the night. And in this warm weather spends most of her day out in the garden, playing sonatas by herself on the clavichord or going over the scores for the concerts at the weekends. Pity you missed last Sunday's. An orchestra of one-hundred-and-fifty musicians on our lawn! God knows how she squeezed them all in! And the performance they gave — I can't tell you — magnificent! I never knew Brückner's Eighth was so intelligent and rich and elegant. And there was your mother in this very formal black silk dress and golden shoes — *soigné*, that's the word — conducting with such assurance, with her eyes closed, and her whole body swaying, and away off in some private world of her own, just as you go off into your own world sometimes, too, don't you?

Oh, she's in buoyant form, your mother. Glowing — that's what your mother is. Incandescent — that's what she is.

315

A small, stocky NURSE *enters left with towels across her arm.*

NURSE So they let you down here to see her, did they?

TOM Do you want me to leave?

NURSE Nobody was to be let in. But now that you're here. I'll come back in five minutes and then I'll have a few tales to tell you about Miss Bridget.

TOM She looks great, nurse.

NURSE Wait till you hear my side of the story. Five minutes — that's it.

The NURSE *exits.*

TOM In a previous life she was a terrier — a bull terrier — a pit bull terrier. We won't let her near your hair, will we? And certainly nowhere near David, the ferret, will we? And what else is there? My new novel? Yes, yes, yes, I was waiting for that question. We've had a surfeit of your cheeky jokes on that subject over the year, haven't we?

He picks up the briefcase and turns it upside down.

Empty. The novel is finished, Miss Connolly. 'I don't believe you!' Finished. 'After how long?' Five years. 'Difficult years?' Oh, yes, five very difficult years, my darling; five years of — desperation?

'And it's with your publisher?' Gaudeamus. 'And he has read it?' The best thing you've ever done, Tom. It's intelligent and rich and elegant — (*Very rapidly, very wearily*) And heartening and true and compelling and disturbing and witty and deeply, deeply, deeply moving, Tom. Five years in the writing? Nothing, Tom, nothing. Do you know the effect it had on me, Tom? It made me feel humble.

(*Quick, flat laugh*) So — The novel is finished and all those difficult years are over and there's no more to be said, is there? (*Pause*) What else is new? Oh, yes, the *really* big news! Thank God they have you in a soundproof room. (*Very privately*) The man who has been with us for the past five days, the agent from that university in Texas, the man who wants to buy up all my manuscripts — yes, David Knight! — the very man! — Mister God himself! — You see, you remember the things you want to remember — well, when I go home this afternoon, David Knight is going to give me his answer. He's going to take me aside and put his arm around my shoulder and he is going to say to me, 'Your papers, Tom, are beyond price. Well done, thou good and faithful servant. Please let me reward that excellence and that faithfulness with the ransom of a king.'

From very far off and very faintly we hear the sound of 'On Wings of Song' on the piano.

And then, my silent love, my strange little offspring, then I will come straight back here to you and fold you in my arms; and you and I will climb into a golden balloon and we will soar above this earth and float away forever across the face of the 'darkly, deeply, beautifully blue sky' —

Pause.

Now, won't that be a great bit of diversion!

The NURSE returns, carrying a plastic bag.

NURSE And would you look at her now, good as gold, and not a peep out of her.

TOM I love her hair that way, Nurse.

NURSE And upstairs only an hour ago she was flailing about and roaring like a stuck bull. Weren't you, ducks? Isn't that why we had to put you down here? Could be heard in Belmullet, couldn't you?

(*To* TOM) I'll give you these soiled clothes. God,

she's had a bad four days. You're a bold girl — that's what you are!

TOM Daisy'll bring them back at the weekend; or I will.

He puts the soiled clothes into his briefcase.

NURSE Naughty — naughty — naughty. Right — bath time. Off we go for a good scrub and nobody needs one more than you. Give me a shove, will you?

TOM Sorry.

As they push the bed off left:

NURSE Still writing away at the books, Mr Connolly?

TOM 'Fraid so.

NURSE That's nice. It's novels, is it?

TOM Novels.

NURSE Ah, that's lovely. And how many have you done already?

TOM Oh, I don't know. A dozen — fifteen maybe.

NURSE And are you working at one now?

TOM Trying to. For the past five years.

NURSE Good for you. Keep at it. Nothing I like more than a good novel. Steady on, girl! You don't want to be kept down here for another week, do you?

The moment they exit the stage is suddenly flooded with an opulent and somnolent August sunshine and with the sound of Elizabeth Schwarzkopf singing 'On Wings of Song'.

We see the living room (upstage) and the lawn/garden (downstage) of an old and graceless nineteenth-century house, now badly decayed.

A French window connects the two areas. It is wide open and some of the glass panes are broken, a few missing. The living room is two steps above the lawn. It is a comfortless and neglected room and furnished mostly with the leftover belongings of previous tenants.

On the floor along the back wall we can see Tom's papers very neatly laid out in a line, one beside the other; mostly manila folders, but also a few box files and shoeboxes. Perhaps about thirty items in all.

There are books in a bookcase and in small piles on the floor. Also clearly visible through the open door is a sideboard with a record player and a haphazard collection of CDs, tapes, old 78s. Also on the sideboard are a few bottles and some cloudy glasses.

What was once the lawn/garden is now a rectangle of ground about to revert to a field: bald in patches, overgrown at the verges. A few seats and deckchairs. Two wooden boxes and a large plank of wood — these will later be made into a table.

DAISY is sitting on a deckchair in the centre of the lawn with her back to the living room, listening to the music coming from the house. Her eyes are closed, her face raised to the indolent sun. She has a cigarette in one hand and a glass in the other. She is in her early forties. She pays little attention to her appearance. Her hair, clothes, body are not neglected, just forgotten about. Her feet are bare — espadrilles on the ground beside her deckchair.

DAVID enters the living room from stage left. He carries a few manila folders which he places carefully on the ground beside the other manuscripts. He is in his thirties; dressed with care and precision in a dark suit, shirt, matching tie, polished shoes. He stands listening to the music. Then he goes to the open French window.

DAVID I know that, Daisy, don't I? Schumann, is it?

DAISY (*Opening her eyes*) Sorry, David — I was almost —

DAVID That piece; it's Schumann; isn't it Schumann?

DAISY Is it? I'm useless at —

DAVID Shhh. (*Listens briefly*) Yes, I do know it. It's his *Waldesgespräch.*

DAISY I think maybe — is it not — ?

David moves down to the lawn.

DAVID 'It is late now, it is cold / Why do you ride through the forest alone?' Love that ethereal sound of his. You would think it was floating up there, suspended, wouldn't you?

DAISY Yes.

DAVID And what a life he had. Total nervous collapse when he was only forty-four. Threw himself into the Rhine.

DAISY I never knew —

DAVID Died in an asylum in Bonn two years later. And yet he produced that elegant, controlled sound. (*Brisk*) Well. Last file examined. Job completed.

DAISY Good for you.

DAVID Took longer than I thought but I enjoyed it. So you'll be rid of me tomorrow morning; the house to yourselves again.

DAISY The week flew, David. And I've never seen Tom's papers so well organized.

DAVID Just a matter of housekeeping.

DAISY Yes; I suppose if I were any —

DAVID Is it all right to leave the files there or would Tom want me to bring them back up to his study?

DAISY They're fine there for the time being.

DAVID OK. I'll have a final look through my notes and then maybe we'll all have a farewell drink.

DAISY Have a gin. I'm having one.

DAVID A clear head for the last lap. Anyhow I've been warned off spirits. Where is Tom today?

DAISY Gone into the town — the hospital.

DAVID Ah.

DAISY He'll be back soon.

DAVID In time for the party.

DAISY It's not a party, David. Just my parents and the Fitzmaurices.

DAVID I'll be glad to see them again. I had a great week with them after Christmas.

DAISY I know. And they don't know you're here. A surprise.

DAVID You know I bought all Garret's manuscripts?

DAISY I know that.

DAVID Well, my masters in Texas did. Shipped them out a few months back. Great archive; very full. When you see it all laid out (*Tom's papers*) that's a lot of manuscripts, too, isn't it?

DAISY I have nothing to compare it with.

DAVID Oh, yes; a very substantial archive. Almost forty years of Tom's life there.

DAISY And I suppose substantial is — good, is it?

DAVID A complete archive is good. You always hope to get a complete archive. But of course it's not a question of bulk. Do you like Schumann?

DAISY Schumann? Yes, I think I —

DAVID Something austere about that voice, isn't there? Chilly, really.

DAISY Maybe it is a bit too —

DAVID No, that's appropriate for Schumann.

DAISY Is it?

DAVID Oh, yes; chilly and aloof. Right — up for the final reckoning.

> As DAVID *is about to leave* TOM *enters the living room from the right. He carries his abused briefcase. As soon as he sees* DAVID *he smiles resolutely and assumes a vigour and an enthusiasm he does not feel. He goes out to the garden to* DAISY *and* DAVID.

TOM 'Under the wide and starry sky / Dig the grave and let me lie' — as Robert Louis Stevenson has it. 'Here he lies where he longed to be / Home is the sailor, home from the sea.'

DAVID (*To* DAISY) One happy man.

TOM 'Happiness isn't for us. Our fate is to work and work and work. Happiness is for the people who come after us.' Who wrote that, David?

DAVID I've told you, Tom: I'm no good at that game.

TOM Make a stab.

DAVID Can't.

TOM Nineteenth century.

DAVID Help me, Daisy.

TOM Russian.

DAVID Give me another clue.

TOM 'And look at those beautiful birch trees; so still; so self-aware. They are waiting for something to happen.'

DAVID A wild guess — Tolstoy.

TOM Sorry.

DAVID (*Leaving*) I told you — no good. Educate me later.

TOM (*Calls*) We'll start the revels as soon as you're ready, David.

> Now that DAVID *is gone* TOM *becomes urgent and intense.*

Well? Mister God, what did he say?

DAISY Just that he's finished.

TOM I know he's finished! What's his verdict?

DAISY He said nothing. He's completing his notes.

TOM What notes?

DAISY His assessment of the stuff, I suppose.

TOM No hint? No indication?

DAISY He said it was a substantial archive.

TOM Substantial.

DAISY Yes.

TOM Just substantial.

DAISY Very substantial.

TOM Very substantial.

DAISY And almost forty years of your life went into it.

TOM My God, the man can count!

> DAVID *suddenly appears in the living room.* TOM *becomes enthusiastic again.*

DAVID One small detail, Tom.

TOM Yes?

DAVID (*At the French window*) Your first novel came out the year you graduated or the year before you graduated?

TOM Year before.

DAVID Thought so. Thank you.

TOM I was a mere twenty.
DAVID Right.
TOM A prodigy.
DAVID Indeed.
TOM Prodigious.
DAVID Thanks.

As DAVID *exits again* TOM *calls after him:*

TOM Chekhov, David.
DAVID What's that?
TOM The quotation — both quotations — both Chekhov.
DAVID Yes? I told you — no good.
TOM Silly game — stupid game. 'Some for renown on scraps of learning dote / And think they grow immortal as they quote.'
　　God! It's an addiction! I'm ill!

DAVID *has gone.* TOM'*s anxiety returns.*

I heard him say 'chilly and aloof'. What novel was he talking about?
DAISY He was talking about the music.
TOM What music?
DAISY I was playing a CD.
TOM The music was chilly and aloof?
DAISY The singer — the singing.
TOM The singing was chilly and aloof.
DAISY That's what he said.
TOM What a phoney he is! And that's all he said?
DAISY That's all.

She goes into the living room to get another drink.

TOM Fine. So that's his answer — he's just not interested — he's not going to buy. Fine.
DAISY He didn't say that, Tom.
TOM How did he say 'substantial'?

He follows her into the living room.

Did he say 'This is a very substantial archive' or did he say 'This is a very substantial archive'? Oh, Christ, listen to me!

DAISY Have we any wine? Is there any in the kitchen?

TOM Depends on how much you haven't drunk, doesn't it? Sorry, Daisy. I'm beginning to buckle. I think maybe there's a bottle of red in the cabinet.

He goes out to the garden again.

DAISY Do you want a drink?

TOM Give me a vodka.

DAISY Vodka's finished.

TOM Whiskey, then.

DAISY None left.

TOM Gin — wine — any damn thing. I told her all ferrets drink like fish. I never know what gibberish I'm saying to her.

DAISY *comes out. She is carrying some envelopes.*

DAISY What did you say?

TOM That's her laundry (*in briefcase*). It would need to be soaked right away. A bad week apparently.

DAISY Don't tell me, Tom. (*Brief pause*) Yes, do, please.

She closes her eyes and stands absolutely still.

TOM She hasn't eaten for three days. (*Pause*) She has begun roaring again. (*Pause*) They have her back in the padded cell.

DAISY God —

TOM They asked me to authorize six more electric shock treatments. What do you answer? 'No, I won't give my consent'? (*Pause*) They're to begin next Monday.

DAISY Oh, please, Tom, please, please, please; she's only a —

TOM For God's sake, Daisy, one of us has to face up to it!

DAISY Sorry — I'm sorry — It's just that —

TOM (*Gently*) I know — I know — I know. Jesus, what a hell-hole that place is. (*Pause*) That damned car almost didn't take me home. One of these days it's just not going to go anymore. (*Pause*) Thanks (*drink*).

They both sit.

Where are your parents?

DAISY Out for a walk.

TOM They seem well.

DAISY Yes.

TOM And when do you expect the great Fitzmaurices?

DAISY They should be here soon.

TOM With their usual panache and fake enthusiasm. Oh God, what a bloody week! Five days of smiling and grovelling and scrutinizing every syllable that charlatan uttered. 'Substantial archive, Tom. But I'm afraid my masters in Texas will feel it doesn't fit comfortably into their current acquisition plans.'

DAISY He thought it was Schumann. He was wrong.

TOM What?

DAISY I knew it was Mendelssohn. I suppose I should have spoken up, shouldn't I?

TOM But the really galling thing is that I gave him absolute freedom to examine every private detail of my entire career: every stumbling first draft, every final proof copy, every letter, every invitation, every rejection.

DAISY He'll hear you.

TOM My entire goddamn life for Christ's sake! Touch it, feel it, sniff it, *weigh* it! And then, Mister God, please tell me it's not altogether worthless.

DAISY He's only an agent. He's of no importance.

TOM He should never have been let into the house in the first place. Tell me — how was he allowed in, for God's sake?

DAISY You wrote and asked him, Tom.

TOM Just hold on a second, Daisy. It was —

She hands him the envelopes.

DAISY They're threatening to cut off the electricity next
       Friday and they won't reconnect the phone unless
       we pay thirty pounds.

TOM   The truth of the matter is that you —

DAISY We're broke, Tom. We have no money at all. Your
       royalties have dried up completely. The hospital
       eats up anything you make from journalism. You
       just can't get on with that novel you've been work-
       ing at for five years. It's seven years since you pub-
       lished anything and —

TOM   *The Tumbril* came out two years ago.

DAISY *The Tumbril* was first published fourteen years ago.

TOM   So I'm washed up? Jesus, how would I survive with-
       out your encouragement?

DAISY I'm not criticizing you, Tom — honest to God, I'm
       not. What happened was that we heard that David
       had offered Garret Fitzmaurice a small fortune for
       his papers and what you said was: 'If he's forking
       out big money to Fitzmaurice for his rubbish, what
       must my stuff be worth? I'll flog the lot to him and
       get the head above water for once.'

TOM   (*Glancing at envelopes*) You prefer living in debt — is
       that your point?

DAISY Of course you want to get your head above water,
       Tom, because that would release you from all those
       puny, immediate anxieties. And you need that free-
       dom — I know you do. But I think you had another
       reason for writing to David. You want to establish
       something. You want to know will he offer you more
       than he's supposed to have offered Garret.

TOM   Now there's a rare divination. Gin has its merits then,
       hasn't it?

DAISY We have no experience of this sort of thing, but I just
       know he's going to offer you a lot less — if he buys
       your stuff at all. Not because Garret is a better writer
       — of course he's not and you know that. But he's
       more prolific than you; and he has a big audience;

and his work is much more immediate, much more
— of today than yours. And all these things must
influence David's assessment.

TOM I think you should drop this, Daisy.

DAISY So my hope would be that he makes you a worthy
offer — just for your sake, only for your sake. Because that acknowledgement, that affirmation might
give you — whatever it is — the courage? — the
equilibrium? — the necessary self-esteem? — just to
hold on. Isn't that what everybody needs? So for
that reason alone I really hope he does buy the stuff.

TOM Thank you. Now let's end this, will we?

DAISY And I might as well plunge on now. I had another
thought, too. And it came from something David
said almost as an aside. He said that a complete
archive was always more valuable.

TOM So?

DAISY You haven't let him see the manuscripts of the two
novels you wrote after Bridget got ill first.

TOM What are you talking about?

DAISY You know the two. You've shown them to nobody; I
know that. But they are part of the archive. And you
could insist that nobody would have access to them
for so many years.

TOM Daisy —

DAISY Can't you imagine how those two novels might well
adjust his attitude to you and to all your material?
If he's unsure about buying that could certainly tilt
the balance. Two novels by Tom Connolly that nobody even knows about! He might suddenly find
you at least as interesting as Garret Fitzmaurice —
maybe more interesting! (*Laughs*) Maybe more valuable! God, Tom, wouldn't that be a howl! Imagine
Garret's face! Imagine Gráinne's face!

TOM What a strange creature you are.

DAISY And they are part of the 'Connolly canon', aren't
they? Of course they are. Don't you agree?

TOM Very, very strange.

DAISY Anyhow, that's what I think — in my befuddlement.

Yes, let him see them. They're in two yellow folders on top of the wardrobe in our bedroom.

TOM This isn't about money at all, Daisy — is it?

DAISY Yes, it is. I want a red sports car; I want a diamond this size; I want to travel the world in my own yacht. Look at that baffled face! You're not suddenly jealous of your 'good name', are you? Your moral standing in Ballybeg, are you? Just give him the damned things, Tom. Don't anguish over it. Writers don't have to be saints. For God's sake, look at the writers we know — most of them are shits. Don't you agree?

JACK, Daisy's father, enters the garden from stage right. He is in his late sixties. A small, dandyish man with a faintly theatrical air. He is dressed in inexpensive but carefully chosen clothes — white linen jacket, salmon slacks, a raffish bow tie, very distinctive black-and-white shoes.

JACK (*To* DAISY) All my life I've known never to trust the countryside. Or country people. (*To* TOM) You're back, Tom?

TOM About ten minutes or so.

JACK We went for a gentle walk. (*To* DAISY) You might have warned me you live on the edge of a quagmire, Daisy.

DAISY What quagmire?

JACK Look, Tom. (*He points to one of his shoes*) Disaster.

TOM What happened you?

JACK One step off the avenue into a damned field — left foot soaked.

TOM (*To* DAISY) Where is this?

JACK Where the driveway turns right.

DAISY (*Laughs*) Quagmire! That's just a piece of soft ground, Father!

JACK Sank up to the knee.

DAISY It's only a spark of dirt. You and your silly shoes!

JACK They happen to be very special, these shoes, missy. (*To* TOM) Made from the skin of a boa constrictor.

TOM Snakeskin?

JACK Absolutely. Only pair in Ireland.

TOM (*To* DAISY) Is this true?

JACK Special present from the boys in the band when we broke up six years ago. Would you like them, Tom?

TOM Not my style, are they?

JACK Beautiful shoes; I'd love you'd have them.

DAISY Nobody but you would appear in things like that, Father.

> JACK *takes the shoe off.*

JACK My own fault, I suppose. As I used to tell the boys: the moment you leave the city behind you, put on your galoshes and carry a big cudgel.

TOM I've a pair of slippers in here.

> TOM *goes into the living room and brings out the slippers.*

JACK Have you? Thank you most kindly.

MAGGIE (*Off*) The clothes on the line are dry, Daisy.

DAISY (*Calls*) Sorry?

JACK The clothes on the line are dry, Daisy.

MAGGIE (*Off*) Will I bring them in?

JACK Will I bring them in?

DAISY (*Calls*) If you would, Mother.

JACK (*Calls*) If you would, Mother, please.

DAISY Please — sorry.

JACK (*To* TOM) Their go-between. Always was. Unsuccessfully.

TOM Those (*slippers*) should fit you.

JACK Great. Thank you.

> *He sits beside* DAISY.

You're looking just beautiful, my Dais. Isn't she?

DAISY Father.

JACK Give me a big kiss.

He kisses her on the forehead.

Vibrant.

DAISY That's me.

JACK And such an elegant dress.

DAISY How far did you walk?

JACK (*To* TOM) I know what I hate most about the country-side — apart from country people — I hate the *smell* of it. (*To* DAISY) Just down to the bridge. More than your mother was fit for. Is that the Ballybeg river down there?

DAISY They call it a river. It's really a big stream.

JACK From down there this house looks huge. (*To* TOM) You must be here well over a year now?

TOM Two years last December.

JACK And you can see right up the valley. Absolutely. You were at the hospital?

TOM Yes.

JACK How are things there?

TOM As ever.

JACK She's probably content enough in her own way, Tom. It's the only life she's ever known. (*Pause*) And she has no pain, no discomfort.

DAISY Yes.

JACK And it sounds a much better place than the last one. (*Pause*) We could drop in on our way home tomorrow; but I suppose there isn't much point, is there?

TOM From the distance the house does look well, doesn't it? Originally it was a shooting lodge — away back in the 1880s; then it was a manse; then it was a youth hostel; and then we moved in. I was working it out last week; this is the fourteenth place we've lived in since Bridget was born; and they get more and more isolated and more decayed and of course cheaper — not unlike myself. But better days ahead. 'The past unsighed for, and the future sure' — as Mr Wordsworth has it.

MAGGIE, *Daisy's mother, enters right, carrying a basket*

of clothes. She is about the same age as JACK, *her husband, but because of her disability she looks older. She leans heavily on a stick and moves slowly and with difficulty.*

MAGGIE I heard the Mendelssohn earlier. You used to play that piece.

DAISY Did I?

MAGGIE Don't you remember?

DAISY I think I do. I'm not sure.

MAGGIE You could play that whole song cycle before you were nine. And beautifully, very beautifully.

JACK Absolutely.

MAGGIE Practised four hours every day; and with such dedication. Oh, you were a very determined young lady.

DAISY (*Laughs*) What in God's name became of me?

JACK (*To* TOM) And sometimes she'd sing the songs, too, in some gibberish German she concocted herself.

MAGGIE (*To* DAISY) You remember *that*, don't you? (*To* TOM) Of course he (*Jack*) thought she was brilliant.

DAISY Gibberish German! I never did!

MAGGIE Oh, yes, you were more than promising once.

JACK (*To* TOM) Much, *much* more than promising.

MAGGIE Threw it all up for bigger things, didn't she? What's that?

DAISY It's gin, Mother.

MAGGIE Ah.

Brief pause.

JACK (*Quickly, to* TOM) Concert pianist material — absolutely.

MAGGIE So you never play now?

DAISY No piano now.

MAGGIE Pity.

DAISY And you?

MAGGIE *holds up her arthritic hands.*

MAGGIE Darling —

DAISY Sorry.

MAGGIE Where do you keep the iron?

DAISY Rest yourself, Mother. I'll do it tomorrow.

MAGGIE (*Laughs*) D'you know — I'd forgotten that: 'I'll do it tomorrow.' The piano was your one discipline. Everything else — 'I'll do it tomorrow.'

DAISY Always a lazy lump.

MAGGIE No, not lazy.

DAISY A slut even then?

JACK *is examining one of his shoes.*

JACK (*To* TOM) Nobody can make shoes like the Italians. The British used to be the best but they lost the touch. Something snaps here and the gift's gone. Seen it happen to lots of musicians, too — especially jazzmen. Nothing physical. All in the head.

TOM You're playing the piano as much as ever, aren't you?

JACK Semi-retired.

MAGGIE Still working too hard for his years.

JACK Afternoon teas in the Imperial Hotel on a Wednesday, and Sunday evening in the Grand, and that's it. No more pupils and absolutely no night work. Enough to keep the muscles flexible.

MAGGIE You went to see Bridget?

TOM The weekly duty.

MAGGIE A difficult duty.

TOM Occasionally.

Pause.

DAISY How's the arthritis?

JACK She's gone back to Gerry Plummer for some reason.

MAGGIE He delivered you, Daisy.

JACK Even though she has no faith in him herself.

MAGGIE We're exactly the same age; qualified the same year. And *he* swims in the open sea for an hour every day.

JACK In the winter, too. Absolute fool. Where's he from?

MAGGIE   Somewhere down the country.

JACK   See?

> *He spreads his hands as if to say 'That explains everything'.*

MAGGIE   All he ever wants to talk about is our class of forty years ago, as if he were still in competition with them. He told me last week that nine of them are dead, two are in jail for drug smuggling, and one was executed seven years ago in Paraguay for murdering his wife. I suppose we should count our blessings, shouldn't we?

JACK   You wouldn't have shoe cream in the house, Daisy?

DAISY   Don't think so.

JACK   They may dry out. Eventually.

DAISY   The arthritis, Mother.

MAGGIE   Well, according to Gerry, it's 'making progress'.

DAISY   Does that mean it's getting better or —

MAGGIE   Wouldn't dream of pressing for an answer.

JACK   The fool doesn't know.

MAGGIE   Ambiguity's preferable.

DAISY   Shouldn't you go to somebody else?

MAGGIE   He wants me to see a friend of his he thinks the world of.

JACK   A creature from the wilds of Mayo, for God's sake!

DAISY   Maybe he's good, Father.

JACK   For God's sake, he swims *two* hours every day.

MAGGIE   Wouldn't dream of seeing anybody else. More assessments, more appraisals — spare me. (*To* TOM) Some things better not to know, aren't there?

TOM   Are there?

MAGGIE   Oh, yes. (*She produces a quince from the basket*) You have great gooseberries back there. And your quince is beginning to fall.

DAISY   Is that quince? I didn't know what those were.

MAGGIE   You have a wonderful crop. You should gather it.

DAISY   I suppose so. I'll do it tomorrow.

MAGGIE *holds up an admonishing finger.* DAISY *laughs.*

Today.

TOM   Where did you say those yellow folders were?

DAISY   On top of the wardrobe in our bedroom.

TOM   I'll have a quick read. Excuse me.

JACK   Maybe we could do a tour of the whole estate later, Tom?

TOM   Of course. Some estate.

He exits through the living room.

JACK   Tom's a bit quiet, is he?

MAGGIE   Makes a lovely jelly — quince.

DAISY   It's been an anxious few days.

MAGGIE   Though I prefer the jam; nice edge to it.

JACK   The agent chappie *is* going to buy the manuscripts, isn't he, Dais?

DAISY   We may get his answer today; tomorrow at the latest.

MAGGIE   I'll send you some old jam pots.

JACK   He wouldn't spend a week here if he weren't going to buy, would he?

DAISY   Maybe not.

JACK   So it's reasonable to assume he is going to buy, isn't it?

MAGGIE   You know nothing about those things, Jack!

JACK   All I asked was —

MAGGIE   You may be a cocktail pianist of some modest competence but you know nothing about the sale of literary papers! Nothing! (*To* DAISY) Of course he's going to buy. A university in Texas, is it? I like the sound of Texas. Texas sounds lavish. Texas sounds prodigal.

JACK   May I help myself to a drink?

DAISY   There's more wine in the kitchen cabinet.

JACK   Anybody else?

DAISY   I'm fine.

MAGGIE   Not for me.

JACK   Then I'll put up the table for the party.

DAISY Father, it's not really a —

But JACK *has exited through the living room.*

MAGGIE How often do you go to the hospital?

DAISY Only occasionally. Cowardly, I know.

MAGGIE That's something Tom does very faithfully; always has.

DAISY Yes.

MAGGIE I don't enquire, Daisy; not because I don't care — you know I do. But because I've nothing medical or maternal to offer that might — assuage.

She squeezes DAISY'*s hand briefly.*

How do you think he's looking?

DAISY Father? Dapper as ever.

MAGGIE As ever.

DAISY Complaining about the 'smell' of the countryside.

MAGGIE Every so often he improvises a new affectation. He thinks it makes him interesting.

DAISY How has he been?

MAGGIE Not bad. Indeed very good. Just one little incident and that was about a year ago. I tell myself he's cured — reformed — whatever the word is. Isn't that silly? Maybe as he gets older the compulsion — or whatever it is — gets less compulsive. I've stopped analyzing it all years ago.

DAISY What was it the last time?

MAGGIE Not money, thank goodness. Although why do I say that as if what he did was virtuous? I suppose because the theft of money in the past has always been especially squalid. You'd never guess: two packets of biscuits, wholemeal, from the grocery shop at the end of the street. Just lifted them off the shelf and walked off with them sticking out of his pocket. He's so — inept. Of course the police know him well; and I pleaded with the shopkeeper — his wife used to be a patient of mine; and no charges were brought.

DAISY Oh, Mother.

MAGGIE Cried copiously — as he always does. Apologies. Remorse. Promises. But as usual was able to purge the episode so completely from his mind that the very next day he went back to the shop for cigarettes and was very indignant when the shopkeeper refused to serve him. Wouldn't life be simple if we could all summon amnesia just like that? But perhaps he's feigning it. For his sake I hope he's not feigning.

DAISY Mother, if I can —

MAGGIE Of course the persistent dread is that one day he'll steal something big; and I'll not be able to fix it; and they'll send him to jail. Can you see that vain little creature in a prison cell? He wouldn't survive a week in jail.

DAISY That won't happen.

MAGGIE I suppose not. He'll probably always be just a petty, petty thief, won't he? I used to be so humiliated in the old days when you were a child, Daisy: *Doctor's Husband Charged with Pilfering*. And the constant moving from place to place — bit like yourself. Never a proper practice. Always the itinerant locum. And even now, when he's not with me, or when I don't know where he is, or if he's late home, that not-knowing, that uncertainty, that still crushes my spirit. Then he appears, smiling his winsome smile; and I'm suffused with such relief — no, such joy, Daisy. I know it's absurd, yes, such *delight* — that all I can see is the laughing boy who flooded my head with song more than forty years ago. Gerry Plummer says that the arthritis has begun to inhibit the flow of blood to the brain and that I've begun to dote. Your father's right about Gerry: he is a fool.

DAISY Mother —

MAGGIE Enough of that. Tell me about the Connollys.

DAISY What is there to tell?

MAGGIE I have a sense that you're a bit low.

DAISY Me? I'm fine.

MAGGIE And that his work is in some — difficulty.

DAISY Writers are always in difficulty, especially writers of 'integrity'. And Tom's a writer of integrity, isn't he? Literary probity. High-minded. Oh, yes.

MAGGIE You hardly ever phone and you never write.

DAISY *gets quickly to her feet and goes into the living room for another drink.*

DAISY I'm useless. I'm sorry.

MAGGIE Stop saying I'm useless.

DAISY Sorry.

MAGGIE And stop saying sorry. It must be desolate up here in the winter?

DAISY Tom likes the solitude.

MAGGIE I was thinking of you, Daisy.

DAISY When he's away at a conference or doing a reading, it can be a bit — silent. But I listen to music. And there's the weekly shopping spree to the town — you've no idea how much planning goes into that. And then there's the occasional visit to the hospital to see Bridget, my twenty-two-year-old child. Time passes, Mother.

MAGGIE You should take an interest in the garden.

DAISY I tug at the odd weed. Sure you won't have anything?

MAGGIE Do you read?

DAISY Trashy romantic novels. Devour them. Shameful, isn't it?

DAISY *returns to the garden.*

MAGGIE Or knit? You were very skilful at crochet.

DAISY I need a therapy, Mother — is that it?

MAGGIE An interest. And this is new.

DAISY What is?

MAGGIE Spirits in the afternoon.

DAISY 'Be thou a spirit of health or goblin damned.' Damned

337

quotations. Tom has infected me.

MAGGIE It's doing you no good, darling.

DAISY Do I look that decayed?

MAGGIE That's not what —

DAISY I suppose I do. Yes, of course you're right. But when we sell all that stuff and build the posh bungalow on the bank of some great river, then I'll get a grip on things again; practise the required disciplines.

MAGGIE Indeed.

DAISY I can, you know. I know I will.

MAGGIE Absolutely, as your father says.

DAISY To the miraculous and resolute tomorrow.

MAGGIE Your father's right: Tom does seem quiet.

DAISY Waiting for the Big Answer. It has us all a bit — hushed.

MAGGIE Not that he and I ever had much to say to one another. Your father thinks he's a great fellow.

DAISY He does, doesn't he?

MAGGIE I always thought him difficult.

DAISY You never made a secret of that, Mother.

MAGGIE Because I thought he never considered you — appreciated you. Like all artists he's icy and self-centred and always outside. Have you any love for him?

DAISY One of Mother's forthright questions.

MAGGIE Have you?

DAISY I think I have.

MAGGIE But you've thought of leaving him?

DAISY Oh, yes. Many times.

MAGGIE But will you?

DAISY I don't know. Perhaps. Ask again tomorrow. We may well be wealthy tomorrow and they say money changes everything, don't they?

> JACK *enters the living room, singing 'Daisy, Daisy, give me your answer, do!' He leaves the bottle of wine on the sideboard and goes out to the garden.* MAGGIE *gets to her feet.*

MAGGIE All right — I won't do the ironing. I'll leave these inside.

JACK 'I'm half-crazy all for the love of you.' Who is that most graceful young woman?

DAISY Sit down and behave yourself.

JACK (*Sitting*) Aah. Warm sun — glass of wine — beautiful daughter. Could a man ask for more?

DAISY Clean shoes.

JACK (*Privately*) I lied to you; they're not boa constrictor.

DAISY Never!

JACK Just said that to impress Tom.

DAISY But they do look — distinctive, Father.

JACK (*Whispers*) Imitation leather. And English — God! By the way, your phone's not working.

DAISY Is it not?

JACK Tried to call you last night. Absolutely dead.

DAISY The line must be down again. The arthritis has got suddenly worse.

JACK She really needs two sticks to get around but insisted on leaving one behind her coming here. I don't know what will happen. She shouldn't have gone back to that fool, Plummer. She left the last man because he gave her straight answers.

DAISY What straight answers?

JACK She'll be in a wheelchair in six months.

DAISY My God, is that true?

JACK I think it is. What's to become of us then, Daisy?

DAISY What do you mean?

JACK I'm not fit to look after an invalid, am I?

DAISY With help you are.

JACK Maybe.

DAISY Of course you are!

JACK Maybe you're right. Let's wait and see.

> *He glances into the living room: is she listening? Then he produces an envelope from his pocket and thrusts it into* DAISY's *hand.*

For you. Not a word.

DAISY What are you doing, Father?

JACK A few pounds. Buy yourself a treat.

DAISY Father, I can't —

JACK Shhh. A loan I gave an old trumpeter pal last year. Paid me back on Monday.

DAISY Please —

JACK Thought I'd never see it again.

DAISY Father, I can't take money from you.

Pause.

JACK (*Formally*) It's a repaid loan, Daisy. That is the truth. As God is my judge. (*Quickly*) Not a word. Just do as you're told.

He kisses her on the forehead.

DAISY Thank you.

JACK Did you know that the man who wrote 'Daisy, Daisy' also wrote (*sings*) 'I'll be your sweetheart if you will be mine'? I always play both songs for the old ladies having their afternoon tea in the Imperial. And their faces always light up. And they applaud — they think I know something secret from their past. But people are always reaching out in hope, aren't they?

He jumps to his feet, strikes a theatrical pose and sings:

'It won't be a stylish marriage / We can't afford a carriage — '

DAISY *now joins in with him:*

TOGETHER 'But you'll look sweet / Upon the seat / Of a bicycle built for two!'

MAGGIE *comes out from the living room.*

340

MAGGIE What a talented pair.

JACK Now — where do you want this table to be set up?

DAISY Somewhere over there maybe?

JACK That's where it will be. (*To* MAGGIE) What did you do with the provisions we brought?

DAISY What did you bring?

MAGGIE Four tomatoes and a slice of ham.

DAISY Thank you, Mother.

MAGGIE Provisions — God!

JACK How many will there be?

DAISY Six — seven.

JACK You won't have enough chairs, Dais.

DAISY There are seats in the old potting shed, I think.

> DAVID *appears at the top of the steps.*

DAVID Getting ready for the party?

DAISY It's not a party, David.

DAVID Tom asks if you'd join him. Now, if you're free.

DAISY Where is he?

DAVID In his study. And I'll have a drink now if I may.

DAISY Help yourself.

> DAISY *joins* DAVID *in the living room.*

So you're finished?

DAVID Just about. I'll get it myself.

> DAISY *puts on a record — 'Goodnight Irene' — and stands at the door to see her father's response to it.*

JACK Oh my God!

DAISY I've been saving it for you.

JACK The man from the swampland!

DAISY An old 78.

JACK Where did you get it?

DAISY In a tea chest in one of the stables.

JACK Oh my God, that is just divine.

DAISY *exits left.* DAVID *carries his drink out to the garden and watches* JACK *assemble the table.*

DAVID Can I help you with that?

JACK If I had something to level up this end.

MAGGIE Is this (*stone*) any good?

DAVID That might do it.

DAVID *joins* JACK.

JACK Huddie Ledbetter — do you know him? They called him Lead Belly.

DAVID I know the name.

JACK Twelve-string guitar man. Musical aristocrat.

DAVID Yes?

JACK And a saint. What a life that man had! Jailed for thirty years when he was still in his twenties. Chain gang, beatings, starvation — unspeakable stuff.

DAVID Jailed for what?

JACK Murder.

DAVID Who did — ?

JACK And eleven years later what did they do? Flung him back in again.

DAVID Why?

JACK Attempted murder. Even in his fifties they were still hounding him: back in again only ten years before he died: grievous bodily harm. Isn't that (*music*) heavenly?

JACK *continues working at the table.* DAVID *drifts over to* MAGGIE.

MAGGIE The saintly Mr Ledbetter seems to have had a very full life. When do you go home to Texas?

DAVID I live here. I work on this side of the Atlantic.

MAGGIE I see.

DAVID I go over a couple of times a year — just to keep an eye on them.

MAGGIE It's a library in a university?

DAVID   Special Acquisitions Department. I'm helping them build up a new archive of writers' stuff.

JACK   If they could only get Tom's papers, what a coup that would be for them!

MAGGIE   (*Quickly*) That end's about to topple, Jack.

JACK   I was in a bookshop in town last week and asked the man what Tom Connolly novels they had in stock. None. 'Got three hundred Connollys in last Thursday — gone by Saturday. They just devour Connolly in this city.' Might get a brick out here.

    He exits right.

DAVID   The library's hoping to concentrate on Irish writers. That's why they headhunted me.

MAGGIE   I would like to have visited America. Should have while I was still mobile.

DAVID   Tom tells me your granddaughter has nervous trouble?

MAGGIE   Yes.

DAVID   She has been in hospital since she was twelve?

MAGGIE   For quite a long time.

DAVID   How bad is she?

MAGGIE   Not too well, I'm afraid.

DAVID   But she never gets home?

MAGGIE   I don't think she does.

DAVID   Will she ever be out?

MAGGIE   David, aren't you being a little too — ?

DAVID   I'm sorry — I'm sorry — I sound as if I'm prying — dear God I'm not prying — that's the last thing in my head. Just that I had a little bit of a setback myself some years ago. And I know you're a doctor.

MAGGIE   Retired. What sort of a setback?

DAVID   I'm fine now. Absolutely fine.

MAGGIE   Good.

DAVID   My friends tell me that since I got better I've become more opinionated and even more boring than I ever was. But my doctor says that's a normal compensatory device at this stage and that the stronger I get, ironically I'll revert more and more to my usual — hesitancy.

MAGGIE This was in America?

DAVID London. Working for an antiquarian bookseller; specialist in seventeenth-century books on French history and literature.

MAGGIE That was an unusual job.

DAVID Fascinating. Absorbing. And I became expert at it — I really did. More expert on printing and especially binding than my Hungarian boss. So expert that dealers and buyers from all over Europe bypassed him and consulted me! Honestly! And I had a German girlfriend, Marinella. And an enormous apartment right down on the bank of the river. And we were to be married that Easter. Oh, yes, so fascinating, so *absorbing*, that there were times when I found myself still working at two in the morning, three, sometimes four.

MAGGIE That wasn't very sensible.

DAVID And then one Tuesday evening, on my way home from the Harleian Library, a funny thing happened. My legs suddenly melted. And I found myself sitting on the pavement. And I couldn't remember my name. (*Laughs*) Three weeks before I knew who I was! Ridiculous, isn't it?

MAGGIE Frightening, David.

DAVID No warning whatever. Out of the blue just like that. Frightening? Oh, yes; more than a little frightening.

JACK *enters.*

JACK It's going to be delightful eating out here with these damned flies. Did you know that most country flies are malaria carriers?

DAVID But that's all in the past. I'm perfect now; never better. Keep working — that's the answer. And this work fascinates me. And the Texans in their innocence think I'm a genius at it. Oh, yes, I love this job; fascinating work, absorbing work.

Sudden boisterous, enthusiastic noises from off right
— the arrival of GARRET *and* GRÁINNE FITZMAURICE.
Their calls sometimes overlap.

GARRET   Hello — hello — hello!

GRÁINNE   Hello — hello — hello!

GARRET   Anybody home?

GRÁINNE   Anybody home?

GARRET   Dais-eeeee!

GRÁINNE   Tom!

MAGGIE   What's that racket?

GARRET   Tom!

GRÁINNE   Dais-eeeee!

JACK   The pubs must be closed.

DAVID   It's the Fitzmaurices!

MAGGIE   Who?

GARRET   Stop hiding from us!

GRÁINNE   (*Sings*) 'Where are you — ?'

DAVID   Garret Fitzmaurice, the novelist, and Gráinne.

MAGGIE   Ah.

JACK   Whoever they are, they aren't going to take us by
stealth, are they?

GARRET   (*Sings*) 'Come into the garden, Tom — '

GRÁINNE *joins him:*

TOGETHER   'For the black bat, night, has flown — '

JACK   Could they be sinking in the quagmire?

GARRET   Hello — hello — hello — Tom — Daisy!

GRÁINNE   Daisy — Tom!

GARRET *and* GRÁINNE *enter right (not through the
living room). They are about the same age as* TOM
and DAISY *and their dress is more considered and
more 'arty'.* GARRET *carries two large plastic bags,*
GRÁINNE *has an enormous bouquet of dramatic
roses which she carries with considerable effect.
They bring with them an aureole of enthusiasm and
heartiness and energy — and they are aware of that;*

> *a double act more intuitive than rehearsed. They are also a little overwhelming at times — and they are aware of that, too.*

GARRET We had to leave the car down at the road because the potholes on that — (*He sees* DAVID) I don't believe it! Look, love!

GRÁINNE It's not! It couldn't be!

GARRET But it is! David Knight, by the Lord Harry!

GRÁINNE David Christopher Knight — and no other!

GARRET Well, if this isn't one transporting joy!

GRÁINNE A delight beyond words!

GARRET Embrace me, David.

DAVID Good to see you, Garret.

GRÁINNE Wonderful, wonderful surprise! I want a hug, too!

DAVID Gráinne.

GRÁINNE And I want a kiss, a kiss, a kiss.

GARRET Excessive as ever — isn't she?

DAVID Great to see you both.

GARRET And the style of the man!

GRÁINNE I could devour him.

DAVID Come on.

GARRET (*To* GRÁINNE) Is that the international executive look, love?

GRÁINNE That is the intercontinental executive look.

DAVID Enough of that. You don't know each other, do you? Gráinne and Garret Fitzmaurice — Maggie and Jack Donovan, Daisy's mother and father.

GARRET Ah!

MAGGIE How are you?

GARRET Another great joy. Delighted to meet you both — at last.

GRÁINNE At last indeed; at long last. When did you arrive?

MAGGIE At lunchtime. It took us six hours to get here.

GRÁINNE Oh my God, you must be exhausted!

MAGGIE Jack is a cautious driver.

JACK Jack was given wrong directions at least twice. I didn't catch your last name?

GARRET Fitzmaurice.

JACK Sorry?

DAVID Gráinne and Garret Fitzmaurice. I spent a week with this pair earlier this year.

GRÁINNE Only five days, David.

GARRET Days of unqualified pleasure. And lest I forget — your namesake is fulfilling all our expectations.

DAVID My — ?

GRÁINNE Christopher! The red setter! (*To* MAGGIE) A new pup we got while David was with us.

GARRET Champion written all over him.

DAVID Good.

GARRET Even though I'm not at all confident about the papers that came with him.

GRÁINNE We called him Christopher after David Christopher.

GARRET And tell him about our errant Persian, love.

DAVID I remember that cat — Nemesis!

GRÁINNE Nemesis. Major domestic scandal.

GARRET Go on.

GRÁINNE Eight kittens last Monday and not a Persian among them — seven orange, one jet black.

GARRET And *those* papers were supposed to be perfect. (*To* MAGGIE) We couldn't unload eight ambiguous kittens on you?

MAGGIE Sorry.

GARRET Because if we can't get a home for them, she'll drown them.

GRÁINNE Who'll drown them?

GARRET Didn't you say you would, love?

GRÁINNE Never ever said that.

GARRET Where did I get that from? I beg your pardon.

GRÁINNE He invents compulsively.

GARRET (*To* DAVID) And you remember Jupiter? Tell him about Jupiter, love.

DAVID The swan! How is he? (*To* MAGGIE *and* JACK) Gráinne's pet swan.

GRÁINNE Fully mature — with a splendid orange bill and a powerful neck and black, sinewy legs.

GARRET What a decorous description. (*To* MAGGIE *and* JACK) Jupiter as in Jupiter and Leda.

GRÁINNE Hisses furiously every time he sees Garret. We don't know why, do we? (*Laughs*) At least it can't be because he has read his work.

GARRET Perhaps he just sees through me, love?

GRÁINNE Perhaps. And do you remember that degenerate parrot of his?

GARRET (*To* MAGGIE *and* JACK) It must sound like a menagerie, does it?

GRÁINNE He has taught him a mouthful of new words — all obscene.

DAVID Garret!

GARRET Not obscene — maybe indelicate?

GRÁINNE My husband is scrupulous with language.

GARRET Fastidious, love. And we're boring the Donovans with our domestic prattle.

MAGGIE It does sound like a menagerie. And have you children?

GRÁINNE No.

GARRET No, we don't have a family, unfortunately.

GRÁINNE We did consider children. But we gave our life to letters instead — didn't we?

GARRET We're Bridget's godparents — you know that?

MAGGIE I knew that. (*Aware that* JACK *has been left out*) We knew that, didn't we?

GARRET Not that we're as attentive to her as we should be.

GRÁINNE And of course we've known Tom and Daisy forever.

GARRET And we've heard so much about you both that we feel we know you, too.

GRÁINNE You're retired now.

MAGGIE Yes, I am.

GRÁINNE And I can tell you the precise date — July 28th — a Tuesday.

MAGGIE How do you know that?

GRÁINNE Daisy and I had arranged to meet that day but I had to cancel because Garret's publisher was giving a party in Dublin.

MAGGIE Yes?

GRÁINNE July 28th. Yes. The day his *Soft Underbelly* came out.

GARRET *Soft Underbelly* is the title of a novel of mine.

348

GRÁINNE I'm right, amn't I?

GARRET She loves to set up situations where she can make that very witty joke.

JACK I am completely lost here.

MAGGIE They're talking about the title of Garret's book.

JACK Still lost. But carry on. *Their* shoes seem perfectly dry.

GARRET And we know quite a bit about you, Jack, too.

JACK Yes?

GRÁINNE A lot, in fact.

> GARRET *stretches out his arms and mimes playing a piano.*

JACK Sorry?

GARRET Daisy says you're brilliant.

> JACK *turns to* MAGGIE *in pretended bewilderment.*

JACK What does — (*copying* GARRET's *mime*) — mean?

MAGGIE (*Quickly*) Yes, we're both retired now — well almost. A life of leisure from now on.

GRÁINNE And long may you enjoy it.

DAVID That's something novelists don't do, Garret — retire.

GRÁINNE And they should, shouldn't they? Why do they keep stumbling on long after they're dead creatively?

GARRET To put it elegantly. We don't formally retire, David. But I hope we have the good sense to know when silence is appropriate.

> GRÁINNE *slaps her wrist.*

GRÁINNE Careful, Gráinne, darlin'.

GARRET Do you know is the delectable Daisy going to feed us some time?

MAGGIE I think so.

GARRET Let me leave this stuff inside.

> *He is about to go into the living room but stops when he sees Tom's papers.*

What are Tom's papers — ? (*To* DAVID) *That's* why
you're here!

GRÁINNE Of course it is.

GARRET It just never entered my head that —

GRÁINNE Have you been here long?

DAVID Most of the week. Leaving tomorrow.

MAGGIE We're leaving tomorrow, too. Can we give you a lift?

DAVID Tom's going to run me to the station.

JACK In his car? You'd be quicker walking. This (*table*) is
fit only for firewood.

GARRET So you've been assessing the Connolly archive. Well,
I'm delighted. I really am delighted.

GRÁINNE It's a lot of stuff, David.

DAVID A big archive, isn't it?

GARRET I told you Tom was worth looking at, didn't I? So
you got in touch with him?

DAVID Actually he wrote to me.

GARRET Good old Tom. Tom is a considerable writer. No,
that's ungenerous. Tom Connolly is a terrific writer.

GRÁINNE Much more stuff than you, Garret.

GARRET Most of it's material he's unhappy with himself, I'm
sure; wouldn't want published. What a desolate time
that man has had this past number of years: lost his
agent; fought with his publisher; antagonized all
those people who might throw him a bit of work.
And all because — goddammit! — all because he
just could not write! I've been through it — utter
desolation. For Daisy, too. Maybe more especially
for Daisy. Oh, yes, Tom Connolly deserves a break.
I'll tell you something, David Christopher: nothing
would give me greater pleasure than that he and I
would be laid out together in that Texan library. And
that will happen, won't it?

DAVID That decision rests with my Texan masters.

GARRET You know it doesn't.

DAVID All I do is recommend.

GARRET You're being coy, David.

GRÁINNE Garret, you're —

GARRET You made the decision on my stuff; and a swift and

350

generous decision it was. Wasn't it, love? (*To* MAGGIE *and* JACK) Paid off the house — new car — Canaries next November I'm not ashamed to say. (*To* DAVID) So just answer me: you are buying, aren't you?

DAVID Perhaps.

GARRET Perhaps yes or perhaps no?

GRÁINNE This is none of your business, Garret.

GARRET Darling, I —

GRÁINNE Where are our host and hostess?

MAGGIE Upstairs, I think. Let me find them.

JACK I can do no more with that (*table*). Maybe it will hold. (*To* DAVID) Did Daisy say there were seats somewhere?

DAVID In the potting shed. I'll get them.

> DAVID *exits right.*

JACK I'll leave these (*bags*) inside for you.

GARRET That one's heavy, Jack. There are bottles in it.

> JACK *holds out his hands and flexes his fingers.*

MAGGIE Yes, Daisy plans to eat out here later.

GRÁINNE Lovely. I'm ravenous.

> MAGGIE *and* JACK *go into the living room — where* JACK *leaves the bottles — and exit left.*
>
> GARRET *and* GRÁINNE *are now alone.* GARRET *immediately dashes to the doorway and looks at the manuscripts.* GRÁINNE *slumps into a deckchair and closes her eyes in exhaustion.*

GARRET (*In the doorway*) What a load of stuff! There must be a dozen books there he couldn't get published. David's never going to buy all that, is he? No, he's not! What d'you think? (*Out to garden again*) You can't put a price on a man like Tom, can you? And, if book sales are to be a guideline, that gives Tom no leverage at all.

GRÁINNE Oh dear God, I'm so tired.

GARRET What he'll have to do is figure out some sort of category for Tom and that might give him a yardstick. But what category? Minor writer? Minority taste? Significant minority writer? Major minor writer? For God's sake, never minor major writer? What did he say to you? — 'A big archive, isn't it?' What does big mean? Big means nothing, does it? Is nobody going to offer us a bloody drink? And what a prickly little bollocks that father is — 'I didn't catch your last name'. Did you hear him, for Christ's sake? God, I really could do with a drink. Are you all right?

GRÁINNE (*Quietly*) That performance, that ugly, bitter act we put on when we're with people, Garret — suddenly I know I can't do it any longer.

GARRET What are you talking about?

GRÁINNE In the early days it entertained our friends; and we liked that. 'Wait till you see the Fitzmaurices at each other's throat.' But we've moved beyond that now, haven't we? Now we welcome occasions like this so that we can wound each other as deeply and as viciously as we can, don't we?

GARRET Here we go again!

GRÁINNE But we know, too, that audiences impose limits on how far we can go. And we're secretly glad of that limitation because we're both still a bit nervous that without that restraint we might deliver the final thrust, that mortal wound. And up to now we've been afraid of that conclusion. You know I'm right. Yes, I did set up that awful *Soft Underbelly* joke once again because I wanted to humiliate you — 'Wanted to humiliate you'! — What a way is that to live, Garret? Is that any way to live?

> *He goes quickly to her side and squats down beside her seat.*

GARRET It's not your fault, love. It's mine. Mine entirely. That stupid remark I made about drowning the kittens —

where the hell did that come from? Then you hit back at me about having no children and then we both tore at each other about —

GRÁINNE Don't be so anxious, Garret. It doesn't matter.

GARRET I'm sorry, love. It's altogether my fault.

GRÁINNE No, it's not. I'm as ugly as you.

GARRET I'm such a shit, Gráinne. Who knows that better than you? Am I forgiven?

GRÁINNE When I knew you first I thought your weakness was attractive.

GARRET Do you forgive me?

GRÁINNE I was going to provide the practical strength for both of us and you were to concern yourself just with being creative. A pretty idyll, wasn't it? And for a long time I had that strength, Garret.

GARRET I need you, love.

GRÁINNE You think you do. I know you think that.

GARRET Please don't talk like this, Gráinne.

GRÁINNE But if I weren't in your life maybe you'd find your own resiliences. They won't make you a stronger man but perhaps they'd make you a better writer.

GARRET You're not saying you're thinking of — ?

GRÁINNE You aren't at all the writer you might have been — you know that yourself. Too anxious to please. Too fearful of offending. And that has made you very popular: people love your — amiability. But I thought once you were more than that. I think you did, too.

GARRET *stands up.*

GARRET Jesus, Gráinne, you certainly can deliver that mortal wound.

GRÁINNE Perhaps if you were on your own you'd become tougher and maybe you'd fulfil completely whatever you have. I hope you do. You know in your heart I hope that.

TOM *and* DAISY *enter the living room and come straight out to the garden.* TOM *carries two yellow folders under his arm.* DAISY — *loosened by drink but by no means drunk* — *is in an elated mood. All four greet each other warmly.*

TOM	There you are!
DAISY	Garret! Gráinne!
GARRET	Hello — hello!
TOM	Are you here long?
GRÁINNE	Only just arrived.
TOM	Why didn't we hear the car?
GRÁINNE	Left it down on the road.
GARRET	Wouldn't subject it to your potholes. Daisy, how are you?
DAISY	Good to see you, Garret.
GRÁINNE	(*Embracing*) Tom.
TOM	Welcome.
GRÁINNE	Daisy.
DAISY	Welcome to you both. Delighted you could come.
GRÁINNE	Thank you. These (*flowers*) are for you.
DAISY	They're just beautiful. Thank you. So beautiful. First things first — who's for a drink?
GARRET	By God I am!
GRÁINNE	And me.
TOM	And me.
GRÁINNE	Let me give you a hand. Who's for what?

GRÁINNE *and* DAISY *go into the living room.*

GARRET	We brought some stuff. Your father left it in there.
DAISY	You've met him?
GARRET	Charming man — isn't he, love?
GRÁINNE	Met your mother, too.
GARRET	Both charming, aren't they? (*To* TOM) Aren't they?
TOM	Yes.
GRÁINNE	Orders, please.
TOM	We've no vodka, have we?
GARRET	Yes, we have. And wine. And gin for the lady.
DAISY	Thank you both.
GRÁINNE	May I have your orders?

GARRET (*Softly to* TOM) Bit cranky today. Vodka for me, love.

TOM Me, too.

GRÁINNE Daisy?

DAISY Gin for me.

GRÁINNE I'll try some wine.

DAISY Only gin for yours truly.

GARRET And David Knight's here!

TOM David Knight's here.

GARRET How was that set up?

TOM He wrote and asked could he come.

GARRET He made the first move? Good! And he has looked at the stuff?

TOM For four long days.

GARRET And he's going to buy?

TOM spreads his hands.

For God's sake, he'd kill to get his hands on your stuff, Tom! Wouldn't he, love?

GRÁINNE Can't hear you.

She emerges with her own and TOM's *drink.*

GARRET I'm saying David would kill —

GRÁINNE That's if Tom is happy to sell.

GARRET Who's talking about happiness, love? That's why David is here — to buy!

GRÁINNE Can you manage, Daisy?

DAISY Daisy most certainly can manage.

She comes out with her own and GARRET's *drink.*

GRÁINNE Garret got the cheque for his papers six weeks ago.

TOM Great.

GARRET I'm still in shock.

GRÁINNE So now his real worth is established.

DAISY Mr Fitz — one vodka.

GARRET You're an angel. (*To* GRÁINNE) What does that mean?

DAISY Welcome to you both and thank you most kindly for

the load of stuff you brought.

GRÁINNE Lovely to see you both.

GARRET My Pythia is being Delphic today — aren't you, love?

DAISY What are you talking about, Garret?

TOM 'I am Sir Oracle / And when I ope my lips, let no dog bark.'

DAISY Do you know when he uses quotations? When he wants to hide what he's thinking.

TOM 'Or am embarrassed, impatient, fretful, ill-at-ease — '

DAISY Oh, shut up! I was thinking about you people just the other day —

GARRET Gráinne and me?

DAISY No, no, you writer creatures, and it struck me — smack!

She hits her forehead with exaggerated theatricality.

That's where it struck me —

TOM Daisy —

GRÁINNE Listen to her.

DAISY It struck me how wretched you are. You're unhappy in the world you inhabit and you're more unhappy with the fictional world you create; so you drift through life like exiles from both places. (*To* GRÁINNE) We waste our lives with wraiths.

TOM 'If this were played upon a stage now / I would condone it as improbable fiction.'

GARRET *laughs.*

DAISY Stop hiding, Tom.

TOM Am I not here?

DAISY Only part of him is ever here.

TOM (*To* GRÁINNE) How much more present can I be? — (*To* DAISY) Do you want?

DAISY Indeed maybe there's enough. Maybe more of you would be too rich for us at this stage of our lives.

GARRET *laughs.*

GARRET (*To* GRÁINNE) This is *our* act, love! (*To* DAISY) You're plagiarizing our act, Daisy!

DAISY (*Mock heroic*) I speak from deep in a bruised heart. (*In mock Italian*) — da bruised heart.

GARRET Da bruiseda hearta, no?

DAISY *and* GARRET *laugh.*

DAISY Great! Da bruiseda hearta. We were at a writers' conference in Kilkenny — when was it? — three years ago? — four? —

GRÁINNE Good to see you both.

TOM Seven.

DAISY Was it seven? It's all slipping away, children. Anyhow, my last big outing before we withdrew into our isolation. And I need a refill. (*She refills her glass and keeps talking*) And I noticed that most of the writers' wives or mistresses or whatever used language like that all the time.

GRÁINNE Like what?

DAISY The bruised heart.

GARRET Da bruised —

DAISY One talked about her 'laughing soul'. Another said her spirit was 'fidgety and uncertain'. I heard one of them say to another, 'My kernel felt suddenly animated, Dorothy'. And it struck me —

GARRET Smack!

DAISY Careful, you! — It occurred to me that — I don't know — it just seemed to me that their thoughts and their vocabularies were lifted out of the books of their husbands or lovers. They hadn't even a language of their own.

GARRET They were wraiths, too?

GRÁINNE Listen.

DAISY And I thought to myself: you're not quite as reduced as that yet, Daisy, are you? Not quite — are you?

GARRET (*Sings*) 'Daisy, you're a darling, a darling, a darling — '

DAISY But I'm serious, Garret — (*Pause*) I think I am —

(Pause) Oh, shut up, Daisy —

> GRÁINNE *goes to her bag and produces a small packet.*

GRÁINNE For the godchild.

TOM What's this?

GRÁINNE For Bridget. Her birthday's on Thursday fortnight.

DAISY God — is it?

TOM Thank you, Gráinne — Garret.

DAISY May I open it?

GRÁINNE It's only a token.

GARRET She got it in London.

DAISY Oh, Gráinne, it's beautiful. *(To* TOM*)* A comb with very intricate silver mounting.

TOM Very pretty.

DAISY She'll just love that.

GRÁINNE Always working with her hair, isn't she?

TOM The only thing she has any interest in.

DAISY Just beautiful. Thank you.

TOM Thank you both.

GRÁINNE Have you seen her recently?

DAISY I haven't, I'm —

TOM This morning.

GARRET Well?

TOM As usual. No change. There'll be no change. Ever. *(Sings)* 'Change and decay in all around I see — '

> GARRET *joins him.*

TOGETHER 'O Thou Who Changeth not, abide with me.'

> *Pause.*

DAISY I'm ready to go again.

GRÁINNE We're fine for the moment, Daisy.

GARRET I'm not fine.

TOM And I'll have one.

GRÁINNE All right — why not?

DAISY *goes into the living room.* GRÁINNE *follows her. As she passes* GARRET:

GARRET Jesus, you're not still sulking, are you?

GRÁINNE *looks at him calmly, briefly — then follows* DAISY *into the living room.* JACK *and* MAGGIE *enter the living room from the right. He carries a tray of dishes. She has a plate of food.*

JACK Where will I put these?

DAISY Out on the table, Father.

MAGGIE And this?

DAISY On the table, too, please.

JACK Why does she call it a table? It's a disgrace.

TOM (*To* JACK) Do you want a hand?

JACK No, thanks. I'm very good at this.

MAGGIE He is, too.

JACK People have told me I look like a waiter. I suppose they mean to be nice, do they?

DAVID *enters right with chairs under his arms.*

DAVID That potting shed's full of interesting stuff.

GRÁINNE (*Calls*) A drink, David?

DAVID If you have some wine? (*To* MAGGIE) No spirits. I'm still on pills.

MAGGIE (*To* DAVID) A long time since those have been sat on.

DAISY (*Calls*) They belonged to the rector, Mother.

MAGGIE (*To* JACK) They what?

JACK Belonged to the rector, Mother.

MAGGIE (*Calls*) What rector?

JACK (*To* TOM) What rector?

TOM This was a manse at one time.

MAGGIE Really?

GARRET First a rector — now a wraith.

MAGGIE Is it haunted?

GARRET Tom and I are the wraiths.

MAGGIE Yes?

JACK I'm told that being a waiter is the most boring job in the world. So do you know what most waiters do? Pretend they're ballet dancers.

He illustrates this with one quick movement.

TOM Jack!
JACK Honestly. Just as cocktail pianists pretend to themselves they're concert pianists.
MAGGIE Do you pretend that?
JACK That's true.

DAISY *and* GRÁINNE *emerge with the drinks.*

DAISY David.
DAVID Lovely.
DAISY Father.
JACK God bless you.
GRÁINNE Two vodkas for the wraiths.
GARRET Thank you most kindly, sweet lady.
GRÁINNE Daisy.
MAGGIE Another gin, darling?
DAISY Amn't I shameless, Mother?
GARRET Tom, what in the name of God are you clutching under your arm?

TOM *takes the yellow folders from under his arm and looks at them. Everybody looks at* TOM.

They're manuscripts, aren't they?
TOM Yes.
GARRET You've finally finished the novel! Terrific!
TOM If only. Two old manuscripts, I'm afraid.
GARRET Is there some mystery here?
TOM Maybe you'd have a look at them, David.
DAVID Where did these come from?
TOM I overlooked them. Sorry.
GARRET I do smell a mystery, don't I?
DAVID Early stuff?

TOM Yes. Well — early-ish. (*Looking around*) Nothing mysterious about them. Just two more dog-eared manuscripts.

He hands them to DAVID.

GARRET Novels?

TOM Novels.

GARRET Never published?

TOM Never.

GARRET Every writer worth his salt has one of those.

GRÁINNE You haven't — have you?

DAVID Better have a look at them now, shouldn't I?

TOM There's no hurry. They've been around for a long time.

JACK And when you do decide to publish them, Tom, I'm sure they'll be a great success.

DAVID When were they written — roughly?

DAISY He began the first the day Bridget was committed to the hospital. A glorious 1st of May, I remember. And he went at it with such a fury that he had it finished by Hallowe'en.

GARRET Wow! Six months?

DAISY Then he went straight into the second without a break and he finished that in five months. I never ever saw him work with such concentration. For a whole twelve months! I don't think he even knew I existed for that whole year.

MAGGIE That must have been very exciting for you, Tom.

GRÁINNE Have they titles?

TOM I called the first *Bridget* — a sort of working title. I never got round to naming the second. And for some reason I never showed them to anybody.

GARRET You've read them, Daisy?

DAISY Oh, yes.

GARRET And your agent saw them — you had an agent then, hadn't you?

TOM I showed them to nobody, Garret — just nobody.

MAGGIE (*To* DAISY) Apparently you don't count — do you not?

TOM   And the reason I showed them to nobody was that I was never sure how I felt about them.

GARRET   That's perfectly —

TOM   I suppose because they're both pornographic novels.

Silence.

GARRET   Come on, Tom! You're joking, aren't you?

TOM   No.

GRÁINNE   Is he serious, Daisy?

DAISY   Yes, he is.

MAGGIE   Oh, darling, they're not — are they? (*Pause*) Answer me!

DAISY   They are, Mother. Hardcore porn — as they say.

GARRET   You *are* serious? You bloody are!

TOM   Yes.

MAGGIE   Oh my dear —

GARRET   Holy Jesus, Connolly the pornographer! Well, isn't he the deep one.

DAVID   That certainly is interesting, Tom. Very, very interesting.

Brief pause.

JACK   As you all know I'm very ignorant in these matters. But I'm sure they're both splendid books, Tom. And when you do decide to publish them I haven't a doubt in the world they'll both be enormously successful. None whatever! Absolutely!

Quick black.

ACT TWO

The sound of Schumann's 'Remembrance, Opus 68' pours out from the living room.

Several hours have passed. The meal is over. Glasses, soiled dishes, paper napkins, empty bottles are strewn over the table and across the lawn.

Because of the heat, the food, the drink, the hours together — the atmosphere and the conversation are desultory and lethargic.

JACK *appears to be asleep on a deckchair down right. A straw hat covers his face; his dandy shoes on their sides at his feet, still wearing the slippers Tom gave him.*

MAGGIE *down left is topping and tailing gooseberries.*

Squatting on the grass between JACK *and* MAGGIE *are* TOM *and* GRÁINNE *who are playing a game of* Scrabble. GARRET *moves around restlessly.*

In the living room DAISY *is idly looking through records and tapes.*

GARRET *is slightly intoxicated — and voluble.* DAISY *is slightly intoxicated — and pensive.*

GARRET   What in the name of God can David Christopher Knight be doing up there for the past three hours? No pornography could engage him for that length of time, not even the pornography of Tom Connolly — could it? So what can the Christ-bearer be at? I cannot for the life of me imagine. My imagination affords me no explanation whatever.

TOM   (*To* GRÁINNE) You're not going to like this.

GRÁINNE   What outrageous word is it going to be this time?

TOM   Hold on.

GARRET   But then my wife avers that my imagination is a puny little instrument anyway — don't you, love? — and that a life of pandering has made it punier and littler. Now there's a title for my next book! — *The*

Pandering Imagination. Shouldn't be too hard to set up some jokes around that.

GRÁINNE (*To* MAGGIE) Do you know of any word with the letters q, v and y?

MAGGIE God help you.

GRÁINNE (*To* TOM) Z-y-m — ? What's that?

TOM Just a minute.

GARRET A barrister told me once that he always knew what verdict a jury would bring in. If they're out a long time the verdict will be 'Innocent'. If they're back quickly, 'Guilty'. Now when David Christopher went through my papers he decided instantly. I suppose that makes me guilty — doesn't it, Daisy?

TOM Z-y-m-o-s-i-s.

GRÁINNE That's not a word!

TOM 'Fraid so.

GARRET Not hard to predict your verdict, Tom: after this interminable absence it has to be 'Innocent as a Baby'. And that's appropriate: Garret — 'Guilty', Tom — 'Innocent'. Right, love?

TOM 'The blood-dimmed tide is loosed, and everywhere / The ceremony of innocence is drowned — '

GARRET 'The best lack all conviction, while the worst' — blah-blah-blah. For Christ's sake, we can all hide! May I have a little wine?

Nobody responds.

I may.

He goes to the table.

GRÁINNE Anybody ever heard of 'zymosis'?

TOM (*Hands her a dictionary*) Go ahead. Look it up.

MAGGIE He's right, Gráinne: an infectious or contagious disease.

TOM And also — for your information — a process of fermentation.

GRÁINNE God, aren't you one great bore!

GARRET The difference between Tom and me is that he *occasionally* entertains but I am always and *only* an entertainer. I cater just for the rehearsed response. But that is an honest function, too. And maybe necessary, love. You really shouldn't be so goddamned chaste.

DAISY stands at the door and announces formally:

DAISY The piece you have just heard was 'Remembrance' by Schumann. Some of you may have thought it was Mendelssohn. But you would have been wrong. And the reason you heard echoes of Mendelssohn is that Schumann wrote the piece when he heard that Mendelssohn had just died. Thank you.

She goes back into the living room.

GARRET Thank you most kindly, Missa Daisy. I think you and I should start talking Texan, Tom.
MAGGIE (*To* JACK) We would have had that announcement in pidgin German in the old days. Is he asleep? Jack!
GARRET I have a really imaginative proposal. With the money you get from Texas why don't the four of us go to the Canaries next November? What d'you say, Tom?
TOM What money from Texas?
GARRET It's in the bag and you know it is. Daisy?
DAISY Yes?
GARRET Tenerife for two weeks — what do you say?
DAISY Anybody know this?

She puts on Fats Domino singing 'Blueberry Hill' and comes out to the lawn.

GARRET Christ, we're full of spontaneous enthusiasms, aren't we?

A few moments after the music has begun JACK lifts his straw hat from his face and holds it at arm's length. He listens to the music for a few seconds.

365

JACK Mr Domino calls!

> *He sends his straw hat spinning across the lawn.*
> *Then he gets to his feet, goes to* DAISY, *takes her in*
> *his arms, and dances with her. The dance must not*
> *last more than a few seconds and it is done in a style*
> *somewhere between high theatricality and self-*
> *mockery — and with as much elegance as his carpet*
> *slippers and her bare feet will permit.*
> *When the dance ends — and nobody pays any*
> *attention to it —* DAISY *sits on the steps and* JACK
> *goes back to his deckchair, sits down and closes his*
> *eyes.*
> *During the dance the following conversation takes*
> *place:*

GRÁINNE (*Dictionary*) He's right, the beast. 'A contagious dis-
ease.'
   TOM Been waiting to use that word for years.
GRÁINNE Who was ever sick with 'zymosis'?
MAGGIE It's a general term, not a specific illness.
GARRET (*Texan*) Your husband, Ma'am, is one nimble gentle-
man.
MAGGIE Actually he was a very good dancer once.
GARRET Still is, Ma'am.
MAGGIE Yes, he is. I know that.
GARRET (*To* DAISY) And you, Ma'am, I sure appreciate that
purty waist of yours —

> *He breaks off —* DAVID *has entered.*

Well, look who's here! The Great Assessor himself!
DAVID Have I missed the party?
GRÁINNE What can I get you?
DAVID Anything that's going.

> GRÁINNE *goes to the table.*

(*To* DAISY) I heard the Mendelssohn from up there.

MAGGIE I thought it was Mendelssohn, too, David.

DAISY It was Schumann.

DAVID No, no, I know my Schumann, Daisy.

> DAISY *spreads her hands and addresses the whole group:*

DAISY David — David — David — David. (*Meaning 'You're so wrong, David'*)

> TOM *packs up the* Scrabble.

TOM (*To* GRÁINNE) And you were doing quite well for a while.

GRÁINNE Fermentation — for God's sake!

TOM Pity the collapse was so sudden.

> DAVID *leans down to* TOM *and talks confidentially to him. The others behave as if they are not listening — but of course they are.*

DAVID Wonderful, Tom.

TOM Yes?

DAVID Really wonderful.

TOM Do you think so?

DAVID Everything has suddenly fallen into place.

TOM In what way?

DAVID Everything is of a piece — I can see that now. A complete archive — a wonderful archive.

GARRET (*Calls*) We can't hear you, David Christopher!

DAVID (*Laughs*) None of your business, Garret! (*Confidentially again*) Texas will do their utmost to get their hands on it. I promise you that.

GARRET (*Calls*) And we're dying of curiosity!

DAVID Maybe we could talk ugly money sometime?

TOM Yes — later — later —

GRÁINNE (*At table*) Wine, David?

DAVID Please.

GARRET I'm sorry, but I must persist. No vulgar probing but

one permissible-between-friends question. Are Mr
Connolly, the pornographer, and I going to be laid
out together?

DAVID If that decision were mine alone —

GARRET God, he's being bloody coy again! Answer me!

DAVID All right. In the end that decision will be Tom's.

GARRET But you want the stuff?

GRÁINNE Garret!

DAVID Yes, I want it. Very much.

GARRET And you're prepared to pay for it?

GRÁINNE Garret, stop — !

GARRET He wants it. Enough said. It will be his. Congratulations, Tom — Daisy. (*To* DAVID) Where will we be laid
out? The Fitzmaurice-Connolly Room? The Connolly-
Fitzmaurice Room? Yet another imaginative proposal
— let's all go out for the opening! Right, Maggie?

MAGGIE Whatever you say.

GARRET That's your humour-the-drunk tone. You and Jack
— come as my guests. What about it?

MAGGIE (*To* JACK) Would you like to go to Texas?

JACK All those cows and fields? Spare me!

GARRET Wouldn't he (*Jack*) look great in a ten-gallon hat? (*Sings*)
'The stars at night / Are big and bright — '

He claps four times to complete the line.

GRÁINNE You're a lovely dancer.

JACK Yes.

GRÁINNE *gives a plate and a glass to* DAVID.

GRÁINNE There's more if you want it.

DAVID Thank you.

GARRET (*To* TOM) Why are you looking so bewildered?

TOM I suppose because I *am* a bit.

GARRET (*Softly*) It's in the bag, man — I told you. Now go for
the jugular. (*Aloud*) This is an occasion of moment —
isn't it, Daisy? You two should be falling into one
another's arms and sobbing and smiling through your

tears. Aren't *you* pleased, Tom? Daisy, show some goddamn little joy, will you? (*Grabs a bottle*) Well, I'm going to celebrate appropriately and most injudiciously.

DAVID   (*To* DAISY) Lovely (*food*).

GARRET   But priorities in order. Before Texas comes the Canaries. When are we booked for Tenerife, love?

GRÁINNE   November some time.

GARRET   Have it in my diary. In some things I'm a man of remarkable precision.

He goes to his jacket draped across a chair.

TOM   (*To* DAISY — *in doorway*) Aren't you going to join us?

DAISY   Yes.

She does not move.

GARRET   It's here somewhere. Where the hell is it?

GRÁINNE   At this point I think we should head off home.

TOM   It's early yet. What's the rush?

GRÁINNE   It's a long journey and as you can see I'll be doing the driving.

GARRET   (*To* GRÁINNE) Did you take my wallet?

GRÁINNE   For God's sake.

GARRET   It was there — in that pocket — an hour ago. I saw it.

GRÁINNE   He dropped it somewhere.

GARRET   Darling, I took it out of that pocket, got a toothpick and put it back in again.

MAGGIE   And you've been nowhere since, have you?

GARRET   Into that left-hand pocket.

MAGGIE   So it must be around here somewhere.

GRÁINNE   He's always losing it, for God's sake!

MAGGIE   So let's look for it.

GARRET   Gráinne, I have never, ever, lost my wallet.

MAGGIE, GARRET, GRÁINNE, DAVID and TOM begin looking around the lawn and the table. JACK gets to his feet and stands immobile beside his chair. DAISY sits on the steps and does not take part in the search.

DAVID　Were you in the living room?

GARRET　I was in the living room but my jacket wasn't in the living room. My jacket has been here the entire afternoon.

GRÁINNE　We're trying to help, Garret.

DAVID　(*Privately*) I may have to depend on you, Daisy.

DAISY　I don't think that would ever be a wise thing to do.

DAVID　To persuade him to sell. They often stall at the last minute. And he listens to you.

DAISY　'Absolutely.'

DAVID　I know he does. You do, too.

TOM　What are we all looking for?

GRÁINNE　His wallet, Tom. His bloody wallet.

TOM　What colour is it?

GARRET　Brown.

GRÁINNE　It's probably in the car down at —

GARRET　No, it's not! It's here!

He stops beside JACK's shoes and points to the wallet partly hidden underneath them.

Hiding under the famous snakeskin shoes!

He stoops down and produces the wallet.

GRÁINNE　(*Ironically*) Thank heavens for that!

DAVID　Apologies, Garret.

GARRET　What for?

DAVID　You didn't put it back in your pocket.

GARRET　But I did, David. Most verily I did.

DAVID　Well, then —

And now they all know that JACK stole it and hid it. DAISY moves down quickly towards JACK but stops abruptly and stands absolutely still with her eyes shut tight — as she did in Act One. The atmosphere is tense. All eyes are on JACK — for a few seconds.

*He looks utterly lost and bewildered. He looks into
each face in turn, lingering with each for a moment
— hoping for a gesture of support? Bracing himself
against rejection? Before moving on to the next person.*

MAGGIE*'s face is the last his eyes search.*

*When he looks at her face he suddenly collapses in
tears. With his hands hanging loose at his sides and
his gaze still probing* MAGGIE*'s face he sobs quietly
and deeply. The cocky, dandy, dancing piano player
is transformed into a desolate old man.*

*For a long time nobody moves. The silence is broken
by the sobbing. The sobbing may last forever.*

Then MAGGIE*, who has been at the far left, walks
across the stage to where* JACK *stands.*

*Awkwardly and embarrassedly the others look away,
shuffle away.* MAGGIE *and* JACK *stand facing each other.*

JACK I'm sorry — I'm sorry — I'm so sorry, Maggie —

MAGGIE *speaks softly and very slowly.*

MAGGIE Look at that shabby little swindler.

JACK Oh my God, I'm so sorry, Maggie —

MAGGIE That's what shaped my life. Yes.

JACK Maggie, I don't —

MAGGIE And to think that whatever deformed contour my
life had, whatever panic directions it took, whatever
pits of despair it sank to, that's what determined
them all — that little coxcomb piano player; and to
think that was once the boy who flooded my head
with music.

JACK I don't know what came —

MAGGIE I used to ask God: how do I live with that? Give me
your answer, God. But he never told me. And it's
past the time for an answer now. And now what I
want to know is: what will happen to him when I'm
gone, what will become of that petty little thief?

She is now on the point of tears but will not cry.

I suppose he'll go on playing and dancing and steal-
ing for ever, won't he? There's something eternal about
people like that, isn't there?

JACK Oh, Maggie —

*She stands and watches him sobbing. Then — even-
tually — she goes to him and takes his hand.*

MAGGIE Come with me. We'll have to wash that face of yours,
won't we?

*She takes his hand and leads him up the steps and
into the living room. As he passes* DAISY *he puts out
a tentative, apologetic hand. But her eyes are still
closed — she does not see him. And* MAGGIE *leads
him off right.*
Silence. Then DAISY *runs quickly after them.*
Pause.

GARRET Well, good God Almighty —

Pause.

DAVID I suppose it could have fallen from his pocket and
slipped under —

TOM He's not a swindler. He really isn't.

GRÁINNE *is suddenly brisk and in control.*

GRÁINNE Let's get our things and move off.

GARRET Good idea.

*And as if they were in a panic to escape they move
hurriedly around the garden, picking up the party
detritus, the gooseberries, glasses etc.* DAVID *helps
them.* TOM *attempts to help. As they tidy up:*

GRÁINNE I'll leave these (*glasses*) here.

GARRET Give me a hand with this (*table*), David.

DAVID Sure.

As they all busy themselves:

GRÁINNE We got a beautiful sunny afternoon, didn't we?
GARRET Wonderful.
GRÁINNE Never seen Daisy looking better, Tom.
TOM Daisy's fine — fine —
GARRET Daisy's great.
GRÁINNE She is — isn't she?
GARRET Terrific. Will we leave these (*seats*) here?
TOM I'll put them away later.
GRÁINNE Always looks stunning in blue.
TOM Sorry?
GRÁINNE Daisy. Blue's her colour.
TOM Yes — it is, isn't it?
GRÁINNE Your jacket, Garret.
GARRET Thanks. (*To* DAVID) When are we going to see you again?
DAVID We're all meeting up in Texas — aren't we, Tom?
TOM 'If we do meet again, why, we shall smile.' I'm sorry, Garret. I'm really sorry.
GARRET Nothing — nothing. And that seems to be as much as we can do for now. So — let's hit the old saddle.
DAVID Hold on — what about Texas?
GRÁINNE Let's concentrate on the Canaries first.
GARRET She's right.
GRÁINNE Leave that with me. I'll organize the Canaries.
GARRET Great at that sort of thing.
TOM It's in your hands.
GRÁINNE Tell Daisy I'll be in touch with her next week.
TOM Great.
GARRET (*Diary*) 14th to the 28th of November. It's a huge apartment right on the sea.
GRÁINNE She and I will work out the details.
GARRET So be assured it *will* happen.
TOM Maybe we should all —
GARRET Because in matters mundane there is nobody more efficient than Gráinne.

GRÁINNE (*To* DAVID) But in matters of the spirit — utterly crass.
GARRET I wouldn't say that, love.
GRÁINNE How would you put it?
DAVID I think he means —
GARRET Perhaps not always — alert?
GRÁINNE Alert to?
GARRET The unsaid, the silent counterpoint. But maybe I'm being too austere, am I?
GRÁINNE For a man whose popularity was earned by soothing readers with all the recognizable harmonies — 're-hearsed replies' as he calls them himself — Garret's fastidiousness always astonishes me. But perhaps it's just a pardonable little strut before the final collapse. Yours (*jacket*), David?
DAVID Thanks.
GARRET I know we have an audience, love. But surely that's transgressing the necessary boundary?
GRÁINNE Is it?
GARRET I think just a little. Incidentally — 'rehearsed responses'.
GRÁINNE Sorry?
GARRET You said 'rehearsed replies'. It's of no matter. Another little strut.
GRÁINNE (*To* TOM) Crass *and* unscrupulous.
GARRET No, you're not, love. But even popular deserves accurate, doesn't it?
GRÁINNE Popular *deserves* nothing, Garret. Popular is its own reward.
GARRET Like virtue.
GRÁINNE (*To* TOM) If only that crispness had gone into the work.
GARRET So I'm adequately rewarded?
GRÁINNE Oh, shut up, will you? Where's my bag?

She looks for it.

GARRET (*Privately, delightedly*) The Fabulous Fitzmaurices are back on the road!
GRÁINNE I'm going, Tom. We'll slip out this way.
GARRET We're both going.

GRÁINNE   Thank Daisy for a lovely afternoon.

TOM   Pleasure.

GRÁINNE   (*To* DAVID) 'Bye, David.

DAVID   I'll give you a ring.

GRÁINNE   Do, please. I left a casserole in the kitchen.

She exits.

GARRET   (*To* DAVID) And you're to treat this man with unprecedented generosity. After all these years he deserves a big break.

DAVID   I'll do all I can.

GARRET   'Bye, Tom. Thanks for everything.

TOM   Thank you for coming.

GARRET   As for that little episode — (*Points to* JACK's *shoes*) It's already obliterated from our minds.

TOM   Thank you.

GARRET   And your other secret is equally safe with us.

TOM   My other — ?

GARRET   Your pornography!

TOM   Yes, I suppose that is sort of shameful, too, is it? Bad day at the manse, Garret.

GARRET   'Whereof one cannot speak, thereof one must be silent.' Wittgenstein, the philosopher. Obsessed with him at the moment. Thinking of doing something on him — a fiction — a faction maybe — maybe a bloody play! Well — maybe — perhaps.

TOM   German, was he?

GARRET   Austrian. Not the familiar Fitzmaurice territory but nothing wrong with aspiring, is there? Maybe I could talk it over with you sometime?

TOM   I just know the name. Know nothing about the work.

GARRET   Fascinating, complex man. Came to this country three times back in the '30s and '40s. Some amazing stuff about him when he was here. That's what I'd concentrate on — his life in Connemara. If only I could get my arms round *that* material, Tom. Oh, God!

TOM   Get your arms around it.

GARRET Bit too late, isn't it? What do you think?

TOM Get down to it. Be faithful to the routine gestures and the bigger thing will come to you. Discipline yourself.

GARRET Discipline isn't the problem, Tom. Never was. She's right: my covenant with the great warm public — that's the problem. We're woven into each other. I created the taste by which they now assess me.

TOM Remake yourself. Create a new taste.

GARRET Maybe it's not too late, Tom, is it? The 'final collapse' could be postponed, couldn't it?

TOM Stop talking about a collapse, Garret. I'll write you about this. That's a promise.

GARRET Will you? Please?

GRÁINNE returns.

GRÁINNE I'm going.

DAVID 'Bye, Gráinne. 'Bye, Garret.

TOGETHER 'Bye — 'Bye —

> *They are about to exit right when JACK comes into the living room and out to the garden. This is not the man who was led off by the hand a short time ago. This is the cocky, dandy, opinionated fop again.*
> *GRÁINNE, GARRET and DAVID watch in astonishment as he goes to where his shoes are and puts them on.*

JACK Slippers are very comfortable but they do nothing for the self-esteem. I worked with a drummer once who never wore shoes — always slippers. Said they allowed him direct contact with the rhythms of the universe. And they must have — the most brilliant drummer I ever knew. But his appearance! Ended up a complete slob. Dirty, actually. D'you know what we had to do? Raise his kit up on a little platform so that he couldn't be seen behind it.

Are they (*shoes*) dry? They are. Only pair in Ireland. I told you that story, didn't I?

TOM They're just about to go, Jack. They have a long journey.

JACK (*To* GARRET) You live in the country, too, do you?

TOM On a farm south of here.

JACK Ah well — careful of that field on your way out — right-hand side of the avenue — quagmire. That's where these (*shoes*) came to grief. Absolutely. Garret Fitzmaurice — I've got that now. I'll be on the look-out for that name.

He goes to the far side of the garden, picks up a napkin and polishes the shoes. GARRET *and* GRÁINNE *are still speechless. Pause.*

GARRET (*Almost inaudibly*) Jesus Christ —

Now their urgency returns. They have got to get out.

GRÁINNE Say goodbye to Daisy and Maggie.

GARRET 'Bye, Tom. 'Bye, David.

GRÁINNE 'Bye, David.

TOM (*To* GARRET) That Wittgenstein's a great idea, Garret.

GARRET (*With no conviction whatever*) Yes — I know —

TOM Hang on to it.

GARRET Sure — of course — we'll see —

GRÁINNE 'Bye — 'Bye —

They exit right quickly.

JACK Drive carefully.

TOM *busies himself so that he will not have to talk to* JACK.

DAVID I'll leave these back in the potting shed.

DAVID *exits.*

JACK An — uneasy couple, aren't they?

TOM Are they?

TOM *brings an empty bottle into the living room and comes out again.*

JACK Him especially. All that worked-up agitato. *Anxious* company, aren't they?

TOM Is that your opinion?

JACK And they're Bridget's godparents? I suppose it must have seemed the right choice at the time.

TOM Must have.

JACK Is he a good novelist?

TOM He's a good novelist.

JACK Like musicians, you people: totally loyal to each other before outsiders. But among yourselves — ! But you're right. What's the yardstick anyway? Whatever money David offers you, for God's sake? — He's a bit anxious, too, isn't he? — David. If you ask me there's a story there. (*Pause*) Anything I can do?

TOM Nothing.

JACK I was naughty, Tom, wasn't I?

TOM Is naughty the word?

JACK You're angry with me.

TOM I am not angry, Jack.

JACK Do you despise me?

TOM For God's sake, man.

JACK You have good reason to. Indeed you have. Daisy, too. I ruined your party.

TOM It was never a party.

JACK Of course I did. Didn't you see their faces? Couldn't escape quick enough. I'm sorry, Tom.

TOM We got through a lot of stuff (*empty bottles*).

JACK All the same I don't think she should have called me a swindler before everybody. I'm not a swindler, Tom. I'm really not a swindler. She does it to humiliate me. Always did. Always before people. From the very beginning. I think because she felt in her heart that by marrying the jobbing piano player she had humiliated herself.

TOM The others should be outside. There's still heat in that sun.

JACK And I suppose she did — humiliate herself. Brilliant student apparently. Absolutely. If she hadn't married the little piano player, headed for a brilliant career in medicine. At least that was the expectation. But there's always an expectation, isn't there? And they don't always work out, do they? So maybe all I did was provide her with a different set of disappointments. Certainly did that, didn't I? All the same, humiliating me before people — So I sing, I dance, I play, keep it bubbly, act out the fake affectations — Only way I can cope, Tom. All the same —

DAVID *returns.*

I'll get the ladies to come out.

JACK *exits.*

DAVID Could we have a moment now? To talk about the archive.
TOM (*With sudden fury*) I said later, didn't I? Are you stupid? Didn't I say — ? I'm sorry, David. Forgive me. I'm sorry.
DAVID I just wanted to explain the choices you have. We can agree on a price now — well, after I've got approval from Texas — and that cheque will be in your pocket in less than a month, certainly in time for Tenerife or Texas or indeed anywhere else you want to go! Or you may take a portion of the price now and be paid the balance over the next four years. If you agree to staggered payments I can poach from the budgets of the next four years; and then we're talking about a lot of money, Tom. Without breaching any confidences at very least as much as we gave Garret. What do you think?
TOM I don't have to give you an answer this very second, do I?
DAVID We'll talk again in the morning. Just wanted you to know the choices you have.

TOM   And now I know them.

DAVID   Yes.

TOM   Fine.

DAVID   There is one other thing I must tell you.

TOM   David —

DAVID   I am expected to provide all the Irish material. It's
       an order. 'Deliver Ireland, David.' Of course they
       have no doubt that I can, that I will — they think I'm
       brilliant at the job. But if I can't deliver every single
       goddamn name on their goddamn Irish list, Tom,
       then — in their parlance — you'd never believe the
       word they use — then I'm 'sterile'! (*Laughs*) Yes!
       (*Pause*) I can't afford to lose this job, Tom. I don't mean
       for money reasons — of course, of course, that, too. But
       what I really mean is — you know — emotionally,
       the self-esteem — I really can't afford to be let go so
       soon again.

       Pause.

       I'm depending on you, Tom.

       JACK, MAGGIE *and* DAISY *enter the living room*, JACK
       and MAGGIE *come out to the garden.* DAISY *pauses at
       the record player.* DAVID *joins her in the living room.*

MAGGIE   Yes, there still is heat in that sun. Your guests have
       fled?

TOM   Left.

MAGGIE   Without a word?

TOM   They asked me to say goodbye for them.

MAGGIE   Wasn't that gracious of them?

TOM   Did you expect them to sit around, Maggie?

DAVID   (*Privately*) I'm going to make him a *very* generous
       offer.

DAISY   (*Sings*) 'My very good friend, the milkman says — '

DAVID   I need your support, Daisy. Help me. Please.

       She puts on the CD — Fats Waller singing 'My Very

Good Friend, the Milkman'. DAVID *comes out to the garden.*

MAGGIE Must we have that (*music*), Daisy? Didn't I leave gooseberries here?

JACK They're somewhere about —

He sings a line of the song.

Thank you, Dais.

MAGGIE (*To* TOM) I'm afraid I don't know his work — Garret. Is he a good writer?

JACK He's an excellent writer.

MAGGIE Have you read him?

JACK You know I haven't. Just quoting the Master here.

TOM One of the most accomplished writers in the country.

MAGGIE I must read him then. He's not salacious, is he?

TOM Despite the flamboyance he is a very staid man. I'm the pornographer, Maggie.

JACK (*Quickly*) They called him Fats Waller because of his size. Not too subtle, was it? His real name was Thomas George Waller.

DAISY Thomas Wright.

JACK Thomas Wright — how did you know that? (*To* TOM) And without question one of the high kings of jazz. And I'll tell —

He is standing beside MAGGIE *with the gooseberry dish in his hand.*

MAGGIE Can't you just leave it on the ground? Thank you.

JACK I'll tell you something else about Fats Waller, Tom. In his entire life not as much as one day in jail!

MAGGIE What *is* the world coming to?

DAISY comes out to the garden with a bottle of wine. She walks slowly from one end of the lawn to the other and back again — above the others. She is calm and in control and seems to exude an alertness and a keenness we have not seen before. As she comes out:

DAISY The last of the Fitzmaurices' most welcome and most generous wine. Let us share it in peace and in wisdom and may the giving hand never fail and the best of all ways to lengthen our days is to steal a few hours from the night, my dear.

JACK Whatever that means.

DAISY Nothing. David? (*Wine*)

DAVID No, thanks. (*Softly*) I need him, Daisy.

TOM May I have that (*bottle*)? Have a seat here, David.

DAISY *gives* TOM *the bottle and continues walking.*

DAVID I'll go and do a bit of packing. Leave the family to itself for a while. Give you a chance to snigger behind my back.

DAVID *exits.*

TOM David — !

MAGGIE What a curious thing to say.

JACK What's curious about it? I'll have some (*wine*), Tom.

MAGGIE I don't think that young man is very well. Please sit down, Daisy.

TOM (*To* DAISY) You thought there was something odd about him the first day he arrived.

MAGGIE He has come through a difficult time.

TOM How do you know that?

MAGGIE Nervous trouble. He told me.

JACK People confide in Maggie.

JACK *holds out his glass to* TOM.

Thanks. Because she is a doctor. And kind.

TOM Maggie? (*Wine*)

MAGGIE Nothing for me. Darling, you're making me uneasy.

Please sit down.

JACK Odd he may be, but he's keen to get your stuff — mad keen.

MAGGIE Don't interfere, Jack. (*To* TOM) A breakdown, in fact.

JACK My sense is you can name your price.

MAGGIE A really bad breakdown from what he told me.

JACK Make a killing.

MAGGIE Jack, I —

JACK Salt him.

MAGGIE For God's sake —

JACK Take him to the piano tuners.

MAGGIE Stop that at once, Jack! Tossing out your corner-boy advice as if you were knowledgeable — and you know nothing, nothing! Daisy, please!

But DAISY *continues walking. Pause.*

TOM You're right, Jack — he does want the stuff. I suppose I should be pleased. A month ago I would have been thrilled. I would have been delighted only this morning. And I *am* pleased — well, flattered, I suppose. No more than that. For some reason suddenly no more than a little bit flattered.

JACK But you *will* sell?

TOM (*Shrugs*) If he wants to buy.

JACK End to your money worries, Tom.

TOM That would depend on what —

JACK Look at your friends — loaded. Dammit, nothing would please me more than to see you getting a big break. Both of you.

TOM I know that.

JACK Absolutely.

MAGGIE It would mean you could move house.

TOM If we wanted to, I suppose.

MAGGIE Perhaps somewhere less remote?

TOM Perhaps.

JACK The view up that valley is breathtaking, Maggie.

MAGGIE Perhaps something less — spartan?

TOM Spartan has advantages.

MAGGIE For you, perhaps. I wouldn't have thought Daisy's life up here was entirely — fulfilling.

TOM It probably is not, Maggie.

MAGGIE In fact at times very close to the edge, I suspect.

TOM That could be.

MAGGIE But perhaps mere domestic matters don't concern creative people, do they?

TOM Maggie, I would ask you not —

> DAISY *speaks slowly and simply and with calm consideration. She is not responding to earlier arguments; nor is she attempting to persuade; just making her statement — almost thinking aloud — which is self-evident. She continues walking as she speaks.*

DAISY Oh, no, he mustn't sell. Of course he mustn't sell. There are reasons why he wants to sell and those reasons are valid reasons and understandable and very persuasive. A better place for Bridget. Escape from the tyranny of those daily bills and the quick liberation that would offer. Maybe a house with just a little comfort. And, if David's offer is as large as he suggests, then of course the most persuasive reason of all: the work has value — yes, yes, yes! Here is the substantial confirmation, the tangible evidence! The work *must* be good! I'm not imprisoned in the dark anymore! Now I can run again! Now I can *dare* again!

> *Pause.*

Yes, it is so very persuasive. I convinced myself I believed in all those arguments, too — I think because I knew they were so attractive, almost irresistible, to him. But we were both deluded. Indeed we were. A better place for Bridget? But Bridget is beyond knowing, isn't she? And somehow, somehow bills will always be met. And what does a little physical discomfort matter? Really not a lot. But to sell for an affirmation, for an answer, to be free of that grinding uncertainty, that would be so wrong for him and so wrong for his work. Because that uncertainty is necessary. He must live with that uncertainty, that necessary uncertainty. Because there can be no verdicts, no answers. Indeed there *must* be no verdicts. Because being alive is the postponement of verdicts, isn't it? Because verdicts are provided only when it's all over, all concluded.

Of course he mustn't sell.

And now I'm going to pour myself a little gin. And only half-an-hour ago I made a secret vow to give up gin for ever and ever and to switch to health-giving red wine. But there you are — the road to hell — touch of a slut — and so we stagger on —

She goes up the steps and pauses at the top.

To the Necessary Uncertainty.

She goes into the living room.

What would you like to hear, Father?

JACK What's on offer?

DAISY Brahms — Armstrong — Mr John Field —

JACK What about Mr Mendelssohn, for old times' sake?

DAISY Mr Mendelssohn would be welcome — if I can find him.

MAGGIE If I don't keep on the move I seize up. (*To* JACK) Do you feel like a short walk?

JACK Not at the moment.

MAGGIE Did you bring our bags in?

JACK They're at the foot of the stairs.

MAGGIE (*To* DAISY) Where are we sleeping?

DAISY Sorry?

JACK Where are we sleeping?

DAISY In the back room upstairs.

JACK In the back room upstairs.

MAGGIE (*To herself*) Wherever that is. (*As she exits*) There still is heat in that sun.

DAISY *plays 'On Wings of Song', as at the opening of the play.*

DAISY (*Speaks*) '*Auf Flügeln des Gesanges / Herzliebchen, trag' ich dich fort* —'

JACK '*Fort nach den Fluren des Ganges, / Dort weiß ich den schönsten Ort* —' (*To* TOM) And I'll have you know — that is not gibberish. Better keep an eye on her: might get up to something very naughty.

TOM Maybe you should.

JACK Actually she's not at all steady with that stick. She needs two. But — you know — vanity. Sad, isn't it?

He exits, TOM *goes into the living room. He stands on one side of the record player,* DAISY *on the other, both listening to the music. Pause.*

The NURSE *pushes* BRIDGET'S *bed on and places it as in Act One. She exits.*

TOM I hope it's the right decision. Give me your answer, do, Daisy.

DAISY I don't know. Who's to say?

He takes the envelopes (bills) out of his pocket.

TOM What's to be done about these?

DAISY You could always write another porn novel.

TOM (*Wearily*) Daisy.

DAISY Put Garret's name to it. Gráinne's!

TOM Please.

DAISY Mother's!

TOM Daisy —

Pause.

DAISY I could give piano lessons. I could, you know.

TOM Up here? Where are your pupils to come from?

DAISY You're right. Stupid —

He moves to exit left and pauses before he leaves.

TOM What am I going to say to Mister God?
DAISY Who?
TOM David.
DAISY You're the writer. You'll think of something.

> *He exits left.* DAISY *comes downstage and slumps into a deckchair, cigarette in one hand, glass in the other — just as we saw her at the opening of the play.*
> BRIDGET *is in her pool of light. Bring down the living-room and garden lights to half.*
> TOM *enters left as at the beginning, with his abused briefcase, and as before he gazes at his daughter for a long time, his face without expression. Then he suddenly and very deliberately animates himself and goes briskly to the bedside.*

TOM Well! Who is this elegant young woman? What entrancing creature is this 'with forehead of ivory and amethyst eyes and cold, immortal hands'? It's not Miss Bridget Connolly, is it? It most certainly is my Bridget Connolly, beautiful and mysterious as ever. And what's this? Her auburn hair swept back over her *right* ear? Now that's new! And just a little bit saucy! And very, very becoming!

How are you, my darling? Give your father a big kiss.

> *He kisses her on the forehead, sits on the edge of the bed and opens his briefcase.*

I like this room — don't you? Nobody can hear a word we say. Now — this week's treasure trove. Clean underclothes. Three oranges. A new facecloth. One very red apple. A bar of chocolate. *And* — close your eyes — open them again — six fat wheaten scones laden with raisins! There! Your mother at her most creative. Yes, yes, yes, I'll thank her — of course I will.

What news do I have for you today? First bit of news. Last Wednesday evening, when the clock struck seven, Grandma hit the fourteen-foot mark! I know — incredible! And the house-to-clinic-back-to-house race — one minute, thirty seconds! She's done it! Amazing! Set her target — not one second of uncertainty — accomplished it — and now world champion. You must admit — it *is* an extraordinary achievement, darling — isn't it? Of course I'll give her your congratulations. Absolutely, as Grandpa says.

Grandpa? Not good news about Grandpa, I'm afraid. Awful, really. In jail again. In Paraguay. A town called San Pedro. Arrested with a posse of *mestizos* — bandits in fact. Caught carrying an American B52 bomber plane — yes, that's what I said — fifty of them trying to *carry* this enormous plane across the sierras from Bolivia into Paraguay. And in typical Grandpa style made no real attempt to hide it. But can you imagine what a jail in San Pedro must be like? Will there be a trial? Ultimately, I imagine. And ultimately, I suppose, a verdict of some sort — ultimately. But poor old Grandpa. Should have stuck with alcoholic ferrets, shouldn't he? But he'll survive. Have no doubt. He'll survive. What's that — your mother? Buoyant! Incandescent! Do you know what she's doing? Giving master classes in piano. The most promising young pianists from all over Europe, Asia, America. A young man from — say — Prague flies in. She gives him ten hours non-stop intensive tuition. He reels up to the back bedroom for an hour's sleep. Back down again. Ten more hours — bang-bang-bang. He flies home, happy as a sandboy, a concert pianist in the making. Wonderful, isn't it?

It's dark in this basement, isn't it? Do you feel it cold?

My new novel? Yes, yes, yes, I was waiting for that question. We've had a surfeit of your cheeky jokes on that subject over the years, haven't we?

Well, I'll tell you about it. Took it out again yesterday morning. Went back over all the notes. Looked at all the bits I'd written and tossed aside over the past five years. Read very carefully the twenty-three pages I'd already written. And I can tell you, Madam, let me tell you there just may be something there. I don't want to say any more at this stage. But I did get a little — a little quiver — a whiff — a stirring of a sense that perhaps — maybe —

But that's all I'm going to say at this point. I dare not say any more. But if it were to emerge for me, my darling; if I could coax it out; if I could hold it and then release it into its contented rest, into its happy completion — (*from very far off and very faintly we hear the sound of 'On Wings of Song' on the piano*) — then, my silent love, my strange little offspring, then I would come straight back here to you and fold you in my arms; and you and I would climb into a golden balloon — just the two of us — only the two of us — and we would soar above this earth and float away forever across the face of the 'darkly, deeply, beautifully blue sky' —

> *The moment* TOM *says 'just the two of us – only the two of us'* DAISY *gets suddenly to her feet as if she had been wakened abruptly from a sleep. She seems confused and her face is anxious with incipient grief.*
>
> *Then, as soon as* TOM *finishes his speech she calls out softly, urgently:*

DAISY Oh, Tom! — Tom! — Tom, please? —

Pause. Quick black.

Acknowledgements

The editor thanks Jean Fallon and Suella Holland for their invaluable contributions to the preparation of this edition. Acknowledgements are also due to Anne Friel and family, Leah Schmidt and Dinah Wood.

The London Vertigo (after Macklin) was published first by The Gallery Press in 1990.

A Month in the Country (after Turgenev) was published first by The Gallery Press in 1992.

Wonderful Tennessee was published first by The Gallery Press and by Faber and Faber Limited in 1993.

Molly Sweeney was published first by The Gallery Press and by Penguin Books in 1994.

Give Me Your Answer, Do! was published first by The Gallery Press and by Penguin Books in 1997.

In *Wonderful Tennessee* 'The World is Waiting for the Sunrise' Copyright © 1919, Chappell Music Ltd., London. Reproduced by permission of International Music Publications Ltd.

'I Want to be Happy' Copyright © 1920, Harms Inc., USA, Warner Chappell Music Ltd., London. Reproduced by permission of International Music Publications Ltd.

'Jolly Good Company' Copyright © 1931, Campbell, Connelly & Co. Ltd., 8-9 Frith Street, London W1V 5TZ. Used by permission, all rights reserved.

'There Was I Waiting at the Church' Copyright © 1906. Reproduced by permission of Francis Day and Hunter Ltd., London WC2H OEA.

'Down in de Cane-brake' Copyright © 1928, Forster Music Pub Inc., USA. Reproduced by permission of Francis Day and Hunter Ltd., London WC2H OEA.

'Heavenly Sunshine' Copyright © 1970, Al Gallico Music Corp., USA. Reproduced by permission of EMI Music Publishing Ltd., London WC2H OEA.

Collected Plays

Volume One
The Enemy Within · Philadelphia, Here I Come! ·
The Loves of Cass McGuire · Lovers: Winners and Losers ·
Crystal and Fox · The Gentle Island

Volume Two
The Freedom of the City · Volunteers · Living Quarters ·
Aristocrats · Faith Healer · Translations

Volume Three
Three Sisters (after Chekhov) · The Communication Cord ·
Fathers and Sons (after Turgenev) · Making History ·
Dancing at Lughnasa

Volume Four
The London Vertigo (after Macklin) · A Month in the Country
(after Turgenev) · Wonderful Tennessee · Molly Sweeney ·
Give Me Your Answer, Do!

Volume Five
Uncle Vanya (after Chekhov) · The Yalta Game (after Chekhov) ·
The Bear (after Chekhov) · Afterplay · Performances ·
The Home Place · Hedda Gabler (after Ibsen)